V&R unipress

Wittener Schriften zu Familienunternehmen

Band 10

Herausgegeben von
Arist von Schlippe und Tom Rüsen
im Wittener Institut für Familienunternehmen (WIFU)
an der Universität Witten / Herdecke

WIFU Wittener Institut für FamilienUnternehmen
Universität Witten/Herdecke

Götz Müller

Private Equity Investments in Family Businesses

An Empirical Investigation of the Organizational Metamorphosis

With 14 figures

V&R unipress

FSC
www.fsc.org
MIX
Papier aus verantwortungsvollen Quellen
FSC® C003147

Bibliografische Information der Deutschen Nationalbibliothek

Die Deutsche Nationalbibliothek verzeichnet diese Publikation in der Deutschen Nationalbibliografie; detaillierte bibliografische Daten sind im Internet über http://dnb.d-nb.de abrufbar.

ISBN 978-3-8471-0093-5

Printed in Germany.
Druck und Bindung: CPI Buch Bücher.de GmbH, Birkach

Gedruckt auf alterungsbeständigem Papier.

Contents

List of Figures

List of Tables

List of Abbreviations

AUM	Assets Under Management
BIMBO	Buyin Management Buyout
BD	Balance Dimension (of Ambidexterity)
BVK	Bundesverband Deutscher Kapitalbeteiligungsgesellschaften
CAPM	Capital Asset Pricing Model
CD	Combined Dimension (of Ambidexterity)
CEO	Chief Executive Officer
CFO	Chief Financial Officer
CVF	Competing Values Framework
EBIT	Earnings Before Taxes
EBITDA	Earnings Before Taxes and Depreciation
FB/FBes	Family Business/Family Businesses
F-PEC	Family-Power, Experience, and Culture Scale
GDP	Gross Domestic Product
IBO	Institutional Buyout
IFERA	International Family Enterprise Research Academy
IfM	Institut für Mittelstandsforschung (Bonn)
IPO	Initial Public Offering
KKR	Kohlberg Kravis Roberts & Co.
LBO	Leveraged Buyout
LPE	Listed Private Equity
MBG	Mittelständische Beteiligungsgesellschaft
MBI	Management Buyin
MBO	Management Buyout
MNE	Multinational Enterprise
MO	Market Orientation
M&A	Mergers and Acquisitions
OCAI	Organizational Culture Assessment Instrument
PE	Private Equity
ROI	Return on Investment
SFI	Substantial Family Influence Scale
SME	Small and Medium-Sized Enterprise
S&P 500	Standard & Poor's 500

UK	United Kingdom
US	United States
VC	Venture Capital
WIFU	Wittener Institut für Familienunternehmen

1. Introduction

Private Equity (PE) companies[1] have been crowned the new kings of capitalism (Bishop, 2004). PE[2] has been the fastest growing market for corporate finance over the last decades (Fenn et al. 1997), and experts approximate that PE funds in the United States (US) have grown from managing $0.2 billion in 1980 to $200 billion in 2007 (Kaplan & Strömberg, 2009). On a global basis, Metrick and Yasuda (2010) suggest that PE funds manage about $1 trillion, whereas in Germany assets under management (AUM) are approximated to equal €39 billion in 2010, invested in 6.908 companies (Bundesverband Deutscher Kapitalbeteiligungsgesellschaften, 2011).[3] Diverse commentaries published in newspapers or practitioner-oriented research proclaim that the triumphal rise of PE might find a sudden end given that the business environment can be considered more difficult and uncertain (see Backhaus, 2009; Bain & Company, 2010; Beyerle, 2010; Raina, 2009; Nagl, 2009a; Roland Berger Strategy Consultants, 2011). In a similar vein, advocates of the academic discipline, such as Cheffins and Armour (2008), speculate about the further development of PE. The former mentioned authors propose in their paper *The eclipse of Private Equity*, as a rejoinder to Jensen's (1989) *Eclipse of the public corporation*, that the PE industry can fundamentally change. According to the scholars, certain contingencies will impede

1 Private Equity companies refer to investors that do not have any strategic objectives when acquiring companies. Therefore, these institutions have a pure financial interest when investing (e.g., Achleitner, 2002). The underlying definition utilized in this book is discussed in detail in a later segment (cf. subsection 2.2.1). The terms "PE company," "PE fund," "PE house," and "financial investor" are utilized synonymously in this paper.

2 PE investments refer to the investment of equity in private or listed companies by financial investors. The profit of PE companies is either generated by capital gains or the dividend yield over the investment horizon (e.g., Wright & Robbie, 1998). The modus operandi of PE companies is clarified with elevated precision in a following segment (cf. subsection 2.2.2).

3 The estimated number of unreported cases is assumed to be substantially higher given that the statistics are merely based on the investments from the 218 members of the Bundesverband Deutscher Kapitalbeteiligungsgesellschaften (BVK).

the further development, for example, unstable debt markets, potential regulatory changes, and the availability of targets.

Family businesses[4] (FBes) can be considered a rich source of potential targets for PE companies. The significant contribution of FBes in economic and societal terms represents a widely acknowledged factum. For example, FBes are characterized as the driver of the Industrial Revolution (e.g., Kocka, 1982; Payne, 1983); the Rockefellers, Fords, or Mercks, financed by the Goldmans, Oppenheims, or Rothschilds, have undoubtedly shaped our world. While many of these companies have meanwhile been sold to the public, a major fraction between 75 to 80 percent (Simon, 2005) and 95 percent (Wallau et al. 2007) of all companies in Germany, depending on the underlying definition and methodical census, are still considered to be family-owned. Along these lines, it should not be surprising that FBes employ a substantial proportion of the national workforce and generate a considerable fraction of the gross domestic product (GDP), which constitutes a phenomenon beyond German borders. FBes are considered to be different compared to their nonfamily-owned counterparties. Schlippe et al. (2009) summarize these idiosyncrasies of FBes by means of ten presumptions.[5] One of these presumptions holds that FBes are financed distinctively since they primarily utilize internal funds. This issue is usually explained by the desire of FBes to remain independent (e.g., Erikson et al. 2003; Gallo & Vilaseca, 1996; Romano et al. 2000). Besides this aspiration, FBes have more difficulties in attracting external financiers. Unilateral connections with relationship banks do not anymore ensure a sufficient supply of capital, which is to some extent a result of more restricted credit guidelines induced by new legal regulations (e.g., Kolbeck & Wimmer, 2002). Given the fact that the access to external financing is typically deciphered as a critical incident constraining the development of FBes (e.g., Coleman & Carsky, 1999), a severe threat for these entities appears to exist. FBes have thus to become more market-oriented in the consideration of their financing sources. Furthermore, a recent study conducted by McKinsey & Company suggests that companies in industrialized regions "will have to adapt

4 Due to theoretical pluralism associated with the term "family business," the employed definition in this book is derived in the following chapter (cf. section 2.1).

5 The authors propose that FBes reveal the subsequent idiosyncrasies: FBes are considered to be 1. different (arising through the family influence); 2. more successful (as the family constitutes a valuable resource); 3. more vulnerable (as the family constitutes a continuous risk factor); 4. potentially more intelligent (due to the uncoupling from a short-term orientation capital markets demand); 5. differently financed (given that they rely on internal funds); 6. long-term oriented (as they think in generations); 7. resistant to external advice (comparable to families, FBes attempt to solve problems by themselves); 8. more familial (as social relationships are conveyed to the business); 9. more entrepreneurial (due to high personal commitments to innovate); 10. more persistent (if the family and the business optimally interact).

to a world in which capital is more costly and less plentiful" (2010: 2). Consequently, PE represents an interesting financing alternative for this organizational class, and empirical evidence indicates that owners of FBes consider the employment of PE capital for succession planning and corporate growth (see PricewaterhouseCoopers, 2007).

A mutual need can thus be identified, and the returns to the relationship can be concretely evaluated for both systems. On this account, the message for PE companies is obvious: Investments in FBes constitute a viable strategy allowing investors to maintain and possibly extend their prominent status as capitalism's kings. PE companies systematically focus on FBes (e.g., Financial Times Deutschland, 2010a; Maier, 2011; Nagl, 2009b) since attractive public-to-private buyouts are difficult to uncover and accomplish (e.g., Maier, 2010). Likewise, the utility of PE capital for FBes should be comprehensible: In the light of the ever increasing rivalry in global markets, access to financing and financial flexibility can bring about a source of competitive advantage. Besides these beneficial returns, there are also risk factors associated with this arrangement. From the perspective of FBes, a perceived risk factor has been introduced with the "Heuschrecken" analogy implying the accusation regarding a short-term exploitation of corporate resources in place of a long-term exploration.[6] In recognition of the negative examples reported in the media, among them prominent insolvencies of Märklin or Kampa, owners of FBes have become reluctant toward PE (e.g., Nagl, 2009b; Poech et al. 2005; Poutziouris, 2001; Upton & Petty, 2000). Poutziouris (2001), for example, acknowledges an "empathy gap" between family objectives and PE companies although the reserved attitude is reported to have improved recently (see Höppner, 2008; Leendertse, 2009; PricewaterhouseCoopers, 2007; Schalast & Barten, 2008). The search for minority investments constitutes an escalating phenomenon in this respect (e.g., Dierig, 2007; Dostert, 2009; Heckel, 2010; Financial Times Deutschland, 2010b). Finally, the risks of the counterparty, i.e., financial investors, should not be neglected. The consideration to acquire minority positions results in a significant challenge given that purposeful intervention techniques turn out to be beyond the control of PE companies, which deteriorates their monarchic self-perception. Moreover, the distinctiveness of FBes, as shortly addressed above, poses the severe questions whether and how PE companies can apply their business model to this organizational class; in conceptual terms, Huntington's (1996) doctrines of

6 According to Müntefering, "Wir müssen diejenigen Unternehmen, die die Zukunftsfähigkeit ihrer Unternehmen und die Interessen ihrer Arbeitnehmer im Blick haben, helfen gegen die verantwortungslosen Heuschreckenschwärme, die im Vierteljahrestakt Erfolg messen, Substanz absaugen und Unternehmen kaputt gehen lassen, wenn sie sie abgefressen haben" (2004: 6).

clashing cultures[7] represents a suitable image portraying this circumstance. In accordance with this notion, Achleitner and colleagues (2008c) summarize several conflictive dimensions of PE houses and FBes relating to organizational goals, decision-making processes, and self-conception.

1.1 Intention of this Publication

The image of clashing cultures certainly represents a critical threat for both PE companies and FBes. Despite this awareness, the metamorphosis of an entity, which is induced by a PE investment, constitutes an under-researched phenomenon, particularly for FBes (e.g., Cumming et al. 2007; Wright et al. 2009). In other words, a substantial lack of organizational studies, which academically consider, analyze, and derive inferences from the events following a PE investment in a FB, suggests deploying resources on the topic. In line with the previous argumentation, such a research endeavor can generate valuable scientific and practical implications. In scientific dimensions, gained insights might categorically enhance our understanding of the interplay and idiosyncrasies of both systems. In practical terms, evidence of the potential metamorphosis should assist in limiting uncertainty and in enabling decision-making of elevated consciousness for both entities. In essence, the general intent and overall aim of this research is thus to

> *enhance our understanding of the prospective metamorphosis of (former) German family firms in the course of a Private Equity investment.*

Following this research aim, two more subtle research questions are derived in section 2.3, *Research Questions: The Interplay of Family Businesses and Private Equity,* when the progression of this paper will have provided the context to thoroughly develop them. Thereby, delineations, definitions, and descriptions of FBes and PE houses, which are introduced in the next chapter, should allow for an elaborated determination of the questions. Nevertheless, an immediate acquaintance with the overall aim is expected to provide a better understanding concerning the further proceeding of this research.

7 Huntington's (1996) analyses and findings are based on civilizations and culture areas, such as the Islamic and Western Hemispheres. Nevertheless, the image of clashing systems helps to understand the institutional contradictions concerning an organizational level.

1.2 Balancing Practical Relevance and Theoretical Rigor

The followed research tradition resided on the empirical stratum; thus, generated knowledge emerged through observations of real life events, reinforcing the inductive principles of the philosophy of science. To guide this process, case studies were selected as the utilized method in this research. On the one hand, Dyer and Sanchez (1998) call for an enhanced application and revitalization of this method in response to the overwhelming complexity in FB research. On the other hand, Bird and colleagues (2002) suggest that case studies were the dominant scientific instruments in the beginning of FB research and nurtured insights that became institutionalized by auxiliary methods. Case studies were accordingly employed to cope with the complexity and novelty of the researched subject. *Appendix A* is dedicated to an elaborate discussion of and the study's applied methods as well as its design. Moreover, it also concretely describes the researched cases.[8]

Empirical research in the domain of FBes is usually positioned in the discipline of organization science. Thereby, it typically combines a variety of diverse research fields, for example, economics, sociology, or psychology. Klein (2010) points out that an interdisciplinary investigation always bears a degree of risk that such approaches might not be considered normative enough to encounter the entire scope of each discipline, yet she calls to courageously take up the challenge.[9] Deducing from the verbalized research aim, the predominant intention of this paper, however, was to make an effort to examine a real world phenomenon; therefore, it opposed the idea to make a pure paradigmatic contribution to any discipline. Formalizing this issue, Lounsbury and Ventresca (2002) state that organization science is frequently aimed at creating an understanding of how economic shifts have an impact on a researched object; the investment of a PE company in a FB should thus be considered as an analogy to the researchers' claim. Davis and Marquis (2005) refer to such a proceeding as "problem-driven work." They state that problem-driven research does not intend "to provide solutions to the problems faced by business managers" (2005: 334); rather, "problem-driven work is distinguished by its orientation toward explaining events in the world – starting with the question 'why is it that...?'" (2005: 334). The authors contrast this technique to "paradigm-driven research,"

8 It is advisable to read Appendix A in the aftermath of chapter 3 in order to appreciate its content and its diverse connections with auxiliary chapters.

9 According to Klein, "Es scheint ein Kennzeichen unserer Zeit zu sein, sich mit Themen isoliert nach Fachbereichen zu beschäftigen. Damit begibt sich derjenige, der die Integration verschiedener Disziplinen versucht, auf schwierigem Grund. Ein Fachmann einer Disziplin beherrscht den diese Disziplin betreffende Teil i. d. R. besser und kann im schlimmsten Fall den Autor des Dilletantismus überführen" (2010: 2).

which deduces hypotheses from theory and attempts to test generalizability. They argue that the former orientation of research has gained prominence and will continue to do so in the 21st century. Verification of this notion is recognized by Davis (2005), who substantiates the trend in academic journals toward a problem-driven ethos. A similar classification attempt is also promoted by Hodgkinson et al. (2001) as they refer to such proceedings as "pragmatic science."

Comparable to the former authors, Stokes (1997) differentiates between four research doctrines in the field of natural sciences, advancing the one-dimensional continuum of basic and applied research. He suggests that research can materialize in a combination of both societal usage and a search for fundamental knowledge; as a matter of fact, he typifies research endeavors to be based on a paradoxical logic[10] of rigor and relevance. The resulting pattern combining relevance and rigor, defined as the "Pasteur's Quadrant," is characterized to be the most promising method for stimulating both novel knowledge and societal use. Other patterns emerging are the "Bohr's Quadrant," reflecting a combination of low relevance and high rigor, as well as the "Edison's Quadrant," portraying a combination of high relevance and low rigor. Tushman and O'Reilly refer to Stokes' (1997) "Pasteur's Quadrant" in the field of social sciences and formulate their viewpoint that "dissertations are now often driven by disciplinary concerns" (2007: 772) though the scholars strongly suggest that "the source of research questions should be the phenomena, not the traditions or constraints of a given disciplinary point of view" (2007: 772). Although Lewin told us that "nothing is more practical than a good theory" (1952: 169), contemporary voices also substantiate that "nothing is as dangerous as a bad theory" (Ghoshal, 2005: 86). Hence, the development of a robust theory should always be dedicated to the actual phenomenon under investigation, which reinforces Klein's (2010) assertion for the domain of FBes. In consequence, the underlying study aspired to be positioned in the "Pasteur's Quadrant" of the social sciences in order to combine virtues of societal use and a quest for knowledge generation as visualized by Figure 1.

The "Pasteur's Quadrant" characterization of social science research re-

10 Many concepts and situations are interpreted as a paradox throughout this paper, such as Weick's (1976) concept of loosely coupled systems or the characterization of ambidextrous organizations (see Duncan, 1976; Tushman & O'Reilly, 1996). Lewis (2000) directs attention to this emerging phenomenon in the field of organization science. She defines the term as follows: "'Paradox' denotes contradictory yet interrelated elements – elements that seem logical in isolation but absurd and irrational when appearing simultaneously" (2000: 760). Thereby, she illustrates that the ability to think in paradoxes becomes more and more prominent in order "to live and even thrive within the plurality and changes of organizational life" (2000: 774). A recent publication by Smith and Lewis (2011) summarizes the topic and forms an initial theory concerning organizational paradoxes.

inforces the rigor and relevance discussion (see Baldridge et al. 2004; Bennis & O'Toole, 2005; Daft & Lewin, 2008; Daft & Lewin, 1990; Mowday, 1997; Nicolai, 2004; Shrivastava, 1987; Susman & Evered, 1978; Weick, 2001). As indicated above, Tushman and O'Reilly (2007) analyze the problem with the help of a paradoxical lens since they claim that rigor and relevance are not substitutable.[11] However, scholars usually argue that scientific discoveries, which are published in journal articles, fulfill the criterion of being rigor, but they fall short of being relevant. For example, Palmer's review for the 50 years anniversary of the *Administrative Science Quarterly* causes him to find "a group of scholars that might be aptly labeled the 'silent majority' that advocates disinterest in practical matters" (2006: 550). The reasons why the academic community does not manage to bridge spheres are multifarious. In essence, Hambrick (1994) indicates that there is a barrier inhibiting the diffusion of knowledge between theoretical and practical spheres, and even academic disciplines which are prone to practical application, such as the domain of strategic management, are classified to fail the principles of relevance (Bettis, 1991).

Figure 1: Three Quadrants of Social Science Research

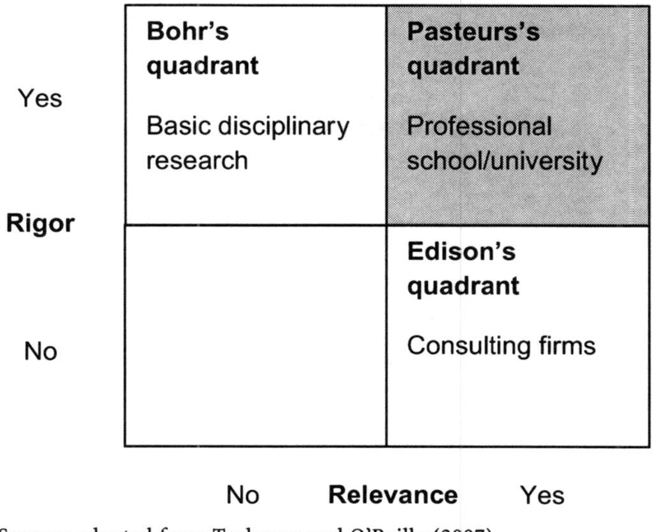

Source: adapted from Tushman and O'Reilly (2007)

11 Moreover, Mayring confirms that such a combination represents the most feasible approach in social science research: "In qualitative orientierter Forschung wird immer wieder betont, dass eine Trennung zwischen grundlagen- und anwendungsbezogener Forschung für die Humanwissenschaft weniger sinnvoll sein. [...] Der Ansatzpunkt humanwissenschaftlicher Untersuchungen sollen primär konkrete, praktische Problemstellungen im Gegenstandsbereich sein, auf die dann auch die Untersuchungsergebnisse bezogen werden können" (2002: 34–35).

From a theoretical viewpoint, Vermeulen provides a deliberation on the topic by building on Hegel's dialectic theory. He argues that "only a systematic change can synthesize both relevance (thesis) and rigor (antithesis)" (2005: 978). In order to reach such a synthesis, Vermeulen states that the most promising research attempts ask "questions that are of importance to reality" (2005: 979); these attempts, however, should not compose "concessions in terms of rigor in developing theory and empirical evidence" (2005: 979). In a later contribution, Vermeulen (2007) advances his viewpoint of asking relevant questions and proposes attempts that further stimulate relevance in academic papers. According to him, such attempts include to address variables under managerial control (see Brown & Eisenhardt, 1997; Szulanski & Jensen, 2006; Vermeulen & Barkema, 2002), to reveal concrete and measurable consequences of variables (see McNamara et al. 2003; Vermeulen & Barkema, 2002), and to create novel constructs (see Cohen & Levinthal, 1989; Levitt & March, 1988; March, 1991). In order to be capable of working both relevantly and rigorously, Vermeulen's (2007) primary argument pertains to the process of actions that stimulate communication between the opposing systems. For this purpose, the author presents the concept of "communication loops of rigor and relevance" and requests the researcher to interlink both spheres. In other words, researchers, being agents in both the academic and practical system, should strive to integrate the paradox of rigor and relevance by initiating discussions with people in organizations "to develop a real understanding of their circumstances" (2007: 759). Besides, these people should maintain the communication with fellow academics.

Measures for Streamlining Rigor and Relevance

Given the fact that case studies should emerge as both relevant and rigor, this paper drew on several criteria to satisfy the requirements proposed by Vermeulen (2007, 2005). The final paragraphs of this section therefore reveal the actual measures taken for streamlining both concepts.

Relevance

Regarding the sphere of relevance, the measures applied in this study predominantly embraced opening and closing chapters. In consequence, aspects of relevance should undoubtedly be found in the introduction, which demonstrated the significance of PE as a financing alternative for FBes and the reservation of proprietors to utilize the former. Unilateral communication with newspaper articles and practitioner-oriented research findings created insights of what seems relevant in the business world. Bilateral communication was accomplished with the help of expert interviews with PE managers regarding their viewpoint on the organizational development and dynamics following an investment in FBes. Precisely, two interviews which were conducted during the conceptualization phase of this study auxiliary assisted in generating awareness of the investigated set of issues. The insights generated in these interviews found application and expression in certain segments of this paper. For instance, the derivation of the guiding research questions was to some extent inspired by these interviews. Hence, Vermeulen's (2005) primary claim to develop relevant research questions was adhered to. Furthermore, variables and constructs were chosen to meet Vermeulen's (2007) criteria that the latter should be controllable, measurable, and novel. The issues are further elaborated in section 2.3. *Research Questions: The Interplay of Family Businesses and Private Equity.*

Rigor

With reference to the dimension of rigor, an outcome of the communication process with the academic community imposed to utilize diverse theories at different levels of abstractness for structuring the concrete researched problem. However, the scope of problem-driven, pragmatic science obligated to avoid proceedings that can be identified as overly normative (cf. Davis & Marquies, 2005; Hodgkinson et al., 2001). Following these implications, the progression of this thesis harmonized with Weick's (1996) evolutionary argumentation starting from the recommendation to "drop your tools" toward a more moderate approach to "drop your heavy tools" (Weick, 1999). By this means, the scholar advises to conduct research which is on the one hand normative in nature but also pragmatic to not lose sight of the underlying problem encountered. There was a good reason to only drop the heavy tools but to remain equipped with lighter ones. Weick's (1993) reconstruction of the Mann Gulch fire indicated that the claim of the firefighters' foreman to drop uniforms and equipment, in order to run away and escape from the fire, resulted in the dissolution of order, chaotic movements, and the death of several firefighters. Weick refers to this incident as a cosmological episode, i. e., a loss of sensemaking, which has triggered the disorganized individual behavior. According to Weick, "As the fire gains on them, Dodge says, 'Drop your tools,' but if the people in the crew do that, then who are they? Firefighters? With no tools?" (1993: 635). This example reveals that dropping one's scientific tools might not be in the best interest of the researcher. Rather, the story conveys that dropping one's *heavy* tools might have hypothetical maintained order and would have potentially enabled the firefighters to escape. In this manner, empirical investigations are supposed to have theoretical backgrounds facilitating the research process (Weick, 1999), but researchers should not be bound to the "straitjacket" (Daft & Lewin, 1990) of some *heavy* tools, disciplines, or organizational theories. This insight reflects a guiding notion throughout the underlying empirical inquiry and is notably revisited in later segments when discussing the topic of organizational change.

1.3 Outline of Chapters

According to Gilbert, knowledge is a social creation and writing is both "a process of discovery as well as a process of clarification and of communication" (2008: 486) for structuring this imagination. The reciprocal relationship between thinking, writing, and communicating leads to the subsequent question posed by Huff, "How can I know my writing will connect with its audience until I see their response to what I say?" (1999: 99).

It seems challenging, if not impossible, to answer this question when taking into account that reviewers of studies usually have the tendency to apply diverse review principles (e.g., Cummings and Frost, 1995; Jauch & Wall, 1989) and correspondingly achieve low consensus regarding their evaluations (e.g., Bowen et al. 1972; Lindsey, 1978; Scott, 1975). Summarizing this communication intricacy, Czarniawska remarks that the academic community achieves at best "an illusion of understanding what the Other is saying" (1998: 274). Nevertheless, the academic community fortunately agrees on certain elements facilitating the communication process between author and audience. For this purpose, Ambert and colleagues suggest that evaluative elements in qualitative research pertain to "the theoretical perspective and linkages to the literature, the analysis of data, matters of reliability and validity, sample adequacy, and, finally, procedures and ethics, including the role of the researcher" (1995: 883). In a similar vein, Daft (1995) describes reasons for the rejection of manuscripts that were submitted to the *Administrative Science Quarterly* and *Academy of Management Journal.* The author mentions that the major shortcomings in both quantitative and qualitative research papers pertain to a lack of theory, research design weaknesses, as well as missing interrelations between the parts of a paper.[12] Furthermore, he suggests that writing skills also constitute an important concern leading to the rejection of manuscripts. To overcome such liabilities, Daft remarks that personal thought processes should be clearly communicated throughout the paper as this openness comprises a "refreshing and positive characteristic" (1995: 178). Among other things, he eventually advises to concentrate on the paper's macrostructure because the "theory has to be congruent with the method, the

12 In a similar vein, Mayring (2002) stresses that the appropriate arrangement of chapters represents one of the most critical inputs for sound research in the field of social science. He predominantly advises to thoughtfully interrelate theoretical with methodical considerations: "Dies aber muss das Ziel sein: die Postulate auf der Theorieebene so zu konstruieren, dass der Zusammenhang mit den später vorgestellten Techniken deutlich wird" (2002: 24).

method with the results, the results with the discussion section, and all the sections with each other" (1995: 179).

Structure of Chapters

With regard to the illustrated suggestions above, a fundamental mechanism enabling the systematic sharing of thoughts is to find an appropriate macrostructure (e.g., Daft, 1995; Mayring, 2002). The selection of an appropriate macrostructure necessitated to purposefully consider the readers addressed. Although the findings of this study should pertain to a wide audience, Morris et al. (1987) suggest tailoring the message to a primary evaluation group. Schatzmann and Strauss even go one step further and indicate that the audience eventually dictates "what substance to include, what to emphasize, and the level and complexity of abstractions" (1973: 118). Following these thoughts, chapters and the overall composition of this book were cautiously organized to predominantly meet academic requirements given that theoretical and methodical deliberations encapsulate extensive segments of this study.

It was briefly mentioned that case study research constituted the utilized method in this investigation, which implies a high degree of variety for selecting the overall construction of this paper. Despite this freedom, this thesis adhered to an ordinary reporting technique for case studies; hence, a "linear-analytic structure" (Yin, 2003) was chosen. This structure approximates standard procedures of most journal articles, which are to define a problem being studied, conduct a literature review, describe methods, present conclusions, discuss the latter, and finalize the paper by deriving certain implications. Yin proclaims that such a macrostructure "is comfortable to most investigators and probably the most advantageous when research colleagues or a thesis or dissertation committee comprises the main audience" (2003: 153). Following the idea of a linear-analytic macrostructure, this book can broadly be segregated into three main building blocks, including seven chapters. Figure 2 summarizes the structure of this study.

Figure 2: Overview of Chapters

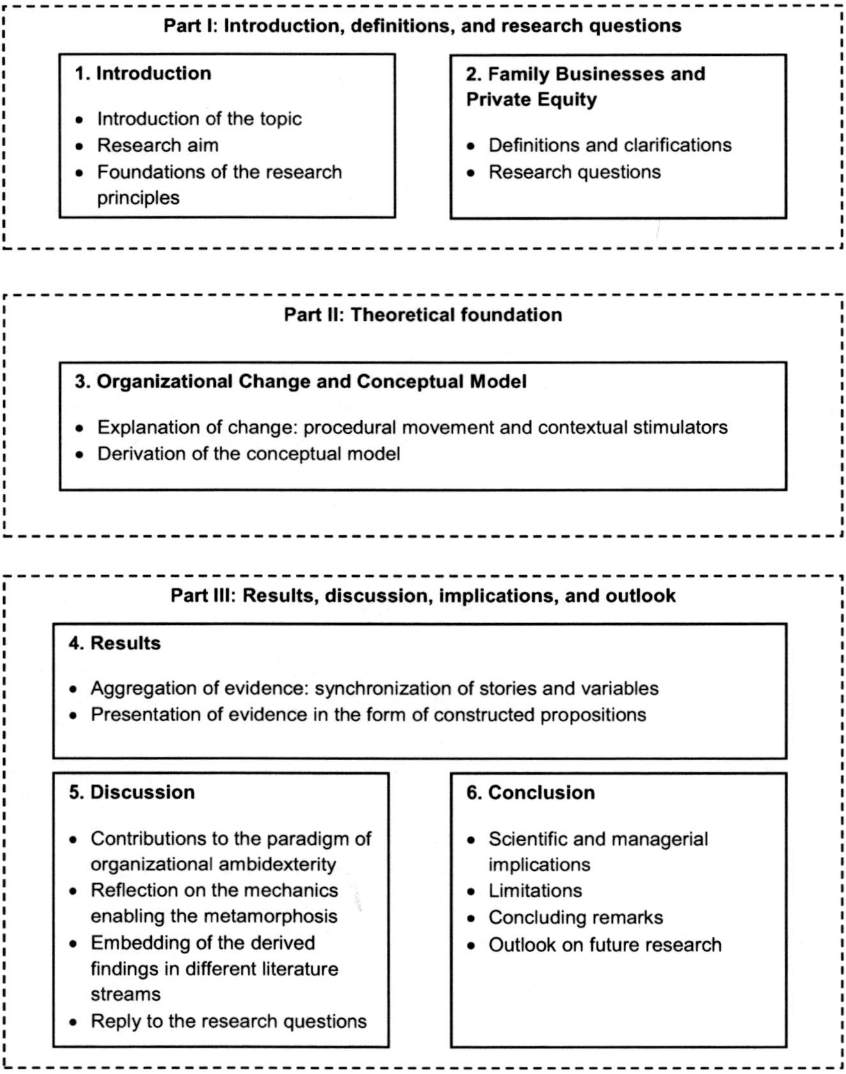

Source: author's illustration

The first part comprises this introductory chapter[13] as well as a further chapter that is devoted to an elaborate description and identification of the

13 The content of this book is formally structured along three levels. The first level is referred to as "chapters." Each chapter possesses of a variety of "sections," which pertain to the second level of order. Eventually, "subsections" are subordinate to sections.

problem studied. For this reason, chapter 2, *Family Businesses and Private Equity*, provides definitions utilized and briefly considers topics regarding FBes and PE companies. In addition, I review the existing literature on the topic of PE investments in FBes in order to more accurately position my research in the identified research gap. The development of the guiding research questions follows that review and also incorporates the results of the two conducted interviews with PE managers, who were specialized in investing in FBes. Accordingly, certain aspects of relevance find application in this chapter.

The second building block of this research consists of the theoretical foundation, to which chapter 3, *Organizational Change and Conceptual Model*, is dedicated to. In the third chapter, I concentrate on topics such as organizational theory, organizational change, as well as the derivation of the conceptual model guiding the research. The underlying logic follows the process that I first intend to show what organizational theory is and how I thought about it in this study. Hereupon, I discuss theories of organizational change and demonstrate the underlying dynamics enabling a corporate metamorphosis. Following this theoretical background, I derive the conceptual framework of this paper and enhance the discussion regarding the content of organizational change. In line with Daft's (1995) recommendation to focus on the interrelations of chapters, the derivation of the framework naturally affiliates to the second chapter.

The third fragment of this investigation consists of three chapters, explicitly results, discussion, and conclusion. Chapter 4, *Results*, portrays the empirical findings. To achieve an integrative fit among the chapters, the presentation of the results is aligned with the constructed conceptual model of chapter 3, *Organizational Change and Conceptual Model*. The primary findings of the results are summarized in the form of propositions, and they are subsequently scrutinized in chapter 5, *Discussion*. In other words, I make an attempt to connect emerging insights to the theoretical perspectives adopted. Chapter 6, *Conclusion*, finalizes this paper and considers the scientific and practical implications that follow from the results and the discussion. Moreover, I highlight the limitations of this paper according to diverse themes and critically assess certain shortcomings. Finally, a concise conclusion recapitulates the dominant achievements of this research and proposes directions for further research.

2. Family Businesses and Private Equity

This chapter is supposed to fulfill one primary concern: It develops and advances definitions and ideas utilized in the first chapter. Terminologies such as FBes, PE transactions, or PE companies are elaborated and defined for application purposes. In order to structure this proceeding, section 2.1, *Family Businesses*, decodes FBes, and section 2.2, *Private Equity*, addresses the domain of PE. Within each of these two sections, a considerable part is devoted to introduce initial ideas concerning the question why modifications in the ownership structure influence the researched object. For this purpose, subsection 2.1.2, *Conceptualization of a Family Business*, typifies FBes by highlighting the importance of the family. Similarly, subsection 2.2.2, *The Value Creation Process of Private Equity*, describes the role of PE houses in inducing change. Finally, in section 2.3, *Research Questions: The Interplay of Family Businesses and Private Equity*, two specific research questions are derived, whose substance, i. e., the employed constructs, is further refined in chapter 3, *Organizational Change and Conceptual Model.*

2.1 Family Businesses

At least two aspects of FBes were addressed in the first chapter: the intricacy to define a FB as well as their idiosyncrasies, which were illustrated by means of ten presumptions about their nature. Both aspects are elaborated subsequently to provide a foundation in terms of the utilized definition and to illustrate the specific situation arising from the coupling of families and businesses. Therefore, subsection 2.1.1, *Definition of a Family Business*, briefly discusses the complexity to derive a definition of the term and concludes with the motivation of the applied meaning. Subsection 2.1.2, *Conceptualization of a Family Business*, indicates how FBes can be modeled and how the models lay ground to an understanding of why an organizational metamorphosis is expected when these entities are subject to a buyout or a minority investment.

2.1.1 Definition of a Family Business

> What is a family business? People seem to understand what is meant by the term *family business*, yet when they try to articulate a precise definition they quickly discover that it is a very complicated phenomenon. Consider the following situations: A business is owned by a family but run by nonfamily managers. A business is owned by a large, multinational corporation but run by a local family. A business is jointly owned by two unrelated partners, each of whom has a son in the business. Are these all family businesses? (Lansberg et al. 1988: 1)

The preceding citation, quoted from the editorial note of the first volume of the *Family Business Review*, properly summarizes the substance of the debate concerning a definition of the term FB. While more than two decades and many volumes have passed since then, "researchers continue to disagree over the definition of a family business" (Chrisman et al. 2005: 555). A thorough definition is, however, considered of basic importance in order to scrutinize auxiliary fundamental issues of FBes, for example, questions pertaining to the issue whether FBes are born or made (see Chua et al. 2004) or the basis of their distinctiveness (see Sharma, 2004).

The three examples mentioned by Lansberg et al. (1988) assist in comprehending the complexity of the phenomenon and facilitate the inference that definitions can hardly ever reflect the multifarious reality. Litz (2008) indicates that most attempts to define a FB in research papers can be classified to be based on single, multiple, or integrative dimensions. Unilateral attempts exclusively rely on aspects of family ownership (see Davis & Harveston, 1998; Littunen & Hyrsky, 2000), family management (see Filbeck & Lee, 2000; Ward, 1990), or generational continuity (see Sharma et al., 1997; Tan & Fock, 2001). Furthermore, there are multilateral conceptualizations which depend on the role of either management or family ownership (see Chrisman et al. 2003; Chua et al. 2001). These approaches acknowledge family influence through dualistic, but exclusive, instances. The combination of both elements, that is management and ownership (see Astrachan, 1994; Kelly et al. 2000; Lansberg & Romano et al., 2000), is identified by Litz (2008) as a multiple conception. Finally, integrative conceptions consider an additional dimension besides ownership and management. This dimension might include particular business specifications (see Astrachan & Kolenko, 1994), for example.

The former classification attempts, despite of being unidimensional, multidimensional, or integrative, enhance our understanding of the applied definitions in empirical papers, which leads to the question of the underlying theoretical basis of such categorizations. By this means, scholars usually differentiate between a components-of-involvement and an essence approach. Chrisman et al. suggest that the "*components-of-involvement* approach is based implicitly on the belief that family involvement is sufficient to make a firm a family business" (2005: 556). Chua et al. (1999) remark that such a classification effort predominantly strives for finding an operational nature of family-owned firms, yet it falls short of analyzing a solid theoretical basis explaining why family involvement makes a difference. In this sense, the components-of-involvement approach mirrors an understanding of family enterprises by means of the principal agent framework. In contrast to the former approach, Chrisman et al. evaluate the essence approach to be "based on the belief that family involvement is only a necessary condition, family involvement must be directed toward behaviors that produce certain distinctiveness before it can be considered a family firm" (2005: 556–557). In other words, the essence approach reflects the second important theoretical perspective, i.e., the resource based view, in which the family is considered a resource for development. Scholars defining FBes by essence typically focus on particular processes that are stimulated by the interaction of both systems, such as the families' influence over the strategic direction (see Davis & Tagiuri, 1989), family firm behavior (see Chua et al. 1999), or familiness (see Habbershon et al. 2003). Concluding, Sharma and Nordqvist posit, "Both the components and the essence approaches are integral for capturing the diversity in family firms" (2007: 2). An approach synthesizing the components-of-involvement and the essence definition can be identified with regard to the F-PEC scale, developed by Astrachan et al. (2002), which is described as "[p]articularly impressive" (Sharma, 2004: 4) for its attempt to integrate ideas. The scale measures family influence with regard to three items: power, experience, and culture. Each item consists of further subscales building a comprehensive identification instrument to explicate FBes. Further studies identify the F-PEC scale as reliable (Klein et al., 2005) but also propose that the concept can still be viewed as immature (Rutherford et al. 2008). Nonetheless, Klein (2010) points out that the scale relies on at least one important characteristic: It overcomes the questionable dichotomy to force an all or nothing authentication of a company to either be or not be a FB. In general terms, Astrachan et al. stress the point that "dichotomizing family vs. nonfamily firms when no such clear-cut dichotomy exists creates more problems than it attempts to solve" (2002: 46).

Definition and Modus Operandi Utilized to Classify Family Businesses

Although scholars suggest that a thorough definition should incorporate the necessary and sufficient conditions, empirical reality makes it difficult to utilize elements from the essence method to identify the researched object prior to the empirical inquiry (e.g., Winter et al. 1998). The former empirical challenge is, for instance, verbalized by Chua et al. stating that a "theoretical definition sets the paradigm for the field of study and the standard against which the efficacy of an operational one must be measured" (1999: 23). The selection of an appropriate empirical definition thus usually results in a compromise because one can at best speculate about the essence nature before entering the field. Due to this circumstance, I utilized Wimmer's (2009) definition for identifying the researched cases in this inquiry.[14] According to the scholar, a FB represents an entity which is owned by one or more families. These families can stand in blood relationship to each other though they do not necessarily need to. The development of the entity under consideration should be intensely shaped by the owning families, which can either occur through operational management or further governance involvement.[15]

The definition proposed by Wimmer (2009) thus properly meets the borderline regarding the components-of-involvement and essence approach given that it concretely conforms to the necessary conditions while it simultaneously converges with sufficient prerogatives on a conceptual echelon, tolerating the classification of FBes prior to the investigation. Hence, the definition does neither dichotomize the field nor does it accept to opportunistically free-ride on the cases selected. In other words, a fairly unconstrained nature of the essence condition permitted to pragmatically enter the field. This was particularly useful since the sample of companies being subject to a PE investment is clearly biased toward companies which can be considered not to be family-owned. For instance, Achleitner et al. (2008a) are merely able to identify 97 minority investments in Germany over a 25 year period prior to their study. Furthermore, Klöckner (2008) reports a total amount of less than 300 buyouts from 1998 to 2007 in German FBes, and the BVK estimates that at least 75 percent of conducted buyouts pertain to corporate divestments, which represents an organizational species that was not acknowledged to qualify as a FB.

With reference to the necessary conditions, the definition shares characteristics with Klein's (2000) substantial family influence (SFI) factor, which rep-

14 According to Wimmer, "Es handelt sich um Unternehmen, auf deren Entwicklung eine Familie oder eine Konstellation mehrerer Familien, die miteinander verwandtschaftlich verbunden sind, aber nicht sein müssen, aus ihrer Eigentümerrolle heraus einen bestimmenden Einfluss ausüben [...]. Dieser Einfluss impliziert nicht notwendigerweise, dass ausschließlich jemand aus der Familie die Führungsrolle an der Unternehmensspitze bekleidet. Er kann auch gegenüber einem Fremdmanagement aus der Position eines Beirates oder eines Gesellschafterrates wahrgenommen werden" (2009: 5).

15 The utilized definition from Wimmer (2009) converges with Chua et al.'s (1999) determination of a FB. The authors state, "The family business is a business governed and/or managed with the intention to shape and pursue the vision of the business held by a dominant coalition controlled by members of the same family or a small number of families in a manner that is potentially sustainable across generations of the family or families" (1999: 24).

resents the power dimension of the F-PEC.[16] This scale was consequently utilized to operationalize parts of Wimmer's (2009) definition. Hence, necessary requirements were identified a priori by means of desk research (cf. Verschuren & Doorenward, 1999) through the analysis of corporate websites, newspaper articles, and third party databases. Sufficient conditions were verified by a combination of desk research and, in addition, by a self identification procedure as utilized in many empirical studies (see Astrachan & Kolenko, 1994; Davis & Harvestone, 1998; Sonfield & Lussier, 2004). To provide an example regarding the pursued approach: In certain cases the companies under consideration presented their family heritage and mission statements that facilitated to distinguish the family shaping influence. Self-identification was supplementarily taken advantage of; in fact, executives were asked whether they could validate that the owning families had influenced the companies' development. The utilization of such a questioning technique, that is the deliberate intent to gather information about the influence of the owning family on the business, partially avoided the general criticism accompanying the self-identification method, which is manifested in the claim that the determination of a FB leads to heterogeneous classification attempts given that informants draw on diverse definitions to classify their businesses (e. g., Chua et al. 1999). The selection of cases is further elaborated and discussed in *Appendix A.*

2.1.2 Conceptualization of a Family Business

Following the pluralism of defining a FB, it comes as no surprise that there is a lack of a unilateral abstraction or conceptualization of this organizational type. Explicating this thought, Zahra and Sharma suggest that "[f]amily firm research has come far but has a long way to go" (2004: 344). In order to shortly summarize how FBes are typified by the contemporary research community, the subsequent paragraphs are supposed to reveal certain established models.

Early scholars who have attempted to further abstract and explain FBes' idiosyncrasies relied on the combination of two subsystems, the family and the business, in order to appreciate the unique character of FBes (e. g., Aronoff & Ward, 1991; Gersick et al., 1997). A recent example of such a dualistic approach is provided by Litz (2008), who proposes that the relationship between the family and the business should be apprehended as a "Möbius strip," a band consisting

16 With reference to Klein (2000), the SFI is computed by means of the following formula: If $S_{Fam} > 0$, SFI: $(S_{Fam} / S_{Total}) + (MoSB_{Fam} / MoSB_{Total}) + (MoMB_{Fam} / MoMB_{Total})$ 1, where S = stock; MoMB = members of management board; MoSB = members of supervisory board; Fam = family member.

of a 180 degree twist prior to having its two ends connected. The description illustrates the idea that a FB exists due to the transfers of elements between the family and the company. The author substantiates that "the family-firm interface becomes increasingly Möbius-like whenever each system's outputs (the family's child and the firm's wages) are transferred *across* the systems to become the other system's inputs, that is, the firm's workforce and the family's income, respectively" (2008: 220). Decoding a FB by means of this constellation, scholars give attention to the paradoxes that emerge through the idiosyncratic rules of each system (see Schlippe, 2007; Schlippe et al. 2008; Simon et al. 2005). The resulting paradoxes are identified to either emerge as a valuable resource or a severe threat for a FB, which depends on the circumstance whether and how these paradoxes are managed. Advantages are contingent on agency benefits and family assets, such as human, social, or financial capital, and drawbacks are contingent on agency costs, specifically altruism, family liabilities, family conflicts, or a lack of appropriate managerial talent (e.g., Dyer, 2006). Nicholson (2008) formally summarizes four dimensions which are the source for potential advantages and risk factors: ownership identity, intergenerational transmission, teamwork between kin and nonkin, as well as genetic wildcard inheritance which "is the succession of family owners or executives who have different psychological characteristics from their forebears" (2008: 105).

The differentiation between agency and family factors implies that the conceptualization of a FB by means of a two system dogma, i.e., the introduced Möbius-strip model (Litz, 2008), lacks a decisive system parameter to better account for the inherent complexity. In response to the shortcoming, Tagiuri and Davis (1996) conceptualize a FB with regard to three interrelating subsystems: owners, family members, as well as the business. The conceptualization has attracted a wide scientific attention (Schlippe et al. 2008) because it portrays the complexity of FBes that operate with fragmented ownership structures due to their large size (Gersick et al., 1997). In empirical terms, Vilaseca (2002) validates the segregation of the family system into owners and family members given that the scholar discovers that all three subsystems possess different objectives and interests. Groth (2008) outlines the logics of each subsystem as follows: The business family represents a social unit in which values of personal recognition and equity dominate; the latter can, however, suffer from the circumstance that certain family members work in the business whereas others do not. Objectives in the ownership system naturally pertain to sound strategic decision-making, executed by certain proprietors. The premise must yet be fulfilled that the business should meet the requirements of the entire family. The logic pursued in the business is survival, but it is contingent on the context condition that family members exert a significant influence.

Besides conceptualizing a FB to be based on three interdependent subsystems, Pieper and Klein (2007) propose that four dimensions should be considered for abstracting the entity: the family, the business, the ownership, and the management. In comparison to Tagiuri and Davis' (1996) three-circle model, the conceptualization thus makes an additional distinction between the business and management sphere. The abstraction assigns a pivotal function to any individual and accentuates their illusive roles in each of the four subsystems. Eventually, the four subsystems are described to be framed by the general environment. In sum, the individual, each subsystem, and the environmental level form a "bulleye," to which the authors refer to as an "indication of where the development of a distinctive theory of the family firm may start from" (Pieper & Klein, 2007: 310).

Figure 3: Dual, Triple, and Quad Conceptualizations of a Family Business

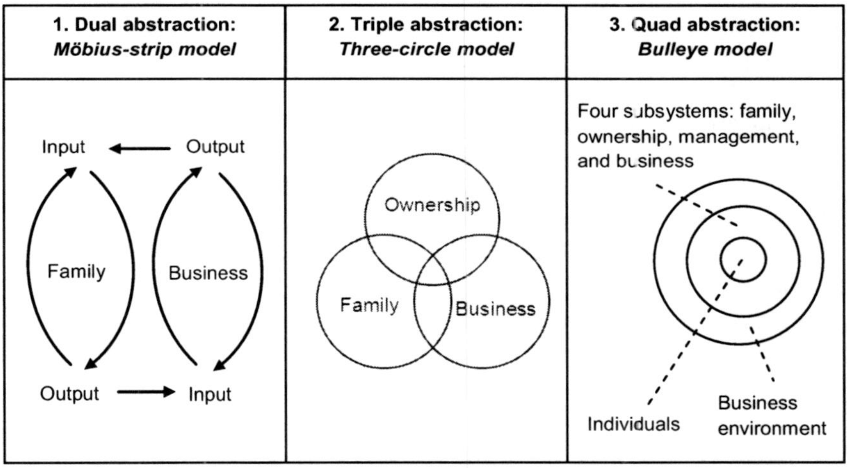

Source: adapted from Litz (2008), Gersick et al. (1997), and Pieper and Klein (2007)

Discussion of the Models With Regard to the Research Intention

Gersick et al. maintain, "The reason that the three-circle model has met with such widespread acceptance is that it is both theoretically elegant and immediately applicable" (1997: 7). Based on this notion, which is probably true for all presented abstractions, the conceptualizations can be utilized to meaningfully and pragmatically underline the research intention of this study, which is to derive an enhanced understanding of the modifications when PE companies invest in FBes.

The most insightful perspective pertains to the one derivable from the three-circle model. According to this viewpoint, the investment of PE companies in

FBes results in two altered situations. In a minority investment, the ownership subsystem is modified whereas the family system remains unaffected. Therefore, the entity can still be considered a FB given that the sufficient condition, that is familiness, and the necessary one, that is family ownership, are not expected to be significantly altered. In a majority investment, in contrast, the corresponding family is most likely to resign from the entire equity ownership and also from the entire family subsystem. Therefore, the family loses its shaping influence. It is questionable whether the entity can still be considered a FB or whether one should speak of a former FB under this circumstance. Furthermore, Pieper and Klein's (2007) bulleye model provides a thorough understanding of the dynamics: The ownership subsystem becomes modified in a minority transaction whereas the ownership, family, and management subsystems are likely to change in a majority investment scenario. Litz's (2008) Möbius strip, however, merely provides an inferior description of the dynamics since it does not contain an ownership dimension. Nevertheless, the latter abstraction highlights the crucial issue that the family identification should remain unaffected in case of a minority investment while the symbiosis of a family and its business potentially breaks apart in most majority transactions.

In conclusion, all three models can be utilized with an escalating precision to initially analyze why the existence of an entity as a FB is put into jeopardy when attracting PE financing. Drawing on any of the proposed models, the understanding of further theoretical issues concerning organizational change, primarily raised in later segments (cf. section 3.1), should thus be facilitated. Both transaction types, minority and majority investments, are explained more intensely in the following section.

2.2 Private Equity

The intention of this section is to provide the basis to understand the PE topic and hence to pragmatically consider the aspects that are important for the development of the argumentation. Concentration is drawn to the differentiation of the various investment types and the nature of PE companies in subsection 2.2.1, *Definitions in the Field of Private Equity.* Hereupon, subsection 2.2.2, *The Value Creation Process of Private Equity,* highlights themes such as the rise of PE and the value creation hypothesis. Finally, the course of action of PE companies is clarified in order to indicate that value creation is connected to changes in portfolio companies during the holding period.

2.2.1 Definitions in the Field of Private Equity

In this subsection, the definitions of the terms "PE investments" and "PE companies" are derived. Contingent on these derivations, both terms are considered with regard to their application in this research. Employed definitions are reverted to in certain methodical segments of this thesis (cf. *Appendix A*).

Differentiation of Private Equity Investments

> What is private equity? The categories of investments that fall within the general rubric of private equity include venture capital; mid-stage company finance; distressed firm investment; LBOs of firms, divisions, or subsidiaries of public and private companies; and going-private deals. (Masulis & Thomas, 2009: 222)

The statement above exemplifies the pluralistic usage of the term "Private Equity." For this reason, Kaserer et al. (2007) distinguish between Venture Capital (VC), which serves as a financing source for young companies, and investments in mature companies, which are achieved by minority and majority investments.[17] The latter investment type is referred to as PE in the following. Companies financed with the help of VC usually operate in emerging industries and have innovative business models. Gompers and Lerner (2001) describe these companies as young and entrepreneurial; these entities are plagued by high levels of uncertainty as they are subject to large information asymmetries between owners and investors. In contrast, PE investments in mature companies are usually associated with lower information asymmetries given that those companies have established a thorough track record in their corresponding markets. Phalippou (2007) estimates that one third of global investment funds are dedicated to VC whereas two thirds focus on PE.

This study concentrates on "Private Equity im eigentlichen Sinne" (Kaserer et al. 2007: 14), precisely minority and majority commitments in mature FBes. A minority investment is defined as a less than 50 percent equity stake in a target company's capital stock, which is supposed to entitle its owner with voting power (cf. Achleitner et al., 2008a).[18] The domain of majority investments

17 Kaserer et al. remark, "Die Begriffe *Private Equity* und *Venture Capital* werden international unterschiedlich verwendet. Während in Deutschland und einigen anderen europäischen Ländern die Begriffe Beteiligungskapital, Private Equity und Venture Capital oft synonym genutzt werden und häufig dabei Venture Capital als Oberbegriff fungiert, unterscheidet man in den USA traditionell zwischen Private Equity als Oberbegriff und Private Equity im engeren Sinne (i. e. S.), sowie Venture Capital als Subkategorien" (2007: 13 – 14).

18 According to Achleitner et al., "Bei einer *stimmberechtigten Minderheitsbeteiligung* […] hält die Private-Equity-Gesellschaft […] Anteile am stimmberechtigten Eigenkapital. Hierzu

emerges more heterogeneously. These investments usually depend on the utilization of high portions of debt, besides equity, causing the classification of majority investments as leveraged buyouts (LBOs). Debt levels approximately range from 60 to 90 percent of the transaction value (e.g., Kaplan & Strömberg, 2009). Why are majority investments levered? With regard to early insights of Modigliani and Miller (1958), it is a common assumption that capital structures do not matter, but leverage seems rational in the world of PE (Axelson et al., 2009). The utilization of equity, which is raised prior to the target selection, combined with debt, raised when the transaction is negotiated, is expected to trigger improved decision-making (Axelson et al. 2009). Majority investments can be further subcategorized with regard to third party buyers involved in the transaction. Thereby, a well-established differentiation in the literature adheres to the following categorization: management buyouts (MBOs), management buyins (MBIs), buyin management buyouts (BIMBOs), and institutional buyouts (IBOs) (e.g., Kaserer et al. 2007). In an MBO, the incumbent management in place and a PE house collectively buy a majority stake in a target company. In an MBI, outside managers and PE companies jointly acquire a business. If external and internal managers collectively acquire a company with the help of a PE company, the buyout is considered a BIMBO. Finally, an IBO pertains to a transaction that is initiated by a PE investor. Empirically, it is sometimes difficult to distinguish which buyout form is actually taking place since the boundaries between the types can become blurred. Figure 4 visualizes the classification attempt of Private Equity investments.

Differentiation of Private Equity Companies

Comparable to the differentiation of PE investments, PE companies themselves can be further categorized. Attention is hence paid to two decisive criteria: legal structure and investing behavior. Both dimensions are briefly discussed before the final segment of this subsection reveals the employed transaction types and the characteristics of the corresponding PE companies.

Legal structure. PE companies are traditionally arranged as limited partnerships and invest in assets by means of several funds, which have a life span between five and seven years. Limited partners supply the funds' money and delegate responsibility for the resource allocation and operational management to the general partners (e.g., Sahlman, 1990). Limited partners are the residual claimants of the funds' profits. General partners are remunerated by an annual

kommt es durch eine Übernahme von Gesellschaftsanteilen bzw. durch eine Erhöhung des Stamm-/Grundkapitals. Der Beteiligungsgeber ist damit Gesellschafter des Unternehmens. Bei der stimmberechtigten Minderheitsbeteiligung hält der Beteiligungsgeber allerdings nur eine Minderheit am stimmberechtigten Eigenkapital, d.h. weniger als 50 %" (2008a: 11).

management fee, a percentage of realized investments, carried interest, and sometimes deal fees for monitoring companies they have invested in (e.g., Metrick & Yasuda, 2010). In principal, every individual and institutional investor can function as a limited partner in a PE partnership; in other words, everybody may invest money in a PE company during the fund-raising stage. Most PE companies, however, have minimum investment levels discriminating against most private investors to participate. Experts estimate that only six

Figure 4: Classification of Private Equity Investments

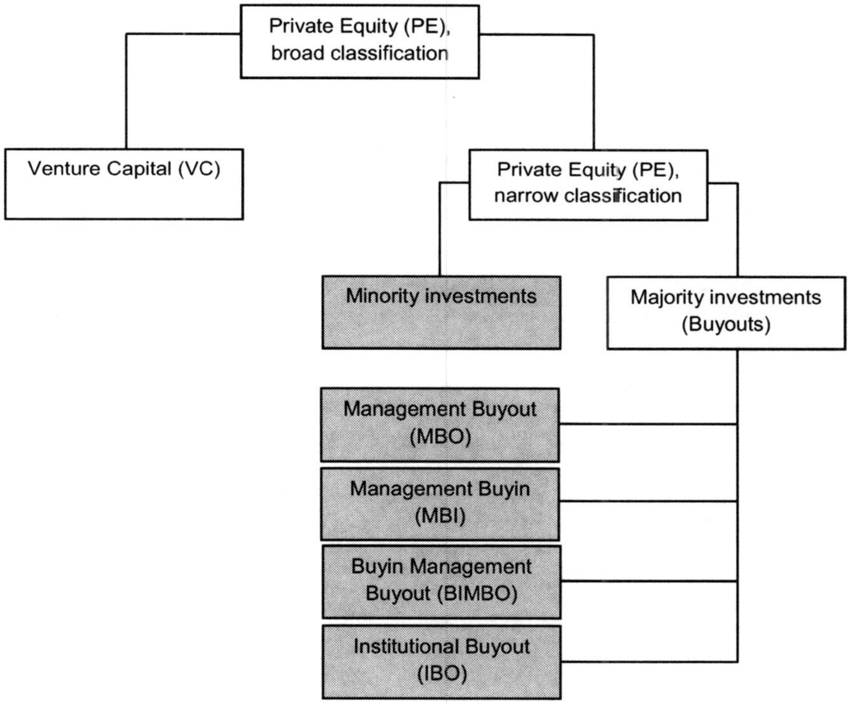

Source: adapted from Kaserer et al. (2007)

percent of the money raised by limited partnerships is provided by private investors (Böhler, 2006). As a response to this obstacle, the rise of new organizational forms, such as quoted investment funds or listed companies investing in private companies, has transformed the PE landscape. Scholars refer to such arrangements as Listed Private Equity (LPE) (see Bergmann et al. 2009; Lahr & Herschke, 2009). An example of the aforementioned listing behavior can, for example, be identified with regard to a KKR fund which was floated in 2006 by raising five billion dollars (Timmons, 2006). LPE permits that limited partners can cash out positions and also enables them to further increase AUM. Furthermore, it fulfills the private investors' appetite for alternative investments.

Investing behavior

Comparable to the legal pluralism having emerged, PE companies can also be differentiated concerning their functional investing behavior (e. g., Goosens et al. 2008). For this reason, Achleitner et al. (2008a) suggest typifying PE companies by means of four criteria. They propose that the holding period, the invested capital, the aspired hurdle rate, as well as the magnitude of intervention with the portfolio company serve as potential elements which allow for a categorization of financial investors. The subsequent classification is based on these criteria: "Mittelständische Beteiligungsgesellschaft" (MBG), "Moderate Private-Equity-Gesellschaft," and "Klassische Private-Equity-Gesellschaft."[19] In essence, the invested capital, the required rate of return, and the magnitude of intervention ascend with respect to the previous classifications. The fourth criterion, holding period, descends along the identified categories. Concretely, "Klassische Private-Equity-Gesellschaften" require the highest rate of return, obtain the shortest holding periods, engage in the largest deals, and most severely interfere in the management of their portfolio companies. The following figure visualizes the categorization attempt.

19 According to Achleitner et al., "*Mittelständische Beteiligungsgesellschaften* lassen sich durch sehr moderate Renditeanforderungen (etwa 15 %), kleine Investitionssummen, eine lange Haltedauer und sehr geringe Einflussnahmen auf das Unternehmen charakterisieren. Neben der Renditeoptimierung verfolgen Mittelständische Beteiligungsgesellschaften (MBGs) bewusst das Ziel der breiten Förderung des Mittelstands. *Moderate Private-Equity-Gesellschaften* stehen für meist mäßige Renditeanforderungen (etwa 15 bis 20 %), mittelgroße Investitionen, eine mittel- bis langfristige Haltedauer und moderater Einflussnahme. Dieser Typ von Private-Equity-Gesellschaft ist oftmals bankennah und zeichnet sich durch einen Fokus auf mittelständische oder familiengeführte Unternehmen aus. *Klassische Private-Equity-Gesellschaften* weisen hohe Renditeanforderungen, große Investitionssummen, eine kürzere Haltedauer und stärkere Einflussnahme auf. Sie haben oftmals einen angelsächsischen Hintergrund und sind international tätig" (2008a: 36 – 37).

Figure 5: Classification of Private Equity Companies

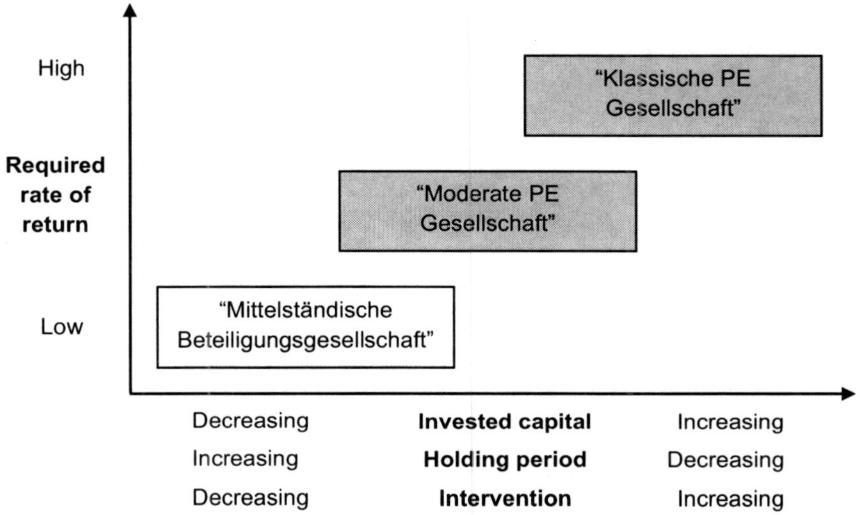

Source: adapted from Achleitner et al. (2008a)

Applied Definitions Regarding Private Equity Investments and Companies

I paid attention to four types of investments in this paper: Minority investments, MBOs, MBIs, BIMBOs, and IBOs were employed to describe the researched cases. The five classification attempts are utilized in method sections to distinguish between the transaction structures (cf. *Appendix A*).

However, I did not differentiate between the legal forms of PE companies in this thesis. In other words, the fact whether a limited partnership or a LPE company was acquiring the company under investigation had no effects on the sample of companies being studied. On the one hand, there was no theoretical motivation for discriminating against any legal form. On the other hand, empirical accessibility was not further restricted.

In contrast, I made a distinction pertaining to the population of PE companies, which was based on the investing behavior. Rationalized by the circumstance that "Mittelständische Beteiligungsgesellschaften" are supposed to promote economic development, the intrinsic political objectives might raise concerns how these can be compared to the business model of market-oriented PE companies. This aspect is essentially vital when reflecting on the theoretical foundation of organizational change, becoming relevant in a subsequent segment of this paper. In consequence, this type of PE companies was not part of the investigation.

2.2.2 The Value Creation Process of Private Equity

The capabilities of buyouts are described in the literature to function as healthy arbitrageurs, and VC is considered to operate as a growth catalyst. Both transaction types have been found to make valuable contributions at a macroeconomic level (see Phalippou, 2007). This evidence, coupled with the observation that PE companies experienced extraordinary growth levels (cf. chapter 1), calls for a plausible explanation since the reasons driving the effect remained unexplored up to this stage. In order to understand this effect, researchers have expended efforts to investigate the return characteristics of PE funds. Kaplan and Schoar (2005) compare the returns of PE and VC funds with the Standard and Poor's (S&P) 500 index. They find that buyout and VC funds outperform the benchmark gross of management fees; however, the set of funds falls short of beating the index net of fees. In a similar vein, Phalippou and Gottschalg (2009) report that PE funds underperform the S&P 500 net of fees by three percent but outperform the benchmark gross of fees by an equal percentage. A study conducted by Hwang et al. (2005), focusing on VC funds only, also indicates positive returns gross of fees and negative returns net of fees. In conclusion, empirical findings emphasize that PE companies seem to create value which is not absorbed by the funds' investors. High management fees of PE companies ranging from 7 percent (Kaplan & Schoar, 2005) to 12 percent (Swensen, 2000) explain this outcome. Moreover, researchers report increased risk profiles of PE companies, for example, a CAPM beta of 1.2 when using stock price returns of LPE (Bergmann et al. 2009). Two consequences follow from these studies (Phalippou, 2007): First, the average PE fund is not worth investing in. This observation constitutes an appealing academic shortcoming given that the rise of PE remains an unexplored issue. Second, although positive abnormal returns are not passed on to limited partners, the business model of PE companies seems to generate value.

Business Model of Private Equity Companies

> To understand the venture capital industry, one must understand the whole 'venture cycle.' The venture capital cycle starts with raising a venture fund; proceeds through the investment in, monitoring of, and adding value to firms; continues as the venture capital firm exits successful deals and returns capital to its investors; and renews itself with the venture capitalist raising additional funds. (Gompers & Lerner, 2001: 152)

Although the scholars refer VC, their description converges with the cycle of majority and minority investments in mature enterprises. Research efforts are thus settled within these stages, and each stage considers certain idiosyncratic problems. Both verdicts formulated in the previous paragraph, describing the unexplored issue of the rise of PE and the notion that PE creates value, are utilized to structure the following argumentation. Figure 6 visualizes the PE cycle and highlights the monitoring stage, which represents the phase this study focuses on.

Figure 6: Private Equity Cycle

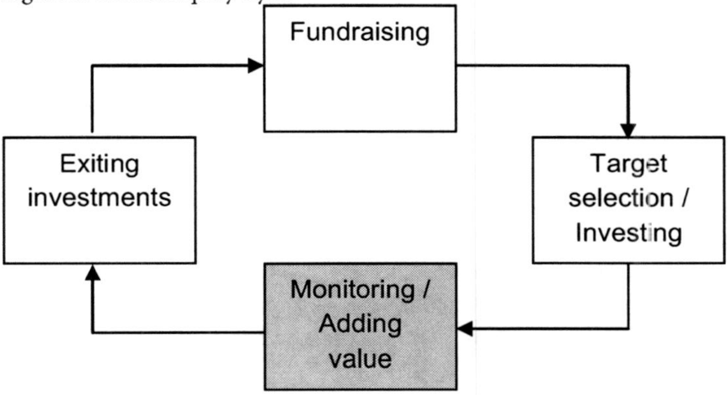

Source: author's illustration

Rise of Private Equity

As indicated in the previous paragraph, an explanation why so many investors give money to PE companies, although these appear to deliver inadequate risk and return characteristics, can be identified to remain unanswered. Nevertheless, research on the fundraising stage is concerned with the following questions: Why and how do these entities evolve? Authors argue that the frequency and extent of raised funds eventually mirrors the state of the economy; in good times investors sense reasonable opportunities to acquire companies whereas they rather focus on already established investments in bad times (Black & Gilson, 1998). Academics furthermore reason that the governance situation of these entities, traditionally arranged as partnerships, provides strong incentives under agency considerations (see Jensen, 1989), which causes their origination. Furthermore, the learning hypothesis suggests that established PE companies have an increased propensity to raise additional funds (Gompers & Lerner, 2001), which explains the growth of established PE companies but again falls short of explaining the appearance of novel companies.

Value creation of Private Equity

The second verdict implying that PE companies create value, inferred from the circumstance that PE funds outperform capital markets gross of fees, corresponds to the remaining three stages of the investment cycle, namely the target selection, the holding period, as well as the exit stage. Value creation should be segregated into two distinct elements. On the one hand, value creation can be artificial; hence, it might only symbolize an investor's ability to exploit market inefficiencies. On the other hand, value creation can arise through an increased performance of portfolio companies following a PE investment.

In confirmation of the artificial value generation perspective, researchers focus on the stages of target selection and exiting. With regard to target selection, scholars pay attention to understand the allocation of capital and argue that value is created via "cherry picking" activities (Popov & Roosenboom, 2009), which is investing in companies with above-average growth prospects (e.g., Engel & Keilbach, 2007; Hellman & Puri, 2000). In this light, Sorenson and Stuart (2001) find that financial investors search for targets in industries they are familiar with in order to proficiently evaluate investment opportunities. Ljungquist and Richardson (2003) show that the time dedicated to the search process increases when the identification of opportunities becomes more competitive. Fierce competition also leads to a substantial increase in the valuations of takeover targets (Gompers and Lerner, 2000). Nonetheless, Bargeron and colleagues (2007) report that PE companies, compared to public companies, pay less money for targets, implying that they have better bargaining and selecting competences. Directing attention to the exit stage, PE companies might in contrast have inferior capabilities in exiting investments. PE investors are found to be reluctant to realize their losses (e.g., Odean, 1998) as they keep "living dead investments" in their portfolios (Phalippou, 2007). Investors are likewise examined to exit promising investments too early in order to build a positive reputation, thereby signaling the quality of their investments to the market. The latter move advances their position for raising capital for new funds (Gompers, 1996).

In contrast, returns might also stem from real improvements made by the portfolio companies, which develop over the holding period. To categorize such value generating advancements, Cumming et al. propose to term these "real returns." The academics imply that "real returns" are based on an "impact on economic efficiency" (2007: 440). Scholars usually refer to three dynamics facilitating a wealth creation in buyout scenarios: financial, governance, and operational engineering (e.g., Kaplan and Strömberg, 2009; Kaserer et al. 2007). Financial engineering and governance modifications are based on three procedures: the incentivization of management through higher equity stakes, board control and more active governance, as well as the employment of increased leverage. These methods are usually associated with majority engagements; therefore, they are not directly applicable to minority investments. The third instrument, operational engineering, should find application under both forms of contracting. Kaplan and Strömberg clarify the term and its importance as follows: "Financial and governance engineering were common by the late 1980s. Today, most large private equity firms have added another type that we call 'operational engineering,' which refers to industry and operating expertise that they apply to add value to their investments" (2009: 132). Klier et al. (2009) even go one step further and suggest that operational engineering represents the dominant source of value creation in the contemporary market environment. They note that PE companies "have increased their operational capacity and now focus more strongly on active ownership and intervention in their portfolio companies" (2009: 7). Additional evidence regarding the concrete nature of real returns is incorporated when deriving the research questions in the following section.

2.3 The Interplay of Family Businesses and Private Equity

Having concisely illustrated fundamental thoughts, courses of action, and relevant literature streams regarding FBes and PE, academic insights on the interaction of both systems can be considered underdeveloped. Buyouts in FBes were long neglected by the research community because the topic did not seem to be particularly appealing. The buyout wave during the 1980s which reached peak with the takeover of *RJR Nabisco* by *Kohlberg Kravis Roberts & Co.* (*KKR*), documented by Burrough and Helyar (1989) in their book *Barbarians at the gate: The fall of RJR Nabisco*, naturally served as an inspiration for both practitioners as well as academics to predominantly direct attention to the phenomenon of public-to-private transactions. From an academic viewpoint, Kaufman and Englander (1993) illuminate the business practices of *KKR* to which they refer to as the restructuring of American capitalism. They posit that "KKR's innovations were its ability to overcome investors' collective action and monitoring problems by arranging takeovers through limited partnerships and by managing acquired firms through shared equity ownership with management" (1993: 52). At the same time, Jensen's (1989) significant paper on the *Eclipse of the public corporation* more formally facilitated the attention concerning buyouts of listed companies. The message delivered by Jensen (1989) was primarily based on agency arguments contending that liberated mechanisms in public-to-private transactions assist in prevailing over the shortcomings of publicly held equity. The scholar reasons that the emergence of PE transforms, innovates, and revitalizes the organizational landscape since it revises the dominating conflict between owners and managers, which is the separation of ownership and control (e.g., Fama & Jensen, 1983).

In family-owned enterprises, though, the former argument is hardly applicable due to the circumstance that agency costs differ from those of public corporations as they might be lower or higher (e.g., Chrisman et al., 2004). Wright et al. argue, "Agency theory has shortcomings when applied to the broad sweep of private equity-backed buyout types, as in some cases pre-ownership change agency problems were likely low (e.g., family firms)" (2009: 353). Following this argumentation, agency problems might often be non-existent in FBes, which is especially true for the first generation (e.g., Blanco-Mazagatos et al. 2007). Nevertheless, they might also be higher compared to public corporations, triggered by altruistic behavior (e.g., Karra et al. 2006; Schulze et al. 2002; Villalonga & Amit, 2006). It is speculative whether this level of complexity serves as an explanation for the wide ignorance of scholars regarding PE investments in FBes, yet it might represent an important factor of relevance. Research in this topic can for this reason be considered more theoretically diverse and complex in comparison with investigations of buyouts of listed corporations. Moreover, there are auxiliary reasons that might have inhibited the concentration on FBes. The difficult data situation that stems from private-to-private transactions should be appreciated as a constraining factor. Furthermore, the general academic tendency which failed to notice the distinctive character of FBes might be another potential explanation for the immature literature of PE investments in FBes. Fortunately, the topic has gained momentum over the past years. The literature review in *Appendix B* summarizes these attempts and provides the foundation for the derivation of the following research questions.

Derivation of Research Questions

Spradley (1980) suggests distinguishing between two levels of research questions in order to functionally organize and limit the scope of any research. According to him, the derivation of a research question can either proceed from general to specific dimensions or from specific to more general ones. He advises to proceed from general to specific questions given that specific questions do not frame early activities but "might emerge later as important" (1980: 76). In accordance with Spradley (1980), the general dimension of the research was verbalized with the objective to "enhance our understanding of the metamorphosis of (former) German family enterprises in the course of a PE investment" (cf. section 1.1). The specific research questions are consequently derived in this section. For this purpose, Punch (2006) maintains that research questions are supposed to fulfill certain quality criteria to be classified as decent interrogations. The proposed five cornerstones impose that questions should be clear, specific, answerable, interconnected, and substantially relevant. Clarity and specificity pertain to universal standards of science. Answerability and interconnectedness are related to the empirical practice of each research. Relevance is defined by Punch (2006) as a criterion that optimally emerges as a combination of praxis and theory. Hence, the research questions, posed subsequently, were derived by integrating the former insights.

1. How is organizational performance influenced in FBes in the course of PE investments?
2. What are the intra-organizational determinants which energize this prospective development?

Naturally, a variety of associated questions could have been formulated in addition for advancing the above postulated interrogations; research questions should, however, focus on the most important studied elements (Spradley, 1980). The above derived questions consequently served as an element that facilitated the generation of results, yet the scope of the research questions did not limit my perspective on auxiliary issues concerning certain themes in FB research. Dyer and Sanchez (1998), for instance, identify the shortcoming that in the leading journal for FBes, the *Family Business Review*, a percentage of less than four percent of published articles was dedicated to themes such as organizational adaptation and change over a ten year period from 1988 to 1997. Recently, Hatum and Pettigrew contend that the existing "family business literature has not directly tackled the issue of adaptation" (2004: 238).

In sum, the binary outline of the research questions, which are subordinate to the research intention, assisted in effectively structuring the empirical progression since they focused my attention on particular data. In doing so, deliberations of Punch (2006) regarding answerability and interconnectedness should have found a solid application. Relevance of the derived research questions naturally resulted from the synchronization of both the immaturity and the momentum effects characterizing the research field. In order to further augment the criteria of clarity and specificity, the above presented research questions are elaborated in the following paragraphs. The explanation considers their characteristics and draws on supplementary empirical contributions from the domain of PE investments in nonfamily-owned firms. Moreover, insights of two conducted interviews with PE managers, who specialized in the field of investing in FBes, are incorporated given that these facilitated the development of the research questions and the utilized constructs. In fact, Vermeulen's (2007, 2005) requirement to maintain a dialogue with practical spheres was hereby realized (cf. section 1.2).

Discussion of the Research Questions

Achleitner et al. consciously observe that "it is of great interest to investigate the impact of private equity investments on the performance of family firms"

(2008b: 25) whereby a comprehensive "analysis of the levers that drive the success of the partnership would increase the transparency of this form of financing" (2008b: 25). In essence, this call for future research papers summarizes the nature of the two proposed research questions: Organizational performance and its determinants are concepts which deserve a further clarification.

Organizational performance

The first interrogation aims at uncovering elements to which Achleitner et al. (2008b) refer as performance. March and Sutton (1997) reflect on the characteristics of *Organizational performance as a dependent variable* and emphasize that the utilization of organizational performance as a dependent construct constitutes a problematical endeavor. The reasons are multifold and pertain to the construct's instability throughout space and time or the oversimplification of a complex world, among other things. Furthermore, the fact that organizations do not always reliably report their "performance" represents a well known dilemma. This behavior was, for example, demonstrated by the accounting scandals of Enron and WorldCom. On the other side of the coin, PE managers expressed that an increased financial performance, driving corporate value, represents the eventual target pursued, and one investment manager remarked that this "is independent of the fact whether our company invests in family firms or public corporations." In consequence, a tradeoff can be identified between academic warnings related to an empirical nihilism trap and the claim of practitioners to consider a performance variable. This dilemma resulted in the compromise not to further define this construct at this early stage of the paper, but certain preliminary thoughts are provided in the following.

Without foreclosing the substance of later arguments, insights from VC-backed companies illustrate that financial investors enhance the innovation activity of their portfolio companies (Kortum and Lerner, 2000). Similarly, Lerner et al. (2008) empirically demonstrate that PE-sponsored companies – this time the researched sample constitutes of LBOs – show an improved product quality and higher numbers of filed patents, which are especially based on the portfolio companies' core competencies. Recently, Ughetto (2010) empirically reinforces the findings presented by Lerner et al. (2008) as he finds evidence that the patent behavior of European manufacturing firms, having changed owners via buyouts, increases by 50 percent compared to the situation prior to the transaction within a relatively short time horizon. Further papers in this area demonstrate that MBOs enhance new product development and facilitate entrepreneurial activities (see Bruining and Wright, 2002; Wright et al. 2001a; Wright et al. 2001b; Wright et al. 2000; Wright et al. 1992; Zahra, 1995). Thereby, these studies refuse the argument concerning a myopic behavior, which often serves as an accusation concerning the business model of PE houses. In contrast, these findings seem to verify that PE-sponsored companies develop in positive terms regarding long-run innovation skills. In a similar vein, studies consistently identify positive productivity gains for companies with PE owners (see Amess, 2003; Amess, 2002; Bull, 1989; Harris et al. 2005; Lichtenberg and Siegel, 1990). For instance, Lichtenberg and Siegel (1990) report median productivity gains of almost six percent, realized in the first three years after a LBO. In order to validate these positive efficiency gains which result from an investment, Ofek studies unsuccessful buyouts and reports "no increase in operating performance following the buyout attempt" (1994: 637).

In sum, these gains, related to increased innovation skills and productivity, represent "real returns" (Cumming et al. 2007), which were introduced in this chapter (cf. subsection 2.2.2). The positive development of these real returns consequently constitutes a central inference for deriving the appropriate performance construct in a later part of this publication (cf. section 3.2). The derivation of the construct additionally draws on the finding that innovation and efficiency levels positively correlate with financial performance (e.g., Bayues et al. 2003; Grifell-Tatje & Lovell, 1999; Roberts, 2001, 1999), which was an important factor that was frequently mentioned by the interviewed PE managers. This relation therefore indicates that a sound synthesis of rigor and relevance should have been established.

Determinants of performance

The second research question, which is closely associated with the first interrogation, aspires to uncover changed conditions energizing the outcome variance. Comparable to the dependent construct, the concrete nature of the independent constructs is also derived in a later part (cf. section 3.2). Nevertheless, this abstract briefly introduces the fundamental idea behind the second research question.

In conjunction with the argument that agency explanations do not necessarily emerge as feasible for analyzing private-to-private transactions (cf. section 2.3), focus was shifted to auxiliary theoretical verdicts from the field of organization science, which were assumed to explain the potential variance in the dependent variable. In this sense, an interview partner from a PE house indicated that the modification of several organizational characteristics constitutes a crucial activity after an investment. According to the informant, the realization of the target's full operational potential usually requires changes regarding key personnel and internal processes. However, he maintained that the interference with FBes also necessitates a careful approach. He raised the issue that the loss of the patriarch and the simultaneous addition of a PE company usually present a severe moment for many employees. Moreover, the loss of the patriarch was reported to not only relate to social issues in FBes but also to aspects of creativity, stretch, and motivation. According to him, "The maintenance and enhancement of sound processes are naturally crucial tasks. The preservation of the family businesses' genes is also a very important aspect. However, you need to improve the companies' performance to make the financing work." Having relied on these insights, the second proposed research question aims at delivering an understanding with regard to certain organizational determinants energizing changes in performance. Literature that directs attention to these dynamics can be considered as almost non-existent as the review of PE investments in FBes demonstrated. Even in the wider research domain of PE investments, studies examining effects leading to improved productivity or innovative skills fall short of delivering valid theoretical explanations. This shortcoming is, among other things, caused by the cited studies' quantitative nature depending on restricted data from surveys or databases. Obtained results from this study, which aspire to highlight underlying reasons, thus possess the quality to intensely enrich the field. With reference to Acharya et al. who declare that "a considerable interest remains in understanding in greater depth the nature of engagement and involvement of PE houses with portfolio companies and providing more robust evidence how these relate to value creation" (2009: 38), this study makes an effort to close the gap.

3. Organizational Change and Conceptual Model

Initial theoretical and empirical evidence was introduced in the previous chapters, illustrating notions how to think about FBes, PE companies, and the interplay of both organizational types. In particular, a brief literature review was executed to highlight and analyze the individual qualities of both systems and the evidence in case of interaction. Hereupon, published phenomena were integrated and the guiding research questions of this paper were developed. This procedure necessitates a thoroughly grounded perspective on organizational change for creating an understanding of the organizational dynamics following an investment. In other words, the superordinate mechanism in place of this chapter, i. e., the central theme, is organizational change. With regard to Pettigrew (1988), organizational change was differentiated between its process, context, and content as illustrated subsequently.

To analyze organizational change, the chapter proceeds as follows. Section 3.1, *Organizational Change,* is organized to discuss change around two central issues as proposed by Pettigrew (1988). Subsection 3.1.1, *Process: Movement of Change*, clarifies how the processes of organizational change become empirically ascertainable. Furthermore, subsection 3.1.2, *Context: Causation of Change*, considers the question why transformation unfolds in organizations. After having clarified "how" and "why" modifications might occur, section 3.2, *Conceptual Model*, expands the illustrated procedural character of change by content; hence, it models an answer to the interrogation pertaining to "what." Initial deliberations regarding the construct scopes, which were provided in section 2.3, *Research Questions: The Interplay of Family Businesses and Private Equity*, are for this purpose translated into guiding conceptualizations. This chapter is finalized by the discussion of the derived framework.

3.1 Organizational Change

Similar to the necessity to reflect on the term organizational theory, organizational change demands an intensified understanding. Evidence presented in the literature review suggested that elements of portfolio companies of PE houses experience a transformation; in accordance with the first research question, this transformation becomes visible by altered real returns, precisely gains in productivity or innovation skills (cf. Cumming et al. 2007).

Inferring from the viewpoint that organizations are subject to a metamorphosis over time, Barnett and Carroll simply characterize change as "a transformation of an organization between two points in time" (1995: 219). Further scholars define change as the adoption of a new idea or behavior by an organization (see Aiken & Hage, 1971; Pierce & Delbecq, 1977). Despite of the definition utilized, researchers generally proclaim that "[c]hange is a complex subject" (Bergh & Fairbank, 2002: 359) and agree that the world of organizations is always in "a state of becoming" (Benson, 1975: 6). Organizational change has been a controversial issue for decades because it has introduced an additional level of complexity to the organization sciences. Weick (1998) points out that the existence of change represented a phenomenon, probably in some researchers' awareness even an anomaly, which diverged from the superordinate objective to explain order. In fact, the academic community widely shares the opinion that organizational change is a phenomenon which is challenging to capture and illustrate (e.g., Mintzberg & Westley, 1992; Orlikowski, 1996; Tsoukas & Chia, 2002).

Van de Ven and Poole posit that explaining "why and how organizations change has been a central and enduring quest for scholars" (1995: 510). Similar to this differentiation, Pettigrew (1988) proposes to distinguish between content, process, and context for classifying organizational change, and James and Connolly contend that this categorization "is a very useful framework for the analysis of change" (2000: 30). Content acknowledges the subject of a transformation: What changes in organizations? Process considers the characteristics of change: How do organizations move from one state to another one? Context is directed to reveal the dynamics enabling the development: Why do organizations change? In consequence, these three interrogations are followed and scrutinized in the subsequent parts of this chapter. The conception of change, relating to the process and the context, is reviewed in this section to indicate how to think about the modifications in FBes in response to a PE investment. In other words, the overall section aims to provide a theoretical background upon which the third dimension, content, is extended in the next section. Subsection 3.1.1, *Process: Movement of Change*, thus deals with various aspects of the change process, for example, the dynamics of modifications, intervention theories, and the role of change agents. Hereupon, subsection 3.1.2, *Context: Causation of Change*, introduces a typology which answers the question why organizations change by revisiting conceptual thoughts made in an earlier segment (cf. subsection 2.1.2).

3.1.1 Process: Movement of Change

The beginning notion that change represents a static divergence of two points in time (Barnett & Carroll, 1995) necessitates a description clarifying how an organization exactly moves from one point in time to the next one. Theorists usually structure this movement on the basis of a binary typology, for instance, continuous and discontinuous change (see Meyer et al. 1993), incremental and radical change (see Tushman and Romanelli, 1985), evolutionary and revolutionary change (see Miller, 1982), or first-order and second-order change (see Watzlawick et al., 1974). Similar to these distinctions, Weick and Quinn (1999) classify change as "episodic" and "continuous." Building on the work of Porras and Silvers (1991), Weick and Quinn define change on the one hand as "episodic, discontinuous, and intermittent" (1999: 362) and on the other hand as "continuous, evolving, and incremental" (1999: 362). According to the authors, episodic change typifies infrequent and intentional changes, which are triggered by a misalignment between organizational structures and environmental conditions. The term "episodic" captures the cyclical nature of the rebalancing process; thus, it is considered to possess a revolutionary character. In contrast, "continuous" change occurs on an evolutionary and emerging progression, which is uncoupled from particular intentions. The categorization of change, as either episodic or continuous, has far reaching implications for auxiliary elements such as the underlying image of an organization, the intrinsic intervention theory, or the role of change agents. Before dealing with these elements, the cause of the proposed segregation deserves attention, which is the observation of organizational change.

The Observation of Organizational Change

Since Berger and Luckmann's (1967) work on *The social construction of reality*, it has become a recognized circumstance that social phenomena cannot be objectively accessed but are always contingent on a certain systemic perspective taken. With regard to this insight, all classification attempts distinguishing between two forms of transformation, as considered above, usually assume two types of observers. Weick and Quinn note, "From a distance (the macro level of analysis), when observers examine the flow of events that constitute organizing, they see [...] episodes of revolutionary change. But a view from closer in (the micro level of analysis) suggests ongoing adaptation and adjustment" (1999: 362). The former citation, differentiating between an inside and an outside observer, yet only considers half of the argument concerning the operation of observation.

The second issue deals with the concept of time. Weisbord (1988) posits that there is no difference in the movement of change noticed when taking snapshots of two discretionary points in time; the frozen situations do not reveal any dynamics. An evaluation, analyzing whether a transformation occurred on a continuous or episodic basis, is therefore difficult to accomplish. In this respect, an observation starts to become less ambiguous when the former cross-sectional viewpoint turns into an interval perspective since many points in time allow for a more profound assessment of the underlying conversion. A more radical assumption regarding the perspective of time is emphasized by Purser et al. (2005). The authors claim that time itself depends on different perceptions, which causes ambiguous observations. To underline their viewpoint, they differentiate between a causal and a flow time. The former follows Newtonian logics, and the latter is "based on cultivating the direct experience of time" (2005: 3). The character of time thus shifts from a stable to an unstable concept, and it transforms into a flexible variable signifying an essential part of investigations (Pettigrew et al. 2001).

The differentiation related to space and time remarkably reminds one of Einstein's theories of relativity. Indeed, the change from a Newtonian state of the world to Einstein's model of spacetime implies that reality is always contingent on subjective observations, which is, for instance, advocated by epistemologists of constructivism.[20] In order to take advantage of these insights, the interviewing technique, highlighted in the method chapter (cf. *Appendix A*), is dedicated to partially subvert the obstacle stemming from different observational perspectives.

20 Jensen notes, "Konstruktivismus ist die Theorie der Realität, die in der Beobachtung (vor allem der wissenschaftlichen Beobachtung) erscheint. [...] Ein Grundprinzip des Konstruktivismus lautet: Jede Behauptung muß einem Beobachter zugerechnet werden" (1999: 31–32). The author further remarks that a rejection of the Newtonian absolutism, relating to space and time, in favor of a relativistic approach, deduced from Einstein, constitutes one of the central building blocks of constructivism. However, he proposes that a physical definition of the term "space" cannot be identically projected to constructivism as constructionists speak of a social space. The same logic applies to the concept of time.

Episodic and Continuous Change

As suggested in the beginning of this subsection, Weick and Quinn's (1999) synopsis on the rhythm of change provides a thorough overview regarding the process of change, illustrating how an organization moves beyond two points in time. What makes the review valuable is the reflection on issues such as the underlying metaphor, the intrinsic intervention theory, and the role of the change agent, which advances an isolated perspective of the rhythmic appearance of change. Table 1 summarizes the key distinctions, conceptions, and argumentations of Weick and Quinn (1999) before these are elaborated in the following paragraphs.

Table 1: Overview of Episodic and Continuous Change Processes

Dimension	Episodic Change	Continuous Change
Organizational Metaphor	Organizations are inertial, and change is infrequent, discontinuous, and intentional.	Organizations are emergent and self-organizing, and change is constant, evolving, and cumulative.
Analytical Framework	Change is an occasional interruption or divergence from equilibrium. It tends to be dramatic, revolutionary and it is mostly driven externally. It is seen as a failure of the organization to adapt to a changing environment. The emphasis pertains to short-run adaptation.	Change is a pattern of endless evolutionary modifications in work processes and practice. It is driven by organizational instability and alert reactions to daily contingencies. Numerous small accommodations cumulate and amplify. The emphasis pertains to long-run adaptability.
Intervention Theory and Change Agent	Change is Lewinian: 1. Unfreeze, 2. Transition, and 3. Refreeze. The change agent is seen as a prime mover creating change.	Change is Confucian: 1. Freeze, 2. Rebalance, and 3. Unfreeze. The change agent is seen as a sense maker redirecting change.

Source: adapted from Weick and Quinn (1999)

Organizational metaphor

An essential difference between episodic and continuous change pertains to the characterization of an organization. Supporters of an episodic process propose that an organizational misalignment with relevant environments is driven by the concept of inertia (see Hannan & Freeman, 1984) or punctuated equilibrium considerations (see Tushman & Romanelli, 1985). In punctuated equilibrium models, organizations adapt to their environment until they reach a state of equilibrium. Along this way, environmental imperatives have already become more turbulent, which in turn necessitates further rebalancing acts. Weick and Quinn (1999) proclaim that inertia might be related to a set of internal mechanisms, such as culture (see Tushman & O'Reilly, 1996), feedback procedures, (see Arthur, 1995) incentive systems (see Kaplan & Henderson, 2005), routines (see Feldman, 2000; Gioia, 1992), or technology (see Tushman & Rosenkopf, 1992). The metaphor of an organization is thus built around the notion of second-order change, implying that certain mechanisms are required to transform inertial practices (e.g., Danneels, 2008). With reference to the dualism of deterministic and voluntaristic change (see Marek, 2010), episodic change is likely to occur at the voluntaristic end. The underlying portrait of an organization therefore reminds one of an organization maintaining decoupled interdependencies. These are static in nature up to a certain point which requires the entity to meet new environmental imperatives.

In contrast, supporters of the continuous transformation paradigm view an organization rather by means of a process viewpoint (cf. Weick, 1979). Weick and Quinn (1999) note that according to these academics, change represents "repeated acts" of improvisation (see Moorman & Miner, 1998), translation (see Czarniawska & Sevon, 1996), and learning (see Sitkin et al. 1998). This procedure noticeably indicates the first-order logic implied. Organizations are characterized in terms of adjusting, rather than transformational, patterns. The interpretation of improvisation, translation, and learning as repeated acts symbolizes the existence of prescribed routines, which manifest themselves at the deterministic echelon. Adaptations in this category are driven by programs of determined or probabilistic internal forces, which are absent in the episodic perspective. Expressed differently, the organization can be classified as highly responsive: Organizations possess tightly coupled interdependencies, and learning itself is identified as a modification regarding the quality of learning to learn (Danneels, 2002).

Analytical framework

Following the divergent views on an organization, the analytical frameworks of episodic and continuous change consequently vary (Weick and Quinn, 1999): In episodic change paradigms, the situation of organizational inertia requires a replacement of existing practices to readapt to new conditions having arisen in the external environment (e.g., Mintzberg & Westley, 1992). The emphasis is therefore on a short-run adaption. This process energizes an organization to pass through several stages, such as development, stability, adaption, struggle, and revolution (Mintzberg, 1978; Mintzberg & McHugh, 1985; Mintzberg & Waters, 1982). The scholars state that the outlined sequence enhances the picture of "periodic bumps" (Mintzberg & Westley, 1992), which merely consider the stages of stability and revolution. To replace existing practices, particular elements are required to initiate the revolutionary process. These elements pertain to internal and external imperatives, for example, management, performance, or environmental considerations.

Continuous change does not rely on replacements (Weick & Quinn, 1999) since "rapid and relentless shifts" (Brown & Eisenhardt, 1997: 1) cause this reaction to be superfluous. In contrast to the socially constructed stimulation of voluntary change, the doctrine of continuous change posits that every modification is already encoded in an organization's genes steering its development. The absence of a punctuated equilibrium allows for drawing the conclusion that organizations move in a sphere that is characterized by permanent disequilibria. Therefore, change does not reach a state requiring revolutionary conversion as the emphasis is on long-run adaptability; in fact, this conceptualization renders initiating forces unnecessary. The modus operandi of continuous change is best outlined as an "ongoing mixture of reactive and proactive modifications, guided by purposes at hand, rather than an intermittent interruption of periods of convergence" (Weick & Quinn, 1999: 379).

Intervention theory and change agent

It is suggestive that the intervention theory behind both systematizations requires two diverse models, specifically a "Lewinian" approach and a "Confucian" one (Marshak, 1993; Weick & Quinn, 1999), which illustrates the battle between a design and an emergence school of strategy and change (cf. Grant, 2005; Mintzberg, 1985). With reference to an episodic perspective Weick and Quinn (1999) indicate that Lewin's (1947) model of change processes seems to appropriately typify the central mindset: unfreeze, change, and freeze. The unfreezing phase corresponds to a preparation for change and a disconfirmation of expectations. Hereupon, the change phase is characterized by a cognitive restructuring through external support. In the third phase, change is made congruent with preliminary mental models in order to return to previous comfort levels. Marshak (1993) points out that Lewin's (1947) model is based on five central postulations. According to the author, the model is characterized by a development that is described as linear in time, positively progressive, and goal seeking. Moreover, it is inspired by an optimal equilibrium conjecture and the necessity that modifications are initiated by externals. The goal seeking behavior, the optimal equilibrium focus, and the inducement by externals converge with voluntaristic approaches. Since episodic transformation needs a constructive component, the role of management demands attention. In the episodic paradigm, the active role of an external party facilitates the understanding of managers as "prime movers" (Kotter, 1996) or as the "origin of origins" (Porter, 1991) initializing transformations (Weick & Quinn, 1999). However, the question remains unanswered how management engages in creating intentional modifications. An interesting research stream in this respect examines the role of conversations and language to provoke modifications (O'Connor, 1995). For instance, Ford and Ford refer to change as a "communication-based and communication-driven phenomenon" (1995: 541), which is initiated by top management. Other literature argues that the task of a change agent depends on his capabilities to sell issues within organizations (see Dutton et al. 2001). Evaluating this procedural task, it becomes apparent that even under the doctrine of episodic conversion the change agent is associated with a diminished role in producing determined outcomes. Accordingly, a "Newtonian *mechanistic* logic" (Farjoun, 2002: 561), implying that managers intentionally define strategy and results, appears to have encountered revision. Rather, managers are considered "less heroic" (Burgelmann, 1983); they introduce change by setting goals but cannot forecast the ways to accomplish these objectives.

In contrast to the Lewinian method of change, Weick and Quinn (1999) indicate that the continuous paradigm, advocated by Marshak (1993), reinterprets the proposed sequence by Lewin and proposes a Confucian mindset as follows: freeze, rebalance, and unfreeze. This intervention theory suggests that freezing an organization is obligatory for understanding an organizational metamorphosis as it makes cognitive maps and stories visible for analysis. Hereupon, the meanings of stories are revised to establish a new reality that minimizes mental obstructions. The purpose of this step is to attach a beneficial meaning to historical events for liberating a new spirit of engagement. Eventually, the unfreezing phase is supposed to provide the foundation for the start of new waves related to improvisation, learning, and translation. Marshak (1993) posits that a Confucian change is based on a cyclical process that cannot reach a desired state; rather, the process is driven by the existence of permanent disequilibria requiring an adjusting stimulus. Diverging from the episodic change conception demanding the replacements of processes, advocates of the continuous school of thought appreciate the redirection of the former as the intervention's predominant objective. The role of the change agent hence turns into a redirector of emerging processes: Management is capable of steering and directing arising elements by reconfiguring mutual cognition. Under this viewpoint, the image of a "prime mover" (Kotter, 1996), initializing change by replacement, converts to a mediator. Weick and Quinn exemplify this discrepancy by declaring that managing change is "to tell people what to do" (1999: 380), but leading change is "to show people how to be" (1999: 380). In consequence, organizational strategy takes on the image of a guided evolution (see Barnett & Burgelman, 1996; Farjoun, 2002; Lovas & Ghoshal, 2000). Similar to the picture of the change agent in Lewin's (1947) model, the change agent cannot be held responsible in the continuous paradigms for precise organizational outputs. The Confucian logic, however, draws an even less paramount picture of top management due to the fact that direct and purposeful interference is considered obsolete in this doctrine.

3.1.2 Context: Causation of Change

The diverse conceptions of the role of the change agent imply, among other things, that the academic community has been paralyzed by a battle of paradigms: management scholars advocating that intended and purposeful action is possible versus organizational ecologists neglecting such practices. According to Lewin and Volberda, the questions whether and how managerial intentionality matters "have occupied center stage in research on adaptation and selection" (1999: 519).

On the one hand, a wide domain of theories and paradigms from the natural end, promoted by the field of sociology, contend that the external environment is the solitary driver for changing organizational landscapes (Lewin & Volberda, 1999). Among the most popular approaches are population ecology and institutional theory. On the other hand, approaches from the rational end, such as economics as well as strategy and organizational design, usually define the management as an important reference point of change (Lewin & Volberda, 1999): Theories rooted in such domains pertain to transaction cost theory (see Williamson, 1985, 1975), industrial organization (see Porter, 1985, 1980), strategic choice theory (see Child, 1972), or contingency theory (see Galbraith, 1973; Lawrence & Lorsch, 1967; Woodward, 1958).

The above illustrated categorization indicates that an intensified debate historically dealt with two one-dimensional frontiers of change: external, deterministic approaches and internal, voluntaristic models. Whereas certain scholars are still indifferent whether the dispute has found an end (Baum, 1996), contemporary thinking infers that both perspectives have a valid claim. For instance, Scott (1987) argues that the approaches should be seen as complementary to each other. He maintains that the perspective of environmental selection is helpful for explaining the relative high death rates of small companies, and he suggests that an adaptive viewpoint accounts for the high survival rates of grown and established companies. Levinthal (1991) enhances this notion and proposes that voluntaristic adaptation and deterministic environmental selection fundamentally represent interrelated processes of change. His suggestion builds on the idea that inertia and learning are two interdependent elements. According to Levinthal, "organizational learning contributes, in part, to organizational inertia, which, in turn is the basis of selection processes. On the other hand, far from being incompatible with adaptive learning, inertial forces are a prerequisite for intelligent adaptation" (1991: 140). In a similar vein, Willke (2005) proposes that certain external stimuli are required to initiate subtle procedures that are afterwards driven by the prescribed principles of a system.[21] In line with these selective theoretical deliberations, empirical studies report that both firm specific singularities as well as the type of environment influence organizational development (e.g., Barnett & Hansen, 1996; Beinhocker, 1997; Burgelmann, 2002; Henderson & Stern, 2004; Levinthal & Myatt, 1994).

Baum and Singh (1994) introduce the idiom "coevolution" for describing the simultaneous operations of adaptation and selection. The term has become a frequently utilized and durable concept in contemporary administrative science (see Henderson & Stern, 2004; Burgelmann, 2002). Further authors refined the term. For instance, Lewin et al. classify coevolution "as the interdependent outcome of managerial actions, institutional influences, and extra-institutional changes" (1999: 535). Institutional influences pertain to the education system, capital markets, or regulatory affairs, and extra-institutional changes are associated with demographics, technological advances or the global interdependence. In a similar vein, Lewin and Volberda propose to

> define coevolution as the joint outcome of managerial intentionality, environments, and institutional effects. [...] Change can be driven by direct interactions and feedback from the rest of the system. In other words, change can be recursive and need not be an outcome of either managerial adaption or environmental selection but rather the joint outcome of managerial intentionality and environmental effects. (1999: 526)

Typology of the Context of Organizational Change

This work proceeds with an abstract typology of the overwhelming pluralism of change theories and thus adheres to Gioia and Pitre (1990), who explicitly warn to follow isolated routes when researching organizational change in order to avoid the risk of overlooking insightful discoveries.

Van de Ven and Poole (1995) make an attempt to overcome the theoretical pluralism of change theories and present a review by constructing a framework consisting of four categories. In order to establish the underlying framework, the authors identified over one million papers discussing the theme of organizational change. While reviewing 200 articles in depth, they discovered about 20 theories related to organizational development and change. Based on the derived insights, they classify these theories according to the subsequent four "motors" (the underlying mechanisms are included in parentheses): life cycle (start-up,

21 Willke remarks, "Veränderung ist – legt man die Theorie selbstreferentieller Systeme zugrunde – nur als Eigenleistung des zu verändernden Systems möglich. Sie ist andererseits ohne externen Anstoß höchst unwahrscheinlich" (2006: 88).

growth, harvest, terminate), evolution (variation, selection, retention), dialectic (thesis/antithesis, conflict, synthesis), and teleology (dissatisfaction, search/interact, set/envision goals, implement goals). The authors' language of motors indicates that each of the four patterns has the capability to initiate change on its own. Van de Ven and Poole (1995) categorize these four orientations along the dimensions of the unit of change and the mode of change as can be derived from Figure 7.

Figure 7: Typology of the Stimuli of Change

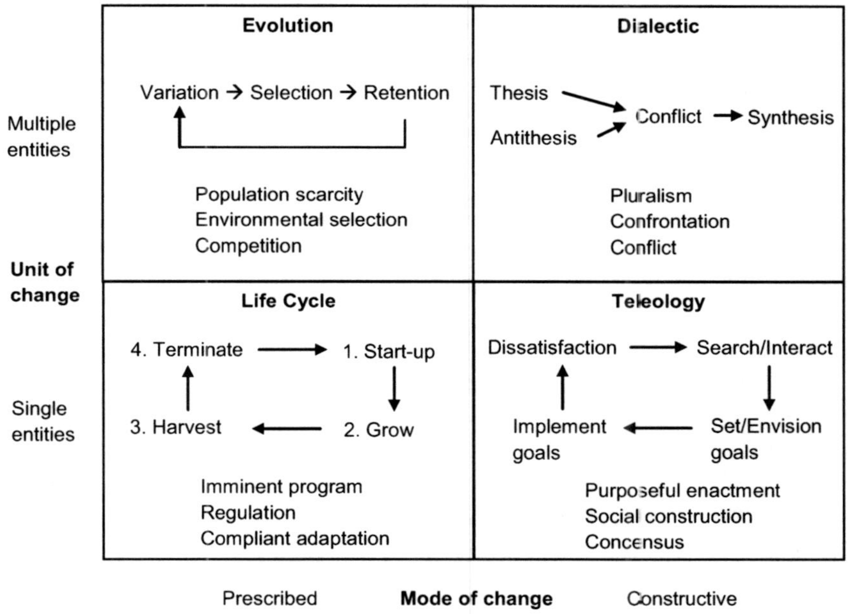

Source: adapted from Van de Ven and Poole (1995)

The unit of change relates to the condition whether single or multiple entities are required to initiate change. Evolution and dialectic paradigms necessitate multiple entities whereas life cycle and teleology operate at a single entity. The second dimension, i.e., the mode of change, is distinguished between constructive and prescribed developments. According to the authors, a prescribed mode of change "channels the development of entities in a prespecified direction" (1995: 522), and a constructive mode "generates, unprecedented, novel forms" (1995: 522). Teleology and dialectic are associated with a constructive understanding of change; theories of evolution and life cycle are guided by prescribed advancements. The four orientations are explicated subsequently with regard to the argumentation of Van de Ven and Poole (1995).

Life Cycle

Inspired by pioneers such as Comte (1798–1857), Spencer (1820–1903), and Piaget (1896–1980) life cycle models describe organizations, human development, or group decision-making shifting through sequences of prescribed stages. The logic pertains to an image of organic growth derived from biology, and scholars portray entities to heuristically change their character from initiation to termination. The process is linear, irreversible, and usually triggered by an imminent program. Therefore, each stage is interpreted as a precursor for the next stage, enforcing a linear and historical ordering of events. The progression is detached from environmental effects that might alter the development because the embryonic code eventually prevails over the development of the organization.

Evolution

In contrast to the metaphor of organic growth from life cycle models, competitive survival represents the most appropriate image in evolution paradigms. Building on the work of Lamarck (1744–1829), Darwin (1809–1882), and Mendel (1822–1884) change proceeds through a probabilistic sequence of variation, selection, and retention, which is initiated by resource scarcity and competition. Although evolution is often applied at a population level (see Hannan & Freeman, 1977), "defined as consisting of all those organizations that compete for resources in the same environmental niche" (Scott, 2004: 8), Burgelmann (1991) introduces the concept of "intraorganizational ecology," and scholars utilize this viewpoint to explain the development at the organizational level (see Aldrich, 1999, Gersick, 1991). Variation refers to the transformation of behavior and patterns ordering a system. Two dominant directions can be identified at this stage. Theorists following a Darwinian logic assume that variation is a blind inheritance through intergenerational forms (see Hannan & Freman, 1977). Scholars accepting a Lamarckian viewpoint, however, reject the image of blindness and propose that learning and improvisation lead to probabilistic variations (see Burgelmann, 1991, Weick, 1979). The latter scholars argue in line with McKelvey (1982) and propose that a definition of organizational generations is rather obstructive. Hereupon, selection processes mediate the induced variations. This mediation procedure attempts to identify certain variations that appear as viable modifications. Finally, retention describes the process when such modifications become embedded and institutionalized.

Dialectic

In dialectic models, building on German schools of thought of Hegel (1770–1831), Marx (1818–1883), and Freud (1856–1939), the key metaphor is opposition and conflict. The logic in this paradigm relates to the existence of opposing forces, thesis and antithesis, which stimulate a discontinuous sequence until values, interests, or classes reach a synthesis. Derived syntheses usually represent an agreement, tradeoff, or compromise of the contradictory forces. Dialectic forces arise through discrepancies of at least two systems, and the derived synthesis of both forces is usually a novel construction. In organizations, the environmental antithesis can be relatively weak, confirming the status quo. Likewise, the antithesis can be particularly strong, which leads to a substitution of the status quo. If forces, however, reach a level of a constructive conflict, organizations adjust their procedures and generate a novel kind of behavior.

Teleology

Teleological models might be the most natural types in management science as they make use of goal setting and planning. Moreover, pioneers such as Weber (1864 – 1920) and Nobel laureate Simon (1916 – 2001) stand in close affiliation to this craft. The metaphor is purposeful action and cooperation. Change follows a sequence of goal setting, implementation, and adaptation until a desired state is reached. In contrast to life cycle deliberations, the process is reversible and not necessarily linear progressive because intermittent goal setting might interrupt the sequence of processes. Having reached a final state, the process starts all over again so organizations usually do not reach a permanent equilibrium. The logic best describing this school of thought pertains to envisioned states and social construction. In essence, organizations might work toward every goal they design though boundaries, such as environmental constraints, are adhered to.

Interplay of motors and processes

Deducing from this categorization attempt, it seems apparent that an understanding of organizational change is highly complex and usually combines diverse motors. Simon (1979), for example, argues that the complexity of a system's behavior constitutes an interplay of simple motors, which reinforces the idea of coevolution. With reference to Van de Ven and Poole (1995), existing theories elucidating organizational change usually consist of a combination of these four ideal-type motors. The scholars show that many different dual motor theories subsist in the field of organization science, for instance, Aldrich's (1979) adaptation-selection model combining life cycle and evolution or Tushman and Romanelli's (1985) punctuated equilibrium model unifying teleological and evolutionary thoughts. Weick's (1979) social psychology of organizing pertains to a theory combining evolution, teleology, and life cycle, but it falls short of including the dialectic stimulus (Van de Ven and Poole, 1995). Van de Ven and Poole (1995) were not able to identify an organizational theory unifying all motors; however, they exhibit with regard to Riegel's (1975) theory of human development that such concepts indeed subsist. With reference to Riegel (1975), human development is determined by the subsequent dynamics: birth to death (life cycle), individual-personality affected by wishes, plans, and skills (teleology), cultural-sociological environments (dialectic), as well as outer-physical events (evolution).

By interpreting the four motors as the originators of transformation, a relation to the process of change, subdivided into episodic and continuous procedures, becomes unmistakably evident. The constructive component of teleological and dialectic doctrines is associated with periodic rhythms whereas life cycle and evolution models have parallels with continuous rhythms. In other words, periodic and continuous sequences emanate from constructive and prescribed change modes, respectively. Thereby, they intrinsically differ in elements such as the applied organizational metaphor, the intervention symbolism, or the role of the change agent. To underline this rationale, it was argued that episodic change requires an inside or outside force to initiate a conversion, which can be conceptualized with the help of teleological or dialectic stimuli. Episodic change was identified to be based on a replacement of existing processes; constructive modifications are described as "discontinuous and unpredictable departures from the past" (Van de Ven and Poole, 1995: 522). Continuous change, however, was outlined to rely on incrementally adjusting patterns; prescribed change enables entities to adapt "their forms in a stable, predictable way" (Van de Ven and Poole, 1995: 522).

Discussion of the Typology With Regard to the Research Intention

Following the insight that life cycle models assume entities pursuing imminent programs, logics, or codes, the nature of this process seems to be uncoupled from a PE investment because the former driven prescribed development is unrelated to any external influence. Likewise, evolution follows a prescribed rhythm for the reason "that one can specify the actuarial probabilities of the changing demographic characteristics of the population" (Van den Ven & Poole, 1995: 518). Although it is impossible to foresee which organizations will survive or fail, the overall population changes according to the specified population dynamics. According to this viewpoint, the motor behind evolution seems to be relatively uncoupled from the event whether a PE company invests in an individual entity. It might be arguable that the existence of PE as a financing class has transformed the competitive landscape because good companies can tap resources for growth whereas bad companies cannot. Such a viewpoint, however, pertains to macro effects and does not explain the transformation of an individual entity financed by PE capital. In contrast to evolution and life cycle motors, it was anticipated in this empirical investigation that dialectic and teleology represented solid frameworks to explain the reasons why change unfolded. In order to explicate this issue, both motors are subsequently discussed with the intention to analyze the empirical problem.

Dialectic

Organizational entities can reconfigure their operations as a response to a passive perturbation stimulated by dialectic forces. Hegel's (1770 – 1831) assumption that we live in a colliding world of contradictory forces, values, and events describe the origins of the processes related to thesis and antithesis. The instrument of power moderates the relationship between these processes and consequently determines the nature of the reached synthesis. Stability is thus ensured as long as the antithesis does not operate with "sufficient power" (Van de Ven & Poole, 1995: 517) to initiate change. In Marx and Engel's (1848) *The communist manifesto*, the consideration of power is verbalized by notions such as the aspired proletariat's dictatorship over the bourgeoisie; the idea of power in this inquiry is probably based on a similar construct, which is ownership. The expected thesis and antithesis are shortly illustrated in the following.

With reference to the colliding systems in this investigation, the idea is put forward that FBes and PE companies maintain different values and objectives, enabling to think in terms of thesis and antithesis. Empirical evidence suggests that financial interest is an important objective in the domain of FBes but not the predominant one, which is usually explained by means of transcending values and beliefs from owning families (see Astrachan & Jaskiewicz, 2008; Chrisman et al. 2010; Chua et al. 1999; Dunn, 1995; File et al., 1994; Hienerth & Kessler, 2006; Olson et al. 2003; Sharma et al. 1996; Tagiuri & Davis, 1992). Summarizing this thought, Sharma et al. reason that the objectives of FBes "are likely to be quite different from the firm-value maximization goal" (1996: 9).

In contradiction to this citation, the potential antithesis can be identified with regard to the nature of PE investors, whose attitude can probably best be explained with an example from Stone's (1987) dramaturgical epos *Wall Street*. The protagonist Michael Douglas alias corporate raider Gordon Gekko, who might be interpreted as *the* personification of financial investors, remarks the following in a speech about his profession:

> The new law of evolution in corporate America seems to be survival of the unfittest. Well, in my book you either do it right or you get eliminated. [...] The point is, ladies and gentleman, that greed, for a lack of a better word, is good. Greed is right, greed works. Greed clarifies, cuts through, and captures the essence of the evolutionary spirit. Greed, in all of its forms; greed for life, for money, for love, for knowledge has marked the upward surge of mankind. (Michael Douglas alias Gordon Gekko, quoted in Stone, 1987)

Walker (1992) suggests that the assertion "greed is good" represents a modern interpretation of Adam Smith's (1723 – 1790) concept of the invisible hand, which eventually demands the maximization of resources. Bottom line maximization should thus be appreciated as a mean of PE investors to generate excess returns, which are formally represented by positive Jensen's alphas (Jensen, 1968).

Despite these polarizing systems' logic, Prym (2010) empirically illustrates that discriminative goals need not necessarily be incompatible in cases when the owning family preserves an equity stake in the company after a PE investment. Concretely, the author illustrates that non-monetary objectives remain in place in FBes when the family continues to hold equity in the company. Non-monetary objectives, however, should be put to jeopardy when the owning family completely walks away from an enterprise, which is caused by the conflict between the inherent objectives and the more powerful ones induced by PE investors: The antithesis should be strong enough to replace the thesis in such situations.

Teleology

In teleological models, management envisions and constructs a predefined goal toward which the entity should develop. Although managers cannot literally define the exact path for achieving the constructed objectives, they have several paths in mind (Van de Ven & Poole, 1995). However, a lack of an ideal equilibrium requires actors to constantly monitor and define new equilibria, which are based on their expectance of future states (Cyert & March, 1963). Therefore, the idea of teleology, though operating at a single entity (Van de Ven & Poole, 1995), is supposed to appropriately symbolize a factor which is eligible for explaining the initiation of change.

The underlying puzzle pertains to the question how new constructions of future states find entry into organizations that are subject to a PE investment. Put simply, it was described earlier that value generation in PE transactions is based on modifications related to the capital structure, governance, and operations; therefore, two initiators of teleological change might be expected when PE houses invest in FBes. On the one hand, operational engineering induced through active involvement via board meetings might be considered a factor of influence. With reference to Klier et al. (2009), this component of PE investors' business model is becoming increasingly important. On the other hand, the investment might passively liberate novel, distinctive initiatives and goals. For instance, the incumbent management might feel a necessity to reconfigure operations in order to meet new financial imperatives. Moreover, new top management personnel might be hired to replace or complement existing executives. Both actions are likely to provoke an alteration regarding the anticipation of future scenarios; they would therefore cause the teleological motor to start operating. As mentioned above, this line of reasoning is continued and advanced in later segments of this chapter.

3.2 Conceptual Model

"Theorizing takes scientists on mental journeys between the world of observed events, such as falling apples, and the imagined worlds of hypothetical concepts, such as gravity" (Folger & Turillo, 1999: 742). The authors continue their viewpoint that bridging spheres between concrete experienced elements and abstract concepts represents an almost irresolvable assignment since the "thick" description of empirical phenomena and the "thin" abstractness of concepts generally disharmonize. According to them, mental journeys, in the form of thought experiments,[22] might constitute a solution to the revealed dilemma. Building on insights of Wilson (1998) maintaining that thought experiments reflect *the* entry point into complex systems, it is inferable that researchers usually build mental frameworks before conducting organizational inquiries. This process transpires intentionally or unintentionally: "The choice is not whether to do mental testing" (Weick, 1989: 529) but to utilize this procedure to derive at better research. Folger and Turillo (1999) suggest that the establishment of a prefactual thought experiment converges with Weick's (1989) idea of theorizing as a "disciplined imagination," which is, in consonance with the latter, a powerful tool to generate abstract descriptions of the complex reality. Discipline is defined as the "consistent application of selection criteria to trial-and-error thinking" (1989: 516), and imagination pertains to the "deliberate diversity introduced into the problem statements, thought trials, and selection criteria that comprise that thinking" (1989: 516). Hence, discipline substantially conforms to the applied method, which is discussed in the subsequent chapter. This chapter deals with the enfolding process of imagination and was inspired by the research intention and the corresponding research questions (cf. section 2.3). Due to the fact that the process of theorizing ideally follows variation, selection, and retention procedures (Weick, 1989), the scholar suggests that variation in this context should be apprehended as an "artificial" creation of thoughts before the investigation takes place. During the establishment of this empirical inquiry "natural" selection procedures emerged by the exposure of the "artificially" created thoughts to empiricism.

In order to structure the conceptual part, I relied on Whetten's (1989) ex-

22 The term "thought experiment" has originally been established by the Danish physicist and chemist Hans Christian Ørsted (1777–1851) and arises from the German expression "Gedankenexperiment" and "Gedankenversuch" (Witt-Hansen, 1976).

perience as an editor of the renowned *Academy of Management Review*, providing a guideline on creating and evaluating conceptual frameworks. According to him, visualizations of the researcher's thinking represent an important clarification and should thus be incorporated into research papers. He proposes that such models have to fulfill four essential elements revolving around the questions (1) "what," (2) "how," (3) "why," as well as (4) "who, where, and when." The first interrogation seeks to explain which factors and concepts, based on comprehensiveness and parsimony, should be included in the framework. Having drawn on Pettigrew (1988) to structure organizational change by means of its process, context, and content, the latter has been postponed to this chapter. Hereupon, the second interrogation attempts to define the logic how the chosen building blocks are interrelated. Whetten suggests that "combining the *Hows* and the *Whats* produces the typical model" (1989: 491). Hereafter, the third interrogation "why" is supposed to justify the selection of concepts and to elucidate the dynamics of the anticipated relations. After all, the fourth interrogations pertaining to "who, where, and when" set the boundaries of generalizability and as such determine the range of the framework. Figure 8 was derived by respecting these considerations. The final paragraphs describe the conceptual framework with the help of the proposed structure of Whetten (1989).

Figure 8: Conceptual Framework

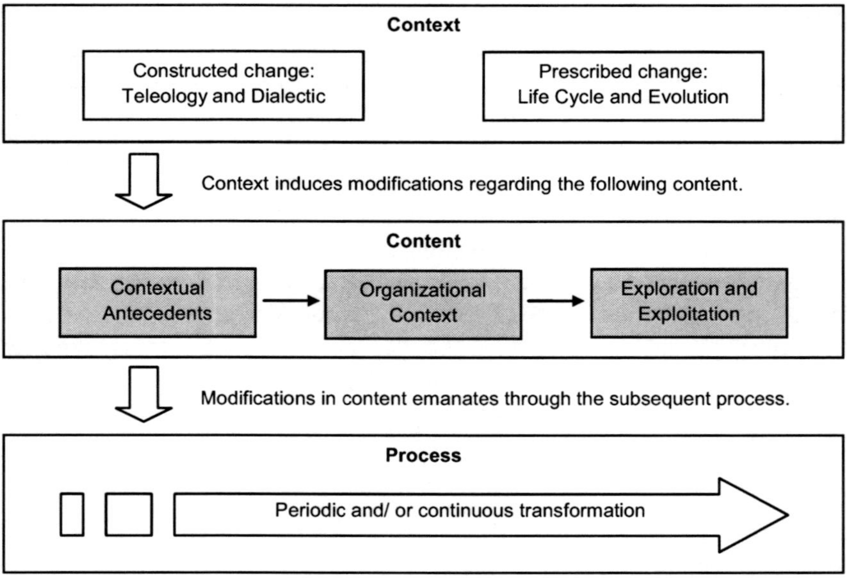

Source: author's illustration

Theory building is principally supposed to comprise the criteria of falsifiability and utility (Barachach, 1989). Construct validity, consisting of clarity and parsimony, and the logical adequacy of arguments are deliberated regarding falsifiability in the following subsections. Likewise, the construct scope and the explanatory potential, reflecting parameters of utility, are implicitly addressed. While the presented model still consists of constructs instead of variables at this stage, the process of operationalization, discussed in the next chapter, enables to consider dimensions such as measurement issues and variables' scopes.

Explanation of the Framework's Content

Scholars researching organizational development report change to occur along multiple dimensions. Kotter (1995) summarizes the concepts utilized in empirical papers and provides a relative exhaustive list consisting of modifications in structure, strategy, culture, knowledge management, quality programs, mergers and joint ventures, technology, or business processes, which implies that organizational scholars can draw on an immense pool of conceptualizations. Given this set of opportunities to model change, the subsequent derivation of the utilized constructs attempts to comprehensively and parsimoniously tap the domain in question (cf. Whetten, 1989).

Derivation of the Constructs Related to Content

The search for an appropriate dependent construct was required to conform to at least three elements. The concept was required to approximate performance indicators which were altered due to PE investments; it needed to be welcomed by organizational scientists; and it should have found application in the organizational change literature. After a meticulous analysis of the appropriate literature, the concept of exploration and exploitation was identified to fulfill these criteria.

First, the concept was selected because it builds on established empirical insights in the research field of PE induced organizational performance modifications, that is advancements in innovation and efficiency, which were summarized by the notion of real returns (cf. section 2.3). The interpretation of exploitation and exploration as an incremental and a radical innovation effort (see Benner & Tushman, 2003; Jansen et al. 2006; Jansen et al. 2005; O'Reilly & Tushman, 2008) lays the ground for inferring a sound proximity between the earlier presented empirical results and the selected constructs. Second, exploration and exploitation possess boundary spanning characteristics in the wider field of organization science (e.g., Raisch et al. 2009; Simsek, 2009; Raisch & Birkinshaw, 2008). Raisch et al. maintain that "[o]ne of the more enduring ideas in organization science is that an organization's long-term success depends on its ability to exploit its current capabilities while simultaneously exploring fundamentally new competences" (2009: 685). Third, the concept directly relates to the issue of organizational adaptation. Gupta and colleagues proclaim that "exploration and exploitation have emerged as the twin concepts underpinning organizational adaptation research" (2006: 693). In summary, these statements underline the rationale that a recent and justifiable theoretical strand, combining comprehensiveness and parsimony, was appreciated in this work. The further paragraphs of this subsection proceed with an elaboration of the concepts of exploration and exploitation. In addition, the auxiliary constructs are derived.

Exploration, exploitation, and ambidexterity

March's (1991) paper on exploration and exploitation introduces the idea of the two constructs. He defines exploration as an element to include "things captured by terms such as search, variation, risk taking, experimentation, play, flexibility, discovery, innovation" (1991: 71). Exploitation is identified to consist of "such things as refinement, choice, production, efficiency, selection, implementation, execution" (1991: 71). According to the scholar, both elements compete for scarce organizational resources. Likewise, Levinthal and March (1993) substantiate that organizations face the need to balance both ideas. Exploratory activities promise future viability whereas exploitative actions ensure survival in the contemporary business setting. In their words, "Survival requires a balance, and the precise mix of exploration and exploitation that is optimal hard to specify" (1993: 105). With regard to these insights, exploration and exploitation are described by many academics as contradictory knowledge generating processes; thus, they are considered to constitute an organizational tradeoff (see Floyd & Lane, 2000; Levinthal & March, 1993; March, 1991). Along these lines, authors argue that exploitation is associated with mechanistic structures, tightly coupled systems, and path-dependence whereas exploration is usually associated with organic structures, loosely coupled systems, and path-breaking processes (see Ancona et al. 2001; Lewin et al. 1999).[23] In contrast to categorize both elements as mutually exclusive, recent literature agrees that they should be appreciated as complementary to each other, eventually describing a paradoxical mindset. Expressed differently, theorists increasingly consider exploration and exploitation as orthogonal variables that can be achieved simul-

23 As suggested earlier, Orton and Weick remark that the concept of loosely coupled systems is often applied as substitutable, which "is typically portrayed as the endpoint of a scale that extends from tightly to loosely coupled" (1990: 205) though it has been intended to possess a dialectic meaning. In essence, the understanding of exploitation and exploration can be considered in analogy to the interpretation methods of loosely coupled systems.

taneously (Cao et al. 2009). Both viewpoints are illustrated and compared by Figure 9.

Figure 9: Continuity and Orthogonality of Exploration and Exploitation

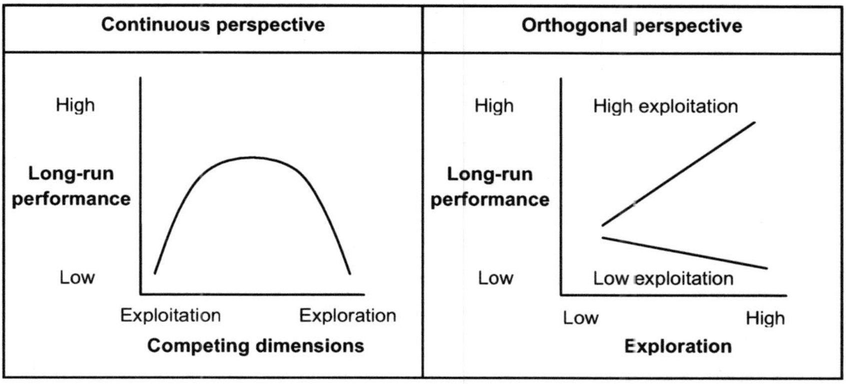

Source: adapted from Gupta et al. (2006)

Early organizational scholars referred to the effective synchronization of this paradox as organizational ambidexterity (see Duncan, 1976; Tushman & O'Reilly, 1996). The term ambidexterity is derived from the ability of individuals to use both hands with equal skill and found application to express the propensity of organizations to simultaneously promote exploitative as well as explorative activities (e.g., Lubatkin et al. 2006). Research in the area of ambidexterity has recently gained momentum; for example, Raisch et al. (2009) report an increase from 10 academic journal papers in 2004 to more than 80 in 2009, which is, among other things, stimulated by novel empirical evidence showing that the effective combination of both activities indeed affects the bottom line, that is companies managing ambidextrously deliver better performance (He & Wong, 2004; Jansen et al. 2006; Lubatkin et al. 2006; Raisch et al. 2009).

As mentioned above, exploration and exploitation have recently been described to signify complementary corporate activities while the verdict was characterized as a dilemma in the beginning. In line with this change, the conceptualization of ambidexterity experienced a modification. Early scholars argued that explorative and exploitative activities might be accomplished by a temporal separation, in which exploration and exploitation are represented by times pertaining to implementation and initiation (see Duncan, 1976), leveraging and developing of business models (see Siggelokow & Levinthal, 2003), or incremental and discontinuous change periods (see Winter & Szulanski, 2001). By overcoming the doctrine to think in terms of static tradeoffs, theorists have commenced to appreciate ambidexterity as a paradox. Along these lines, two general viewpoints have emerged to indoctrinate organizational ambidexterity. On the one hand, scholars propose that a structural separation within entities might function as an instrument to realize ambidexterity. According to this mindset, the synthesis of exploration and exploitation is realized by modifying the organizational architecture to execute both tasks in segregated business units. Tushman and O'Reilly describe ambidextrous organizations as places where incremental and architectural innovations occur and "where the break-through efforts were organized as structurally independent units, each having its own processes, structures, and cultures but integrated into the existing senior management hierarchy" (1996: 76). On the other hand, the most contemporary stream of literature suggests that ambidexterity is stimulated by organizational behavior. In this respect, Gibson and Birkinshaw create the term "contextual ambidexterity" and define the latter as "a meta-level capacity (for alignment and adaptability) that permeates all functions and levels" (2004: 211) in an organization. The emancipation from the concept of structural ambidexterity has inspired further research considering, for instance, the role of leadership (see Beckman 2006; Lubatkin et al. 2006; Smith & Tushman, 2005) and networks (see Gulati & Puranam, 2009; Tiwana, 2007) for creating ambidextrous organizations. Furthermore, papers focus on the effects of environments (see Auh & Menguc, 2005; Jansen et al. 2005; Lewin et al. 1999) and other moderating variables, such as a firm's scope and endowment (see Atuahene-Gima, 2005; Jansen et al. 2006; Lubatkin, 2006), for generating organizational ambidexterity. In fact, Raisch and Birkinshaw remark that the academic community has made the initial steps to migrate "from an emergent to a paradigmatic status" (2008: 403) by bridging research disciplines. In order to classify the arising conceptual heterogeneity, Simsek (2009) illustrates that papers relating to organizational theory (see Benner & Tushman, 2003; Adler et al. 1999), innovation and technology management (see Ambos et al. 2008; Markman et al. 2008; Tushman & O'Reilly, 1996), organizational behavior (see Gibson & Birkinshaw, 2004), and strategic management (see Jansen et al. 2008; Smith & Tushman, 2005) encourage the formation of this paradigmatic status.

Summarizing the various understandings of and viewpoints on ambidexterity, Simsek (2009) illustrates the paths to ambidexterity with the help of a four dimensional matrix portraying harmonic, partitional, cyclical, and reciprocal patterns. As can be inferred from Figure 10, the axes distinguish between a structural dimension, illustrated by means of an independent and interdependent configuration, as well as a temporal dimension, represented by a sequential and simultaneous nature. The viewpoint in this study adhered to a harmonic perspective, which is rationalized while deriving the subsequent construct.

Figure 10: A Typology of Organizational Ambidexterity

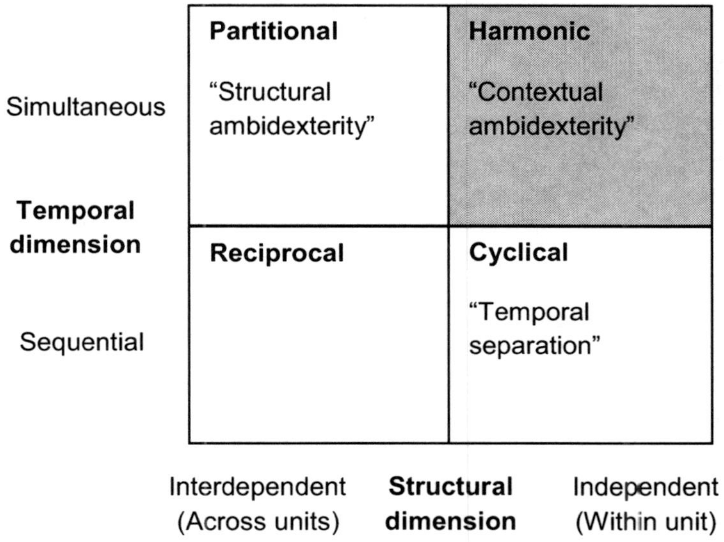

Source: adapted from Simsek (2009)

Organizational context

Consistent with the harmonic conceptualization of ambidexterity, the second construct that emerged was the organizational context; hence, a simultaneous execution of explorative and exploitative activities was conceptualized in this investigation. It should be denoted that the choice for an independent, rather than an interdependent, dimension was deliberate and can briefly be exhibited with the help of Lubatkin et al.'s (2006) declaration that small and medium-sized businesses usually do not possess the resources and administrative procedures for generating ambidexterity by means of structural segregations. Moreover, the one-dimensional character of organizational structure would only deliver a very "thin" abstraction of the "thick" occurrences appearing in the course of a PE investment in FBes (cf. Folger & Turillo, 1999), diminishing utility considerations related to the construct scope and explanatory potential (cf. Bacharach, 1989). In other words, the instrumentalization of the organizational context as an independent construct should have sufficiently provided the basis to "tap the domain of the phenomenon in question" (Bacharach, 1989: 507). In accordance with utility considerations, the explanatory power of the construct in inducing ambidexterity was already demonstrated with regard to Gibson and Birkinshaw's (2004) validated relationship.

The academic community proposes diverse definitions regarding the concept of an organizational context, yet these enjoy comparable attributes. In line with additional scholars (see Burgelmann, 1983; Johns, 2006; Mowday & Sutton, 1993; Papadakis et al. 1998), Gibson and Birkinshaw define an organizational context as "the systems, processes, and beliefs that shape individual-level behaviors in organizations" (2004: 212). It is critical to appreciate the fact that an organizational context represents an organization- wide phenomenon embracing the entire universe of organizational agents. Andriopoulos and Lewis analyze this phenomenon in ambidextrous organizations and maintain that "managing paradoxes becomes a shared responsibility, not only of top management, but across organizational levels" (2009: 696). In a similar vein, Taylor and Helfat (2009) demonstrate the importance of middle management for promoting organizational ambidexterity. The concept hence draws on an exhaustive literature stream describing the significance of middle-level and lower-level managers' ability to contribute to and stimulate strategic activity and change (see Bower, 1982; Floyd & Lane, 2000; Floyd & Woolridge, 1992; Huy, 2002; Miles & Snow, 1978; Schilit, 1987). Although these studies significantly enhance our understanding of the strategic moves that are initiated, they are deficient in explaining the actual causes why management realizes these actions. Ghoshal and Bartlett (1994), in this respect, pose the question why individuals in company A do more for the good of the organization than individuals in company B. They appreciate the organizational context as an answer for clarifying the coupling of individuals and organizations. The researchers conducted a longitudinal field study, in which they accompanied a company over a three years horizon. During this time, they inductively explored the modifications that occurred in the researched company and report that the organizational context, which they define in terms of trust, support, stretch, and discipline, had an impact "on the roles of individuals and their relationship with their organization" (1994: 110). In other words, the study of Ghoshal and Bartlett (1994), serving as the backbone of the concept of contextual ambidexterity, is about organizational change, which consequently reinforces the employment of the concept in this paper. Although the concept of ambidexterity was not developed at the time the study was conducted, the scholars strongly suggest that the organizational context influences organizational learning through the encouragement of mutual cooperation and distributed initiative. Gibson and Birkinshaw (2004) utilize the presented four contextual attributes described by Ghoshal and Bartlett (1994) and limit these to a social and a performance management context.

Contextual antecedents

Although Gibson and Birkinshaw (2004) establish the idea of contextual ambidexterity, they remain widely silent on how to generate contexts facilitating the simultaneous execution of exploratory and exploitative activities.

In empirical terms, Ghoshal and Bartlett (1994) report implemented changes, which eventually shape the organizational context, that are similar to the empirical evidence exhibited by studies from the buyout literature. They concretely illustrate changes regarding the subsequent categories: cost cuts, new accounting systems, focused benchmarking of key competitors, new formal structure, personal style of the CEO, as well as a system of quarterly meetings of senior managers. The announcement of cuts, the introduction of new accounting systems, and the systems of quarterly meetings represent practices applied by financial investors over the holding period (e.g., Acharya et al. 2009; Achleitner et al. 2008a).

In theoretical dimensions, complex systems can only be managed by building suitable contexts, which frame action and behavior (e.g., Anderson, 1999). Anderson summarizes this idea and denotes that managers have principally two options for developing appropriate contexts in complex systems:

> Managers seeking to design and tune such systems, which succeed through their superior capability to evolve complex adaptive behaviors, have two principal levers at their disposal. First, they can alter the fitness landscape for local agents; second, they can reconfigure the organizational architecture within which agents adapt. In both cases, the strategist operates on agents indirectly, taking advantage of the tendency for myriad local interactions to self-organize into a coherent pattern. (1999: 229)

Pertaining to this perspective, strategizing evolves from shaping patterns (Mintzberg and Waters, 1982) to developing contexts in which patterns might emerge (Burgelmann, 1991). Anderson (1999) interestingly refers to March's (1991) concept of exploration and exploitation as the ends to configure means.

Considering the brief empirical and theoretical reflection on the possibilities to build an organizational context, the question from which building blocks it eventually arises remains in place. Gibson and Birkinshaw (2004) comment vaguely on the antecedents of contextual ambidexterity and state that these represent a combination of a company's structural context, culture, and climate. Drawing on recent established evidence, leadership characteristics seem to be an additional parameter for building organizational contexts that trigger exploitative and explorative behavior (e.g., Beckmann, 2006; Cao et al. 2010; Jansen et al. 2008; Lubatkin et al. 2006; Smith & Tushman, 2005). For instance, Carmeli and Halevi (2009) propose that the behavioral integration of the top management team represents a crucial input, which affects, through the mediating role of an organizational context, corporate ambidexterity. The scholars emphasize their viewpoint by reverting to several academic contributions proposing that the characteristics of the top management team signify a decisive variable for building organizational contexts (see Koene et al. 2002; McGregor, 1960; Schein, 1992).

In conclusion, the construct dimension remains undefined and is referred to, in a figurative sense, as "contextual antecedents" at this stage of the paper. Consistent with a reciprocal research process qualitative research provides (e. g., Miles & Huberman, 1994), the construct is defined inductively in a later segment of this paper when the operationalization of the supportive questionnaire is generated (cf. *Appendix A*). When thinking in terms of falsifiability and utility proposed by Bacharach (1989), the postponement should have encouraged elevated levels of construct validity and scope.

4. Results

The intention of this study was to study unfolding organizational dynamics following a PE engagement in German FBes. Former chapters primarily promoted transparency of the cognitive processes and the decisions made to derive the results presented in this chapter. Accordingly, attention can now be paid to the pure findings. Therefore, an interpretative discussion, abstracting from the concrete results, is provided in the following chapter. Section 4.1, *Reporting Technique for Case Studies*, concisely discusses the applied reporting techniques in order to assist the reader in understanding the aggregation of cases and data. Hereupon, section 4.2, *Empirical Observations*, eventually shows the presentation of the evolved results.

4.1 Reporting Technique for Case Studies

> The reporting of qualitative data may be one of the most fertile fields going; there are no fixed formats, and the ways data are being analyzed and interpreted are getting more and more various. As qualitative data analysts, we have few shared canons of how our studies should be reported. [...] The challenge is to combine theoretical elegance and credibility appropriately with the many ways social events can be described; to find intersections between the propositional thinking of most conventional studies and more figurative thinking. (Miles & Huberman, 1994: 299)

It was consistently argued that this study's character can best be considered to revolve around real life organizational problems, which were analyzed by the employment of contemporary theoretical streams (cf. section 1.2). This progression reflects the dichotomy implied by Miles and Huberman (1994) and suggests that the content of this book generally addresses both theorists and practitioners. Following this argumentation, the reporting of case study evidence requires clear structures to satisfy a diverse readership (cf. Huff, 1999). Yin even describes this awareness and the consequential measures as one of the "essential tasks in designing the overall case study report" (2003: 143) since writing is an encoding procedure serving to locate the produced work in the appropriate context for transmission (Richardson, 1990).

A quantity of techniques can be employed to present evidence and case study reports. Referring to the beginning of this section, Miles and Huberman (1994) contend that the reporting of results of qualitative data might be considered along a continuum, polarized by abstractness and concreteness, variable-oriented and case-oriented approaches (see Ragin, 1987), categorizing and contextualizing methods (see Maxwell & Miller, 1992), analytical and synthetic progressions (see Werner & Schoepfle, 1987), as well as variance and process theory (see Mohr, 1982). This line of reasoning is also reinforced by Eisenhardt and Graebner's suggestion that "the challenge in multiple-case research is to stay within the spatial constraints while also conveying both the emergent theory that is the research object and the rich empirical evidence that supports the theory" (2007: 29). Given this continuum, the question undoubtedly originates which point to select for reporting purposes in order to find a suitable balance of the two dimensions. The selected procedure in this investigation directly follows the methodical constructions. In an earlier chapter of this thesis, the thought was presented that, through the utilization of a theoretical framework, the nature of the applied case studies should be considered as an inductive work containing certain deductive elements. As a matter of fact, the deductive elements require that the presentation of data should converge with proceedings that are rather abstract than concrete, rather variable-oriented than case-oriented (Ragin, 1987). Yin recommends, "The typical case study report is a lengthy narrative that follows no predictable structure and is hard to write and hard to read. This pitfall may be avoided if a study is built on a clear conceptual framework" (1981: 64). Nevertheless, Miles and Huberman also posit, "Stories without variables do not tell us enough about the meaning and larger import of what we are seeing. Variables without stories are ultimately abstract and unconvincing" (1994: 302). The scholars thereby confirm Gergen's (2002) assertion that stories are an essential element for conducting widely accessible science. Yet again, Yin (2003) properly describes a reporting technique in which conceptually adjusted cross-case issues dominate individual cases. The scholar argues that each "section would be devoted to a separate cross-case issue, and the information from the individual cases would be dispersed throughout each chapter or section" (2003: 148). In other words, he states that selected individual case evidence should be concisely presented in addition to cross-case conceptualizations in order to draw on the power of richness (cf. Weick, 2007). A beneficial side effect of the inclusion of such stories should be seen in the propensity to make this book more attractive and interesting for an audience beyond academic spheres. Gathered data by means of questionnaires primarily fulfill the function to describe the constructs whereas interview data provide the corresponding stories.

Based on these suggestions and derivations, I have concluded to supplement the presentation of cross-case issues with the information from individual cases. The subsequent section is thus devoted to present the patterns that emerged through cross-case synthesis. This progression leads to the development of certain propositions that are integrated into the running text.

4.2 Empirical Observations

In order to conveniently present the researched matters and the corresponding results, the section is divided into several parts. Subsection 4.2.1, *Summary of Results*, briefly summarizes the results regarding an elevated level of aggregation and abstractness. Thereby, the reader should become familiar with the investigated construct changes and the developed propositions. The epigrammatic display of both issues, i. e., the construct changes and the evolved propositions, should introduce and convey a general understanding of the research content; therefore, it serves as a reference point before these two issues are originated in depth. The latter measures thereupon dictate the substantial fraction of this section. Each construct and its related propositions are discussed in a separate subsection. For instance, subsection 4.2.2, *Propositions with Regard to Ambidexterity*, deals with the construct of ambidexterity. The remaining two constructs, considering the organizational contexts and its antecedents, are also exemplified in discrete subsections.

4.2.1 Summary of Results

Table 2 provides an initial overview of the analyzed case data, which is supposed to facilitate the identification of pattern shifts and causal interrelations, respectively. As mentioned before, the exemplified pattern shifts are derived in depth in the following subsections.

Table 3 summarizes the generated propositions, which are partially based on the presented construct changes. With reference to earlier thoughts, this study's general orientation relied on the inductive principles of science, which implicates that "even though the premises are true and the argument is strong, the conclusion is at best *probable*" (Reichenbach, 2001:179). In the light of this finding, the scholar suggests to make an evaluative judgment whether an argument or proposition can be considered strong or weak, assessing the likelihood that the implied conclusion is accurate. Ferlie et al. (2005), for instance, differentiate between stronger and weaker scientific evidence in their multiple-case study. This insight was taken advantage of for classifying the 13 proposi-

Table 2: Summary of Construct Scope Modifications

Case	Contextual Antecedents*		Organizational Context*		Ambidexterity*
	Internal → External Orientation	Flexibility → Control	Performance Context	Social Context	Combined Dimension
# 1	++	++	↑↑	↓	↑
# 2	+	+	↑	↔	↑
# 3	++	++	↓↓	↓↓	↓
# 4	++	++	↑↑	↓	↑↑
# 5	-	+	↔	↔	↔
# 6	-	+	↑	↔	↔
# 7	-	++	↔	↔	↔
# 8	-	+	↔	↔	↔

* The displayed modifications signify the development of the corresponding constructs. The strength of the observed modifications is differentiated as follows: no significant change (-,↔), fair significant change (+,↑,↓), and sound significant change (++, ↑↑, ↓↓). The construct changes are further explained in this chapter when these are derived.
Source: author's illustration

tions generated in the analytical segment. Five propositions have a weak substantiation, and eight propositions manage to obtain a relatively strong one. Furthermore, Reichenbach (2001) argues that inductive arguments can be subdivided into three types: generalizations, analogies, and causal statements. The propositions developed in this research pertain to generalizations and causal statements. Generalizations synthesize the concrete case evidence and abstract from individual cases. Causal statements make an attempt to explain the variance between the constructs.

As indicated before, the following analysis of case data deals with the creation of the presented propositions. Comparable to the derivation of the conceptual framework (cf. subsection 3.2), the constructs are exhibited in reversed order. In consequence, the first theme illustrated pertains to dependent concept, ambidexterity, while organizational contexts and contextual antecedents are analyzed thereupon. Verbal descriptions and "construct-tables" (Eisenhardt & Graebner, 2007), as exemplified by several studies (see Eisenhardt, 1989b; Ferlie et al., 2005; Gilbert, 2005), are utilized to facilitate the reader's comprehension.[24] Propositions are derived at two distinct levels in order to account for different altitudes of analytical complexity. The initial propositions of each construct recapitulate the observed changes between the time the interview was conducted

24 Eisenhardt and Graebner suggest, "A separate table that summarizes the evidence for each theoretical construct is a particularly way to present the case evidence. These 'construct tables' summarize the case evidence and indicate how the focal construct is 'measured,' thus increasing the 'testability' of the theory and creating a particularly strong bridge from the qualitative evidence to theory-testing research" (2007: 29).

Table 3: Summary of Derived Propositions

Construct Level	Derived Propositions	Scientific Strength*
Ambidexterity	Proposition 1a: *In majority transactions, the level of ambidexterity is subject to a neutral to positive development after an investment.*	Weak
	Proposition 1b: *In minority transactions, ambidexterity remains at a perpetual level after an investment.*	Strong
	Proposition 2: *Evidence portrays an equitable development of both explorative and exploitative activities following an investment.*	Strong
	Proposition 3: *Exploitative advancements predominantly ensue at the product end whereas explorative enhancements are realized at the market end.*	Weak
Organizational Context	Proposition 4a: *In majority investments, performance management contexts develop positively whereas social contexts become vaguely impaired after an investment.*	Weak
	Proposition 4b: *In minority investments, performance and social contexts are not significantly altered after an investment.*	Strong
	Proposition 5: *Performance management contexts appear amplifiable on the basis of sound social contexts.*	Weak
	Proposition 6: *The enhancement of performance contexts predominantly relies on more ambitious targets, encouraging an improved level of transparency and more frequent feedback cycles.*	Strong
	Proposition 7: *Advancements regarding the organizational performance context positively correlate with enhancements in the level of ambidexterity.*	Strong
Contextual Antecedents	Proposition 8a: *In majority transactions, organizations promote elevated levels of stability in place of flexibility and encourage an intensified external focus rather than an internal orientation after an investment.*	Strong
	Proposition 8b: *In minority transactions, organizations are exposed to gradually ascending levels of control in place of flexibility after an investment.*	Strong
	Proposition 9: *Modifications in the composition of the top management team stimulate the conversion to more-externally oriented and controlled entities.*	Strong
	Proposition 10: *An elevated degree of external orientation positively correlates with upper strata of organizational performance contexts.*	Weak

* Scientific strength assesses the substance of gathered data with regard to each proposition derived. Naturally, some propositions could be considered to draw on indications which were verified by an amplified or lessened chain of evidence. In particular, the addition of a "bad investment case" diminished the power of certain propositions given that most constructs progressed in contradiction to the "good investment cases." According to Reichenbach (2001), the distinction made in categorizing the derived propositions' strengths pertains to "strong" and "weak," signifying advanced and attenuated underlying evidence, respectively.
Source: author's illustration

and the time before the PE investment took place. These insights represent the static foundations for generating awareness of the organizational wide changes, which is a proposition type Reichenbach (2001) refers to as generalizations. In a similar vein, generalizations are employed to further illuminate the issue researched, substantiating and advancing the observed modifications. Hereupon, the incorporation of dynamic insights, based on process theory, is utilized to complement these former propositions. This proposition type is associated with causal oscillations (cf. Reichenbach, 2001), which were expected between the three content building blocks. The orchestration of static, yet perceptive, and dynamic propositions should effectively create synergetic knowledge combining "whats," "hows," and "whys" (cf. Whetten, 1989).

4.2.2 Propositions with Regard to Ambidexterity

Throughout this paper, ambidexterity was described as the organizational wide simultaneous execution of explorative and exploitative activities (cf. Tushman & O'Reilly, 1996). Scholars make the point that exploration and exploitation are typified to either take on a continuous character or an orthogonal one (see Cao et al. 2009; Gupta et al. 2006; Uotila et al. 2009). In this study, the disposition of exploration and exploitation was conceptualized to be orthogonal (cf. Baum et al. 2000; Beckman et al. 2004; Lubatkin et al. 2006); this is in contrast to the categorization of ambidexterity by means of a static continuum, illustrating a nature of mutually exclusive choices as initially proposed by March (1991). The underlying reason pertains to the insight that organizations were not expected to utilize their entire resources at an optimal level, suggesting the existence of heterogeneous differentiations of ambidexterity between organizations. In line with previous research (see Gibson & Birkinshaw, 2004; He and Wong, 2004), a multiplicative interaction score of ambidexterity, which is the product of each of the two orientations, was consequently made use of for the questionnaire analysis. Cao et al. (2009) refer to such a procedure as the combined dimension of ambidexterity and contrast this to the balance dimension which represents the continuous nature of ambidexterity.[25]

25 As suggested above, a combined perspective of ambidexterity was adopted to operationalize the interplay of exploration and exploitation (see Cao et al. 2009). A combined, orthogonal perspective necessitates to either add up the individual results for exploration and exploitation (see Lubatkin et al. 2006) or to multiply both items (see Gibson & Birkinshaw, 2004; He & Wong, 2004). The motivation to multiply both dimensions was contingent on the consideration that, although a combined perspective of ambidexterity seemed to prevail over a balance dimension, mathematical products mediate between both doctrines. Adding up an exploration result of five and an exploitation result of one would yield an identical outcome

The gathered evidence validated the applied replication strategy to distinguish the transactions between minority and majority investments: The level of ambidexterity showed tendencies to significantly vary in buyout scenarios, but it remained relatively stable in minority investments. To explicate findings, Table 4 structures and summarizes the results and should therefore be appreciated as the backbone of discovery.

Propositions 1a and 1b

In the buyout cases, ambidexterity experienced a neutral or positive development in four of the five companies researched. The only negative development was observable at *EmergencyIBO #3*, in which the going concern principle was violated. The cases are portrayed in chronological order, and the derived construct changes, exhibited in Table 2, are motivated. In line with Lubatkin et al. (2006), the subsequent description of exploration and exploitation is structured along each enterprise's modifications pertaining to both the product end and the market end (cf. *Appendix A*).

The collected evidence at *EngineeringMBO #1* suggested inferring a fair positive change regarding the ambidextrous construct. The questionnaire evidence showed an increase of the combined outcome of exploration and exploitation from 9.91 prior to the transaction to a result of 13.41. The respondents described that considerable quality and cost enhancements were realized after the transaction. A strategy manager explained that implemented organization wide Six Sigma standards encouraged "minimizing errors, which in turn cause costs to decrease." Although two respondents remarked that the company put an intensified emphasis on the development of advanced products, auxiliary informants indicated that products have ever been adapted by the company to meet customers' demands, which overall implies a relatively stable level of exploitative or explorative product innovations regarding this incident. Concerning the market side of exploration and exploitation, the informants generally proposed that the company did not make any attempts to deeper penetrate into the existing customer basis. Nevertheless, winning customers from competitors and identifying new customers were described as elements which came to the fore. A marketing manager remarked concerning this issue: "Today, one is required to switch to supplementary markets. In general, we deal with the market more intensely compared to the situation before. We also possess more representations at strategically important locations." By this means, the em-

compared to explorative and exploitative activities that are both valued three. Even under the combined view of ambidexterity, it should be apparent that a result of three for each dimension seems to be a more appropriate ambidextrous result, which becomes substantiated by multiplying the elements.

Table 4: Evidence and Classification of Organizational Ambidexterity (1/3)

Case	Pattern Shift*	Interviews	Questionnaires**		
			Variable	Mean Values	N***
# 1	↑	"This [note: improved product quality] is a fascinating topic. If you merely consider the statistics, we significantly improved the quality of our products in 2010. Reasons date back to [year of the PE investment]. We have introduced Lean Six Sigma and considered basic themes such as risk analyses." (operations manager)	**Exploration**	ex post: 3.80 ex ante: 3.20	5/5
			Exploitation	ex post: 3.53 ex ante: 3.10	
		"New customers certainly play an important role, and these are more intensively targeted. Most notably, there are attempts to win more customers from our competitors. Such actions were not really part of our agenda in the past." (marketing manager)	***Ambidexterity***	ex post: 13.41 ex ante: 9.92 **3.49**	
# 2	↑	"New products and services have been introduced. Moreover, we have attempted to modify existing products in order to access a broader group of buyers." (operations manager)	**Exploration**	ex post: 4.00 ex ante: 3.56	3/4
		"We have evidently become more cost-efficient. We have to think twice before spending each Euro. We dedicate ourselves to this [effort] and require commitment from our employees and our suppliers." (strategy manager)	**Exploitation**	ex post: 3.72 ex ante: 3.06	
		"We are now able to generate higher margins since our volume has increased. Due to the [name of the asset], which we gained by acquiring [name of the company], we strikingly strengthened the market position." (marketing manager)	***Ambidexterity***	ex post: 14.88 ex ante: 10.89 **3.99**	
# 3	↓	"For instance, [name of the product and according segment] was swept under the table in order to focus on young, modern [name of the product], which was merely a niche product. It was missed to explore new market segments." (marketing manager)	**Exploration**	ex post: 3.33 ex ante: 3.00	2/3
			Exploitation	ex post: 3.00 ex ante: 3.41	
		"An essential problem why targeted figures were not achieved pertained to costs that occurred due to the postprocessing of production errors. The production site in [geographical location] was not able to properly manufacture tailor ordered goods […]. Error rates significantly increased, which brought about our downfall." (strategy manager)	***Ambidexterity***	ex post: 10.00 ex ante: 10.25 **-0.25**	

Table 4: Evidence and Classification of Organizational Ambidexterity (2/3)

Case	Pattern Shift*	Interviews	Questionnaires** Variable	Mean Values	N***
# 4	↑↑	"When I joined the company four years ago, 75 percent of the revenue was generated in these countries [note: German speaking countries]. […] This [deficit] was changed fundamentally with the entrance of Private Equity." (strategy manager) "The product portfolio was adapted and modernized to meet current demand. Certain new products were added while old products were simultaneously eliminated. The latter consisted of many antiquated products, which nobody was buying anymore and which were unprofitable." (marketing manager) "We have also put increased emphasis on quality management by having introduced new processes regarding this issue." (marketing manager)	**Exploration** **Exploitation** ***Ambidexterity***	ex post: 3.44 ex ante: 2.78 ex post: 3.89 ex ante: 2.94 ex post: 13.40 ex ante: 8.19 **5.21**	4/6
# 5	↔	"We have ever since changed things [note: products]. This is part of our success story. Without this behavior, we would have never achieved success. Back then, we had a focus on [name of the product]; thereupon, we attempted to diversify." (marketing manager) "There are always small changes to the products. There are projects which are already planned today but which will not be launched before 2012 or 2013. Such projects have ever been accomplished." (strategy manager)	**Exploration** **Exploitation** ***Ambidexterity***	ex post: 3.75 ex ante: 3.58 ex post: 3.79 ex ante: 3.75 ex post: 14.22 ex ante: 13.44 **0.78**	4/4
# 6	↔	"Essentially, there was no change pertaining to the business segments we operate in or to the products we manufacture." (financial manager) "I cannot see any changes [regarding the issues of innovation and efficiency]." (strategy manager) "Efficiency gains have ever been continuously realized. I do not think that any change occurred due to the altered shareholder situation. I do not see any differences." (operations manager)	**Exploration** **Exploitation** ***Ambidexterity***	ex post: 3.94 ex ante: 4.00 ex post: 3.33 ex ante: 3.33 ex post: 13.15 ex ante: 13.33 **-0.18**	3/3

Table 4: Evidence and Classification of Organizational Ambidexterity (3/3)

Case	Pattern Shift*	Interviews	Questionnaires**		
			Variable	Mean Values	N***
# 7	↔	"Manufacturing operations, supply chain management, and so on are totally efficient [and have always been this way]. […] We produce a commodity product and such a market environment requires utmost efficiency." (financial manager) "Growth at our company speaks for itself. I have participated in five production site inaugurations over the last [number of years]. That is a gigantic number. We operate at the highest technical level." (strategy manager) "I do not think [that new markets and segments are explored] more aggressively than before. Once you operate in a stagnating market, growth is only attainable through aggressive moves." (financial manager)	**Exploration** **Exploitation** ***Ambidexterity***	ex post: 4.17 ex ante: 4.25 ex post: 3.58 ex ante: 3.58 ex post: 14.93 ex ante: 15.30 **-0.37**	2/4
# 8	↔	"There was growth because existing products simply experienced greater demand. Simultaneously, we generated growth by replacing products with new technology. […] We have always been a very innovative enterprise, and this behavior has not changed." (strategy manager) "Of the products which were blockbusters 20 years ago survived less than 5 percent. The market [we operate in] consists of competitors' [name of the product] which are sometimes 40 years and older. I think that 30 percent of our products are younger than 5 years, and 60 percent are younger than 10 years. 95 percent of our products are younger than 20 years." (operations manager)	**Exploration** **Exploitation** ***Ambidexterity***	ex post: 3.67 ex ante: 3.67 ex post: 3.40 ex ante: 3.20 ex post: 12.47 ex ante: 11.73 **0.74**	5/5

* The shift in the construct is indicated by the corresponding arrows. It is based on a triangulation of data from interviews, questionnaires, and auxiliary sources. An increasing quantity of arrows symbolizes a stronger categorical transformation and indicates no significant changes (↔), fair changes (↑, ↓), and sound changes (↑↑, ↓↓). The direction of the arrows portrays the development of the ambidexterity level when researched compared to the situation before the investment was conducted; for example, a positive development is denoted by arrows tending upwards (↑, ↑↑).
** Mean values signify the surveyed results of exploration and exploitation; "ex ante" represents the point in time before the transaction occurred, and "ex post" indicates the status quo when the company was investigated. The bold figures signify the difference between the multiplicative interaction products of ambidexterity, calculated as follows: Exploitation * Exploration = Ambidexterity (cf. Gibson & Birkinshaw, 2004).
*** N signifies the number of validly returned questionnaires, e.^g., 2/3 indicates that only two of three interviewed managers returned the questionnaires. Although considerable care was taken to collect all questionnaires after the verbal inquiry, certain interview partners were unwilling to fill out the survey.

Source: author's illustration

phasis on new customers conveys an example of enhanced explorative activities at the market end.

The data triangulation at *ServicesMBO #2* suggested inferring a significant change in the ambidextrous concept, which was evaluated to be fair positive. The questionnaire evidence revealed an increase from 10.89 prior to the investment to a product of 14.88 when investigated. The informants consistently remarked that the company has "evidently become more cost-efficient" after the transaction, yet the entity did not necessarily improve in terms of the offered services' quality. The service portfolio was described to have become adapted and expanded in order to better meet the need of customers. Operating in a market which was characterized by extraordinary levels of turbulence and velocity, the interviewed managers indicated that the company has turned into a very nimble market player, which does not invent trends but which is very fast at "jumping on the technology band wagon," verbalized by a strategic manager. A corporate press release indicated in this respect that the acquisition of a company in a related business segment further enlarged the product portfolio, and a marketing manager declared that this move "strikingly strengthened the market position." Likewise, new regional markets were explored by the establishment of additional local subsidiaries, a finding that was substantiated by an operations manager as follows: "By this move, we reach new customers, who were not located inside our operating range in the past." Activities to enhance revenues with existing customers, such as cross-selling measures, were described as relatively unchanged.

The bad investment case, *EmergencyIBO #3*, was subject to a fair negative change pertaining to the ambidextrous construct. The questionnaire evidence indicated that the level of ambidexterity slightly decreased from a combined result of 10.25 before the transaction to a product of 10.00 after the transaction; this movement would not justify inferring a significantly weaker result, but auxiliary data sources further emphasize the dynamic story behind the interpreted pattern change. The informants mentioned during the interviews that the production flexibility was deteriorated after the PE investment, which extensively diminished the quality of finished goods and simultaneously increased the manufacturing costs. This behavior is appropriately summarized by the following citation from an internal document, provided by an interview partner: "Outsourcing of certain production processes to 'cost-effective' third party suppliers developed as an intensive trend. As a consequence, the quality of goods and services became worse and many corrections were necessary." Regarding the market side of exploration and exploitation, an interviewed marketing manager stressed the subsequent point: "My advice was ignored that [name of the company] focuses on a wrong market segment with its new products. We figured out back then that [name of the segment] was seriously declining [...].

This incident was misjudged by the new management." The statement converges with a description from the internal document stating that certain "premium products were no longer pushed by the marketing department although sales people and customers signified demand." In sum, the penetration of existing markets seemed to have experienced a loss regarding exploitative activities, and new markets were not explored with much effort.

The analysis of evidence at *ConsumerMBO #4* pointed out that ambidexterity was subject to a sound positive conversion after the investment. For instance, the questionnaire data showed an increase in ambidexterity from a combined outcome of 8.18 to 13.40. The interviewed managers described that the company under consideration made uncompromising moves to internationalize the company. According to a marketing manager, "I have just mentioned that we predominantly focused on German speaking countries. Nowadays, we strive to reach international markets." Verifying these moves, which were consistently mentioned by all the informants, corporate press releases noticeably underline these explorative activities: Through the establishment and acquisition of companies in the Asian market, the organization "attempts to increase presence and performance" in the latter geographic area. With regard to the market end of exploration and exploitation, the interviewees mentioned that the product portfolio became much more focused; hence, products that did not constitute a core competence were outsourced to third party suppliers. Emphasis was rather put on core products, which were, according to an operations manager, "adapted and improved." On this account, a corporate press release signified that the company was able to obtain a certification "as the first German [name of the product] manufacturer" in its industry with regard to ecological production processes and eco-friendly products.

At *ConsumerBIMBO #5*, the transformation in the ambidextrous concept did not appear significant. The questionnaire evidence did not indicate a considerable variance in ambidexterity since a result of 14.42 was obtained to demonstrate the situation at the time when researched, and a product of 13.44 signified the condition before the transaction. The informants indicated that products have ever been modified throughout the entire history of the company. For instance, a marketing manager suggested that the contemporary product portfolio was based on several "milestones" of the company's heritage. Likewise, the product quality was described as an attribute which has always received uncompromising attentiveness given that inferior quality could affect the final customers' health. The company experienced an enormous company growth prior to the PE investment. Newspaper articles in the *Frankfurter Allgemeine Zeitung, Hamburger Abendblatt*, or *Spiegel* report that the enterprise under consideration grew by double digit figures ten years before the transaction had occurred; revenues were more than tripled in this period. Although certain informants made the point that several new customer segments have recently been approached, domestic and international growth was the dominant strategic orientation in the years prior to the buyout. In the words of a marketing manager, "Penetration of new markets through the optimization and exploration of new sales floors [has ever represented a dominant activity]." This statement does not imply a considerable alteration related to explorative or exploitative actions at the market end.

Paying attention to the minority investments, the evidence appeared comparatively consistent since ambidextrous activities were not considerably modified in all three cases during the holding period.

According to case evidence, the ambidextrous orientation of *IndSpecialityMINORITY #6* was not significantly altered during the holding period. On this account, the case can be considered the company in which the least divergence concerning the two points in time was reported. The interviewed organizational agents indicated that their business model was responsible for the static behavior over the investment horizon. According to a strategic manager, the products relied on "capital intensive" manufacturing methods, and the industry could be considered an "oligopoly." This constellation posed a difficult context for altered activities regarding the product or market ends of exploration and exploitation. An operations manager said regarding this circumstance: "Our core business is [name of the manufacturing activity]. In this respect, there are almost no innovations in this process." Product quality has ever been attempted to be increased because the industry structure necessitates continuous quality controls along the entire supply chain. In sum, the informants strongly pointed out that no considerable efforts were accomplished to modify and improve its products or to focus on new markets. Nevertheless, this situation was appreciated as a significant weakness, so certain informants proposed thoughts to consider adapting their products for new industries in order to reduce the dependence on the oligopolistic structures. Concerning this outlook, a financial manager said, "We have several renewal activities in the pipeline, but these are not yet ready for the market." The questionnaire data also showed a negligible effect regarding the construct's modification: The ambidextrous level was surveyed to have slightly decreased from 13.33 to 13.15.

Comparably, the ambidextrous construct was not significantly modified at *IndCommodityMINORITY #7*. The questionnaire data proposed a trivial reduction from a combined result of 15.30 to 14.93; both orientations signify the highest observations in the sample. Hence, it should not be surprising that shared consensus was established around the subsequent notion: "The company is prepared for the future. We work at the utmost level of efficiency and innovation," said by a strategic manager. The respondents indicated that the market success of the supplied commodity product generally relies on two critical inputs, i. e., efficient supply chain management and manufacturing operations, which both have always been managed at high efficiency levels. In the words of a financial manager: "It is imperative to fully utilize all efficiencies in a bulk business. We have always accomplished this to a high degree." Concerning the market side of exploration and exploitation, press releases and documents from the corporate website reveal that the company's aggressive expansion strategy had commenced long before the minority investment was carried out. In fact, the company has always attempted to locate new manufacturing sides in proximity to the final customer in order to minimize logistic costs. A strategic manager demonstrated that this "very rapid growth" eventually peaked in the establishment of new manufacturing sides, which were partially financed by the minority investment. In conclusion, a financial manager stated that the enterprise, as a result of the transaction, did not seem to "more aggressively" explore new market segments or to penetrate more deeply into the existing customer groups.

The analysis of *EngineeringMINORITY #8* emerged to be complex, which was caused by the reason that the secondary investment did not constitute a decisive turning point for most of the interviewed organizational members. For instance, an informant mentioned via email that it was challenging to differentiate between the two points in time when filling out the questionnaire. Against this background, it is not surprising that questionnaire evidence suggested a reasonably stabilized level of ambidexterity of 11.73 before the transaction and 12.47 when researched. The investment period of the first investor was generally described as very successful as revenues increased by approximately 20 percent annually during this time. In fact, a strategy manager noted: "[Name of the second investor] has not yet put its stamp on the company [...]." This circumstance was verified by an operations manager who argued: "The most fundamental changes took place when we opted for a minority investment with [name of the first investor] back then." Concerning modifications at the product end of ambidexterity, a corporate document indicated with regard to a relatively exhaustive list of company milestones, established over the past 25 years, that "finding solutions" to difficult problems and "optimising applications" have always been part of the innovation process, signifying strong explorative and exploitative qualities. In a similar vein, the company was described to have ever made moves to explore new markets by leveraging its products to diverse industries, a finding that was also substantiated by press releases and corporate information brochures. Likewise, a strategy manager indicated that the company has ever been "internationally well-placed." In sum, ambidexterity has not been subject to a significant transformation in response to the sale of the minority shares to another PE house.

The described modifications pertaining to both transaction structures revealed adequate evidence to formally derive the subsequent propositions:

Proposition 1a: In majority transactions, the level of ambidexterity is subject to a neutral to positive development after an investment.

Proposition 1b: In minority transactions, ambidexterity remains at a perpetual level after an investment.

Proposition 2

An accusation that is frequently brought forward against financial investors, especially concerning their business model, pertains to managerial myopia, which describes tendencies to exclusively focus on the short-term (cf. Miller, 2002).[26] According to this logic, exploration and exploitation would embody substitutable phenomena; hence, PE companies are indicted to promote the exploitation of corporate resources in place of exploring new ones. Based on the generally positive ambidextrous advancements, inferred from *Proposition 1a*, the reasons for the combined development of exploration and exploitation deserve an intensified analysis in order to verify or reject the highlighted insinuation. In this respect, an examination of this phenomenon also allows for commenting on the continuity versus orthgonality debate presented earlier in this paper (cf. subsection 3.2).

The gathered evidence facilitated to appreciate exploration and exploitation as an orthogonal concept, rejecting accusations regarding temporal myopic behavior.[27] The questionnaire data of cases, as illustrated in Table 4, did not reveal any imbalanced movements of exploitative and explorative activities. To be precise, the corresponding questionnaire data implied that an increase in the total ambidexterity result was based on a simultaneous elevation of the two concepts: The three cases which were signified by positive advancements in the ambidextrous construct (*EngineeringMBO #1*, *ServicesMBO #2*, and *ConsumerMBO #4*) were not subject to an asynchronous movement regarding the two constituents. Rather, interviewees constantly suggested that both efficiency

26 A suitable and concrete example regarding the accusation of temporal myopic behavior is briefly elaborated by the following story taken from a management periodical: "Die langfristige Expansionsstrategie sei bei Gardena durch einen kurzfristigen Sparkurs ersetzt worden, um das Unternehmen für einen Verkauf oder Börsengang aufzupeppen – was Detlef Dinsel, Deutschland-Chef von Industri Kapital, bestreitet. Firmeninsider befürchten dennoch, der Strategieschwenk gehe zu Lasten der Traditionsfirma, die es sich nicht leisten könne, bei der Entwicklung innovativer Produkte zurückzustecken" (Papendick, 2004).

27 Having measured exploration and exploitation as an orthogonal concept, the threat of circular reasoning emerges. Being aware of this circumstance, interview evidence seems compelling to prevent fallacious reasoning as informants talked about the duality of performance gains from a theoretically unconstrained context.

gains and innovative activities were progressively realized at the aggregated company level. Although certain respondents occasionally provided some examples in which resource scarcity constituted a problem, the latter contingency was not a frequently mentioned incident. Similarly, the auxiliary cases, portraying a stabilized movement of ambidexterity, did not hint at any imbalanced shifts of the two components; when ambidexterity remained stable, so did exploration and exploitation. Hence, it comes as no surprise that informants consistently rejected the "Heuschrecken" analogy but emphasized the long-term interest of the financial investor in the company.

In sum, the evidence inferred from the observed sample of cases rejected the accusation that PE investors focus on the short-term maximization of resources. In contrast, the investigation of cases delivered convincing evidence to derive the following proposition:

> *Proposition 2: Evidence portrays an equitable development of both explorative and exploitative activities following an investment.*

Proposition 3

Diversity among theoretical perspectives making use of the concepts of exploration and exploitation necessitated to select a certain perspective for measurement. Having relied on Lubatkin et al.'s insights, ambidexterity entailed "exploration and exploitation differences along an innovation's proximity to the firm's current technological/product trajectory […] and an innovation's proximity to the firm's existing customer/market segment" (2006: 655). O'Reilly and Tushman (2008) refine these dimensions and argue that innovation in the technological/product path consists of incremental, architectural, and discontinuous modifications whereas the second dimension, markets, pertains to alterations regarding the dualism of new and existing customer groups. Drawing on these two dimensions, exploitation was thus employed to predominantly describe gains with regard to incremental product innovation (cf. Jansen et al. 2006) and modifications in the current customer base. Accordingly, exploration was primarily attributed with advances in architectural and breakthrough product innovations (cf. Jansen et al. 2006) as well as a focus on new markets. In line with *Proposition 2*, demonstrating that explorative and exploitative behavior in sum progressed symmetrically, the reflected nature of the transformation was augmented by an analysis of the sources of enhancement: Did advancements predominantly relate to alterations in the companies' product/technology repertoire, or did they pertain to positive achievements at the market end? Figure 11 visualizes the underlying idea and the patterns that transpired.

Case data signified an interesting pattern regarding the previously posed question: Intensified exploitative activities predominantly appeared at the product end whereas augmented explorative activities were primarily enforced at the market end. These pattern shifts were observable in the three cases portraying a positive development (*EngineeringMBO #1*, *ServicesMBO #2*, and *ConsumerMBO #4*). In particular, this kind of behavior can be exemplified by reverting to *ConsumerMBO #4*. Exploration in this case almost exclusively comprised activities to focus on new markets in further continents. Thus, there were no discontinuous modifications in the product portfolio. However, the product portfolio was subject to considerable adaption and advancements, and the manufacturing operations were described as more efficient after the buyout. Finally, there were only minor improvements reported that the organization focused more intensely on existing customers, which implies a relatively stable level of exploitation regarding the market end. A similar outline also evolved at

Figure 11: Changes in the Dimensions of Exploration and Exploitation

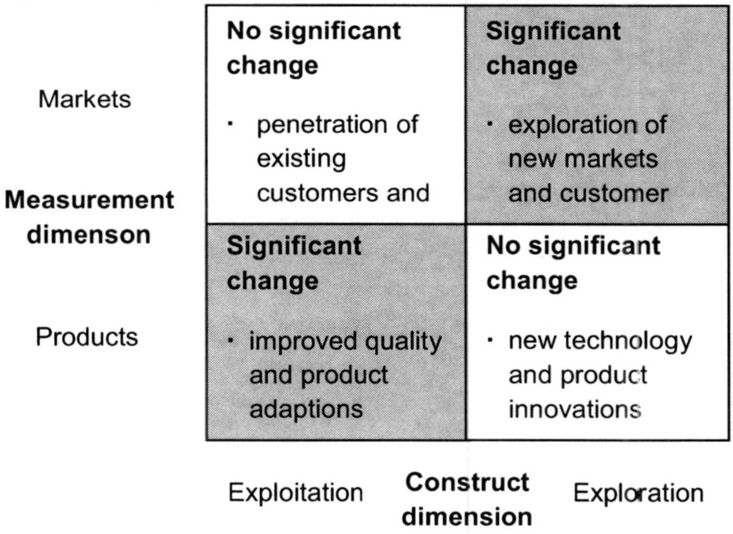

Source: author's illustration

EngineeringMBO #1 and *ServicesMBO #2*, which can be inferred from the presented case descriptions. Evidence from the remaining cases denoted no significant modifications; in fact, stability was not maintained by a substitution between improvements and deteriorations regarding the market and product end.

Summarizing, the picture that emerged seemed robust to derive the resultant proposition:

Proposition 3: Exploitative advancements predominantly ensue at the product end whereas explorative enhancements are realized at the market end.

4.2.3 Propositions with Regard to the Organizational Context

The organizational context was defined as the processes and systems that shape individual action in organizations (cf. Burgelmann, 1983; Johns, 2006; Mowday & Sutton, 1993; Papadakis et al. 1998). With reference to Ghoshal and Bartlett (1994) who describe an organizational context to consist of trust, support, stretch, and discipline, Gibson and Birkinshaw (2004) combine these concepts to derive a performance context and a social context. Birkinshaw and Gibson maintain, "Performance management and social support are equally important and mutually reinforcing. The strong presence of each will create a *high-performance organizational context* that gives rise to a truly ambidextrous organization. However, if there is an imbalance of these organizational characteristics, or a lack of both, a less than optimal organizational context will exist" (2004: 51). This insight substantiates, comparable to the operationalization of ambidexterity, that the organizational context was conceptualized to possess an orthogonal character. Nonetheless, for reasons of analytical concinnity, both variables are treated separately in the following analysis. Empirical results, as will be derived in the following, underlined this approach given that findings verified that both variables progressed unsystematically. Referring to the distinction between buyouts and minority transactions, observations of the performance management and social context were analyzed to diverge between cases. Comparable to the derivation of ambidexterity, key evidence is summarized in Table 5.

Propositions 4a and 4b

In the majority investment cases, the conducted analyses revealed a neutral to positive trend related to the performance management context and a neutral to negative development concerning the social context. The positive increase in the performance management context appeared to be more powerful than the negative development of the social context. The subsequent case descriptions elaborate this issue.

According to the case evidence at *EngineeringMBO #1*, the performance context was subject to a sound positive development, and the social context was found to have become fairly negative. Opening with a quotation from an operations manager provides an initial background to empathize with the situation: "If a company has a CEO who is a merely controlled once a year, this person has more freedom and much less pressure compared to somebody who is supposed

Table 5: Evidence and Classification of the Organizational Context (1/3)

Case	Pattern Shift*	Interviews	Questionnaires** Variable	Questionnaires** Mean Values	N***
# 1	**Per-formance Context:** ↑↑	"Targets increased [in terms of quantity] and also became refined and measurable. Results can thus be documented. […] there are people who tell us how we perform according to these objectives." (operations manager)	**Per-formance Context**	ex post: 3.83 ex ante: 3.13 **0.70**	5/5
	Social: Context: ↓	"Yes, I think [that there is an intensified pressure to perform in the organization]. The huge financial effort, which we have to accomplish, requires more input from every employee." (strategy manager)	**Social Context**	ex post: 3.03 ex ante: 3.23 **-0.20**	
		"You do not have the courage to do many mistakes. Our former CEO promoted the statement that the more one works the more mistakes result. I do not think that this statement is still appreciated today." (marketing manager)			
# 2	**Per-formance Context:** ↑	"Owing to the former shareholders, we were comparatively disoriented. This potentially affected the discipline. Today, we work much more disciplined. […] Objectives are more explicit." (operations manager)	**Per-formance Context**	ex post: 3.50 ex ante: 3.17 **0.33**	3/4
	Social: Context: ↔	"The market situation recovered and we feel much stronger. Colleagues possess a higher expectation. Everybody increases his own standards because there are possibilities which were not present beforehand. […] This is why I require that we aggressively work the market and that we increase our targets." (marketing manager)	**Social Context**	ex post: 3.72 ex ante: 3.50 **0.22**	
		"In my opinion, certain employees seclude themselves […] since they feel a higher pressure to perform. […] Nevertheless, this [incident] has already improved today." (operations manager)			
# 3	**Per-formance Context:** ↓↓	"In the past, decisions comprised personal and entrepreneurial risk because one knew, once things went wrong, somebody was supportive. Decision-making became more cautious, and the band width of possibilities thereby became restrained." (operations manager)	**Per-formance Context**	ex post: 2.75 ex ante: 3.67 **- 0.93**	2/3
	Social Context: ↓↓	"Sarcasm. […] We fought with blunt weapons. We knew better what the customers demanded, and suddenly all of this seemed to be wrong. This deeply affected our work ethics and moral commitment." (marketing manager)	**Social Context**	ex post: 2.25 ex ante: 3.42 **- 1.17**	
		"There had never been so many planning processes which were off target. Everybody forecasted his projects to appear as good as possible, but those objectives were never reached. Targets were set too high. Maybe one should have told these employees that nobody would have bitten their head off in case of a negative outlook." (strategy manager)			

Table 5: Evidence and Classification of the Organizational Context (2/3)

Case	Pattern Shift*	Interviews	Questionnaires** Variable	Mean Values	N***
# 4	**Performance Context:** ↑↑	"Yes, these [objectives of growth and profitability] are extremely pushed in the company. Several divisions, which are responsible for generating revenue and profit, are seriously affected by these targets." (financial manager)	**Performance Context**	ex post: 3.50 ex ante: 3.11 **0.39**	4/6
	Social: Context: ↓	"In my opinion, there was a significant change for the employees. The pace and performance standards that we demand from individual employees, from the whole group, and from each division have been considerably augmented." (strategy manager) "I think there is a trend that many employees refuse cooperation. This means that information is not necessarily circulated or that certain employees, who possess relevant information, intentionally withhold the latter." (operations manager)	**Social Context**	ex post: 2.72 ex ante: 3.17 **-0.45**	
# 5	**Performance Context:** ↔	"The top management level has ever been incentivized by utilizing EBITDA. […] We have not adapted the incentivization regarding separate cash flow based objectives [regarding lower levels]. I consider it difficult to identify the potential individual influence." (finance manager)	**Performance Context**	ex post: 3.71 ex ante: 3.63 **0.08**	4/4
	Social: Context: ↔	"No, [financial objectives do] not really [play a role]. We certainly attempt to fulfill these financial targets. […] We have created an understanding for the meaning of these figures, but these figures are not influential for daily decision-making." (marketing manager) "The working atmosphere is good. We have a very good working atmosphere. There is nobody, who attempts to undermine somebody's position." (operations manager)	**Social Context**	ex post: 3.58 ex ante: 3.83 **-0.25**	
# 6	**Performance Context:** ↔	"From a controlling perspective, we have ever been able to generate high margins. […] Due to this circumstance, there was a lack of necessity to adapt production or marketing targets. […] No particular performance indicators or production piece-rates were introduced." (finance manager)	**Performance Context**	ex post: 3.72 ex ante: 3.94 **0.22**	3/3
	Social: Context: ↔	"We have agreed upon objectives with employees, which serve as the benchmark for performance evaluation. […] Parameters include commitment, flexibility, and the general conduct. We have always had such a system in a similar form." (operations manager) "I would describe this [note: the mutual trust in the organization] as sound and unchanged." (strategy manager)	**Social Context**	ex post: 2.83 ex ante: 3.08 **-0.25**	

Table 5: Evidence and Classification of the Organizational Context (3/3)

Case	Pattern Shift*	Interviews	Questionnaires** Variable	Questionnaires** Mean Values	N***
# 7	**Performance Context:** ↑	"You have to get an overview in which areas there might be internal qualification deficiencies. This is why we attempt to introduce a 20-70-10 feedback control at the holding company. This means, the worst performing 10% of employees need to push themselves in order to keep up." (finance manager)	**Performance Context**	ex post: 3.67 ex ante: 3.67 **0**	2/4
	Social: Context: ↔	"Today, this budgeting process contains undoubtedly more personal input. […] After having participated in this process, one is encouraged to reach the set objectives. Sometimes it is difficult to reach these targets, yet they far from being utopia. These are realistic goals." (strategy manager)	**Social Context**	ex post: 3.58 ex ante: 3.67 **-0.09**	
		"Interpersonal relationships have been modified. […] In the past, all employees were little entrepreneurs, which encouraged and required trustful relations. I do not want to attach a negative meaning to this alteration, simply because it is not necessarily negative. We still collaborate trustfully with each other." (finance manager)			
# 8	**Performance Context:** ↔	"There is a strict discipline in the company. Everybody attempts to communicate mistakes and to avoid the latter. […] Every employee is required to double-check his activities. That is a part of our secret of success, and this has always been this way at [name of the company]." (operations manager)	**Performance Context**	ex post: 3.00 ex ante: 3.27 **-0.27**	5/5
	Social: Context: ↔	"We have recently manufactured a 12 tons [name of the product], but our manufacturing facility and cranes were constructed to meet at most 10 tons. One had thus to find a solution with other departments. By means of teamwork, we identified a third party supplier that possessed a mobile crane being able to lift 25 tons." (operations manager)	**Social Context**	ex post: 3.10 ex ante: 3.10 **0**	
		"Trust of employees in the company has somewhat decreased, but I do not see any difficulties regarding the mutual trust. There are still [unaltered] corporate wide action and planning processes in place." (operations manager)			

* Comparable to the changes in the level of ambidexterity (cf. Table 4), the constructs' modifications, which are based on a triangulation of data from interviews, questionnaires, and auxiliary sources, are indicated by the corresponding arrows.
** Mean values signify the surveyed results of both the performance and the social context; "ex ante" represents the point in time before the transaction occurred, and "ex post" indicates the status quo when the company was investigated. The bold figures signify the difference between the two points in time.
*** N signifies the number of validly returned questionnaires, e. g., 2/3 indicates that only two of three interviewed managers returned the questionnaires. Although considerable care was taken to collect all questionnaires after the verbal inquiry, certain interview partners were unwilling to fill out the survey.
Source: author's illustration

to render account once a month. In the past, he was a king and made his employees run. He himself has to run faster now, and all the rest need to run much faster as a consequence. The dynamics concerning this issue have become considerably higher." Additional interviewees agreed that the company became a place that paid an increased attention to discipline and stretch. This was facilitated at the corporate level through more ambitious targets, which were described as "refined" and "measurable" by an operations manager. An internal corporate document indicated that parameters predominantly possessed a financial nature yet also included elements such as environmental protection or innovation, thereby reproducing the idea of the *Balanced Scorecard* (see Kaplan & Norton, 1993, 1992). Furthermore, incentive systems were renewed for most management echelons, which affected the variable component of remuneration at the personal level. The latter generally reflected an intensified focus on the enterprise's financial targets. The amplification of the performance management context, from a result of 3.13 prior to the transaction to a result of 3.83 when investigated, underlined the positive development. In contrast, the social context experienced a fair negative decrease following the MBO. The quantitative evidence showed a drop from a result of 3.23 before the transaction to a result of 3.03 when examined. The interview evidence provided further insights into the topic. Whereas the respondents generally stressed that trust in the top management and new organizational members decreased, the confidence in former colleagues was not altered. Nonetheless, a more severe issue pertained to mutual support, which was reported by most of the informants to have become considerably weaker. For instance, an informant remarked that there was an increased tendency of people to preserve know-how, instead of leveraging this knowledge. An operations manager replied to the question whether the teamwork was formalized that such an interpretation of the circumstance "would be a positive articulation." Although variance in the respondents' answers portrayed a difficult picture, evidence seemed overall supportive to deduce the above specified pattern change.

The data triangulation at *ServicesMBO #2* suggested a fair positive change related to the performance management context and a stable situation concerning the social context. Quantitative figures revealed an increase in the performance management context from 3.17 to 3.50. The respondents unvaryingly testified that the organization developed into a place in which discipline and stretch were increasingly appreciated and supported. A strategy manager remarked that the new way of thinking made a point in "just demanding more" from organizational members. The conversion was described not to rely on formal processes and procedures, such as altered incentives or personalized targets, but rather on elements that encouraged intrinsic commitment. According to an operations manager, "We are aware that we are all in the same boat and that things need to keep moving. This is why employees try to actively get involved." In contrast to the fair positive development of the performance context, the social context rather experienced a negative transition although the former did not really appear significant. The social context was surveyed to slightly increase from 3.50 to 3.72, but the respondents remarked that mutual support was an issue that emerged problematical after the transaction. An operations manager indicated: "Knowledge is appreciated as a kind of insurance that deteriorates collectivity." However, this thought primarily held in turbulent times after the investment and in the era of the economic downturn but reached a normalized state at the time when interviewed. Underlining this circumstance, a marketing manager pointed out that "egomaniacs" have always been part of the system, reducing mutual trust and support. In sum, the mutual support was described to have progressed unsystematically, but the trust in the top management and the company was described as comparatively unchanged and even as slightly improved.

According to the interview and questionnaire evidence at *EmergencyIBO #3*, a sound decrease in both the performance management and the social context was perceptible. The informants clearly pointed out that there was no more commitment in the organization to meet goals or to exceed the former. "Manipulation," said by an operations manager, of financial and controlling data was described to have become common practice after the investment. This created a situation in which transparent and attainable performance standards were all but existent. Decisions primarily turned into political processes, which, according to a marketing manager, were dominated by certain "rope teams." In the words of a marketing manager, "There was a kind of cooperative atmosphere with the former top management team. This means that things were negotiated without any foreordained conclusion. Thereafter [note: after the transaction], one approached meetings with a certain idea which was always overruled by the top management. I would like to classify these meetings as some kind of 'pseudo discussions' which had a dictatorial nature. [...] Resignation was a natural consequence." Following this quotation, it comes as no surprise that the questionnaire data indicated a considerable decrease in the performance management system from 3.67 to 2.75. Similarly, the social context was subject to a steep decline from 3.42 before the investment to 2.25 when researched. Trust levels in the organization were described as clearly deteriorated after the buyout. An operations manager remarked, "The whole top management team, which was installed by the investor, [...] possessed certain specific knowledge concerning performance standards, leadership, and all these matters. But nobody believed in the things these people communicated, seriously nobody did." A further issue pertained to the integration of formerly separately operating business units. Support across the agents of these companies was described by a strategic manager as relatively sound in the beginning but as "destructed" after the integration, which was initiated by the financial investor.

At *ConsumerMBO #4*, the case evidence manifested to infer a sound positive transformation of the performance management context and a fair negative development of the social context. The questionnaire evidence indicated an increase in the performance management context from 3.11 to 3.50. Likewise, the data showed a decrease in the social context from 3.17 to 2.72. Whereas these quantitative data properly revealed the movement's general tendencies, the strength of the transition seemed to be better rationalized by reverting to interview evidence. The respondents remarked that an increase in "performance standards," "exerted pressure," "pace," and "accountability" combined into a performance management context that was more demanding after the buyout. The subsequent quotation by an operations manager summarizes most of the mentioned elements: "Before, things were ordered to get done today which usually meant tomorrow. Today, things are ordered to get done today which means yesterday. The exerted pressure is completely altered." Remarkably, these qualities were described to have enfolded over the entire organization and thus had an effect on all managerial echelons and administrative divisions. Concerning the social context, the interviewees' observations appeared less strong and more miscellaneous. Generally, these interviewees mentioned that a significant decline in the social context appeared immediately after the transaction. A marketing manager said, "First, there was a breach, [which was] followed by a process of normalization." However, this positive advancement did not materialize organization-wide. Whereas the informants generally agreed that trust in the top management remained at a lesser level, reported support within and between divisions emerged divergently. Certain informants from marketing and financial divisions reported a normalized situation at the time when the interview took place, yet the interviewed employees from production functions pointed out that there was an impaired cooperation within and across divisions. In the words of an operations manager, "Everybody attempts to perform his duties more individually. Integrative problem solving and collaboration has become a lot rare."

The qualitative and quantitative data collected at *ConsumerBIMBO #5* suggested that neither the performance management nor the social context were subject to a significant change. The CEO communicated the issue that people in the organization were not supposed to be affected by the altered shareholder situation. According to him, "It was an objective to push the transaction through without the whole company taking much notice. Even in the later process, employees should not feel a difference. I think that we have acquitted ourselves well until today." The interview partners consistently maintained that there were no modified targets, neither for collective nor for individual performance.

Furthermore, they pointed out that there were no alterations in the fixed or variable component of salaries so that even top management was incentivized by means of identical, untouched parameters. An almost unchanged performance context questionnaire outcome of 3.63 and 3.71 emphasized the stable pattern. Similarly, the social context was characterized to have remained at a constant level. An operations manager said, "Mutual trust in [name of the family shareholder] and in auxiliary employees has not been modified." Besides, the interviewed organizational members indicated that mutual support was not influenced since the BIMBO took place. The questionnaire data supported this viewpoint given that the average result of 3.83, signifying the condition prior to the transaction, marginally decreased to a level of 3.59 when investigated.

In contrast to the large fluctuations in the buyout cases, the examinations of the minority investment cases advocated no considerable alteration regarding the two constituents of the organizational context. The following descriptions elaborate the former derived assertion.

The gathered evidence at *IndSpecialityMINORITY #6* did not indicate a significant transformation of both the performance management and the social context. The quantitative results implied that the performance management context remained at a perpetual level as the mean value of 3.94 before the change of ownership slightly declined to 3.72. Company managers indicated that compensation techniques were not altered as a mean to foster discipline or stretch. Substantiation of this outcome was properly underlined by the subsequent quote by a strategy manager: "We have the motto to let our employees participate in generated profits in successful years. This would be the fourth component, besides base salary, personal evaluation, and the performance of work teams. [...] We have attempted to administer these things right from the beginning." Underlying performance threshold levels were reported to not have been adjusted by a financial manager because the ability to generate high margins has always produced "a lack of necessity to adapt production or marketing targets." Attributes of mutual trust and support, which typify the social context, were also not communicated to have become substantially modified. Although the quantitative data indicated a slight decrease from 3.08 to 2.83, a financial manager "would not speak of a deterioration" concerning the organization-wide trust. However, an informant remarked that confidence in the top management became a bit worse, a circumstance that initiated the installment of a worker's council. Nonetheless, the informant further maintained that interpersonal relationships between divisions generally remained at a high level, and he concluded that personal work ethics were not modified.

According to the sources of evidence at *IndCommodityMINORITY #7*, a fair increase toward a higher level of the performance management context was identified. Moreover, the investigation signified a stable development of the social context. Company managers said that the transformation of certain elements stimulated the endeavor to reach higher performance echelons. Transparency of controlling data, as expressed by the interviewed informants, has increased discipline and stretch. As a strategy manager said, "Today, one is able to recognize deviations [from planning figures] considerably faster, which is caused by the transparency related to performance data. Thereupon, one is usually getting some homework in order to correct these deficiencies." Similarly, a financial manager mentioned that a "20 – 70 – 10 feedback control," with reference to Jack Welch's attempt at General Electric, was introduced, creating an atmosphere in which the "worst performing 10 percent of employees need to push themselves in order to keep up." Nonetheless, certain organizational routines were reported to have remained unaltered. For instance, issues concerning individual incentives and salary components were not modified. The quantitative questionnaire data, however, did not suggest any change in the construct given that the performance management context remained consistently at a high level of 3.67. The social context was described to have experienced some kind of transformation, but the former did not necessarily become worse or better. The respondents consistently mentioned that an increasingly formalized communication lead to a context that still emphasized a trustful cooperation and mutual trust. For example, attributes of organizational equity were reported to not have changed. Moreover, personnel fluctuations were identified as an important element regarding the social context. A strategy manager remarked that one had "to gradually restore confidence" in these employees; a situation which did not justify to speak of a significantly altered social context. The questionnaire data verified this finding given that a result of 3.67 portrayed the condition before the transaction while a result of 3.58 was achieved at the time when the company was examined.

Finally, the collected evidence at *EngineeringMINORITY #8* did not indicate a significant divergence in both the performance management and the social context. As emphasized in the description of the construct regarding ambidexterity, the secondary investment was not a formative event; hence, the most modifications in the constructs were described to have enfolded over a longer period of time. With reference to the collected questionnaire evidence, the performance management context was surveyed to have marginally decreased from 3.27 to 3.00, reflecting the points in time when the second investor acquired the stake from the first one and when the company was examined, respectively. The interviewed managers said that the company formally introduced planning intentions with a horizon of five years long before the secondary transaction took place, which, according to an operations manager, "were providing ambitious targets." Likewise, these agents stated that the remuneration was not subject to any changes. An operations manager explicated, "There were definitively no changes [in the remuneration] at the level of department heads and below this echelon. There have always been fixed and variable components. The variable component is measured by means of management by objectives. These have not been adapted." Although a marketing manager denoted that the economic downturn created a situation in which improved personal commitment was valued, evidence was overall not compelling to infer a modified performance context. In a similar vein, the social context was not subject to a transformation as the quantitative data revealed stabilized average figures of 3.10 for the two points in time. In general, the respondents consistently argued that mutual support and trust were attributes that have ever characterized the organization. For instance, an operations manager said, "Colleagues have always communicated with each other and thought outside the box. That is the situation around here, and this has always been the situation around here. When an employee from the assembly department recognizes that there was a problem in the production department, he assists in finding a solution though it is not in his area of responsibility." Similar stories were provided by auxiliary informants, which agreed on the positive, unaltered nature of the social context.

In sum, the considered cases provided sufficient evidence to infer the following propositions:

Proposition 4a: In majority investments, performance management contexts develop positively whereas social contexts become vaguely impaired after an investment.

Proposition 4b: In minority investments, performance and social contexts are not significantly altered after an investment.

Proposition 5

Birkinshaw and Gibson (2004) conceptualize the binary nature of a performance and social context to be mutually reinforcing for creating high performance organizational contexts. How do the dimensions then relate to each other? Although a negative interrelation of both concepts appeared at first glance, the analyzed evidence rather conveyed the logic that a performance context is extensible on the basis of a decent social context. This move, to build an intensified performance context on a sound existing social context, was also highlighted by Birkinshaw and Gibson (2004) as a potential pathway toward a high performance company. According to the scholars, Renault's transformation in the 1990s signified similar characteristics.

With regard to *Proposition 4a*, the cross-case synthesis indicated that performance management contexts generally progressed positively whereas social contexts at best remained stable. In other words, there was no synchronous movement of both constituents observable. In consequence, the question emerged if an increased performance context unavoidably leads to a decreased social context. The cases in which sound positive performance management context alterations were coupled with fair reductions in the levels of social contexts (*EngineeringMBO #1* and *ConsumerMBO #4*) suggested inferring this line of reasoning. Likewise, the evidence stemming from auxiliary cases (*ServicesMBO #2* and *IndCommodityMINORITY #7*), in which the performance management context was identified to have merely increased on a fair basis whereas the social context remained unaffected, further augmented the former argument. Nevertheless, a statement during an interview, raised by a financial manager from *ConsumerMBO #4*, facilitated a distinctive interpretation: "There is pressure coming from the top management asking why certain things have not yet been implemented, which does not necessarily improve the organizational climate and related issues. But this does not mean that it inevitably becomes much worse." In fact, one can severely question whether increased levels of stretch and discipline stimulate a negative development with regard to trust and support. Considering the situation with the help of a transposed perspective, the story behind the modifications becomes more convincing and reasonable. Decent social contexts appeared to provide a basis on which performance contexts were amplified. Along these lines, the unsuccessful investment case (*EmergencyIBO #3*) implied that a steep decline in the social context was correlated with a sound decrease in the performance management context. Although it is difficult to verify the chronology of the reductions, it would not be surprising that substantial trust and support deficits created an atmosphere that discriminated against performance. Interview data hinted at this reasoning. Without foreclosing too many arguments from further segments, FBes' social contexts appeared to provide an appropriate basis for the formation of extended performance contexts. This line of reasoning is revisited and expanded in section 5.3, *Alterations in Performance and Intra-Organizational Energizers.*

In order to summarize the previous discussion, the following proposition is established:

> *Proposition 5: Performance management contexts appear amplifiable on the basis of sound social contexts.*

Proposition 6

Following the generated insights that performance contexts generally happen to become amplified in buyout scenarios (*Proposition 4a*), which appears to be contingent on the existence of solid social contexts (*Proposition 5*), an intensified clarification regarding the substance of the conversion is necessary. The academic literature usually describes performance management systems to be based on a set of defined practices. For instance, Pollit (1999) maintains that performance management systems catalyze along several processes, for instance, target setting, responsibility assignment, measurement, and internal feedback. Similarly, Smith and Goddard (2002) define a performance management cycle to be based on the subsequent attributes: formulating objectives, designing instruments of measurement, analyzing outcomes, and deciding on appropriate responses. The altered processes of the performance context that were observed in this study happened to be quite similar. To reflect these processes, the subsequent rationalization briefly clarifies the modifications examined.

In essence, business goals and performance parameters were consistently identified as a decisive instrument that facilitated the construct's modification by all respondents from cases that were subject to a transformation in the performance context. Targets converted to become more explicit and ambitious at the organizational level, which were passed through the organization to affect functional divisions, work groups, and individuals. An atmosphere was thereby created that challenged organizational members to increase their input and leave trodden paths in order to comply with the new standards. It was interesting to see that the newly induced and raised performance objectives, which almost exclusively pertained to financial metrics at the corporate level, possessed a self-reinforcing nature that enabled these to spread from top management echelons to middle and lower managerial levels. In this process, top financial metrics were translated into new performance objectives for divisions and in certain cases also for individuals. The interviewees reported that the new targets created a welcomed dimension of transparency, which was often lacking prior to the transaction. For instance, a manager at *ConsumerMBO #4* described the problematic undertaking to collect and provide performance data during the due diligence process; these were at best stored in the minds' of organizational agents. Transparency was further augmented through the utilization of more sophisticated accounting systems. In this vein, the interviewed respondents repeatedly mentioned that the newly implemented tools assisted in creating increased levels of transparency. As a next step, escalated transparency often triggered project and divisional feedback to improve in terms of frequency. In turn, this proceeding made sure that performance standards were upheld. An operations manager from *EngineeringMBO #1* referred to this practice as "meeting hopping." This trinary process related to more explicit and more ambitious performance standards, increased transparency, and enhanced feedback/meeting frequency thus effectively traversed internal organizational boundaries and levels and promoted organization-wide stretch and discipline. Whereas this progression was celebrated more (*EngineeringMBO #1*, *ServicesMBO #2*, and *ConsumerMBO #4*) or less (*EmergencyIBO #3*) successful, *EngineeringMBO #1* was the only case in which an auxiliary mechanism was incorporated to complement this process. Monetary incentives were adapted for individual levels to reflect organizational targets with the aim to accelerate and strengthen the former mentioned dynamics.

The subsequent proposition formally summarizes the observed cross-case patterns regarding the performance context:

Proposition 6: The enhancement of performance contexts predominantly relies on more ambitious targets, encouraging an improved level of transparency and more frequent feedback cycles.

Proposition 7

Finally, the theme is illustrated if and how the constituents of an organizational context are related to the level of ambidexterity. Having primarily relied on the harmonic conceptualization of ambidexterity (cf. Simsek et al. 2009), it appeared compulsory to shed light on the concept of contextual ambidexterity.

Considering the pattern changes in the performance management context and the level of ambidexterity, summarized by Table 3, a positive correlation between these two constructs appeared to subsist in the investigated cases. On the contrary, the relationship between changes in the social context and modifications in the level of ambidexterity were rather unsystematic. The social context should, however, not be interpreted to render unnecessary as implied by *Proposition 5*, but evidence suggested that it was not directly decisive for triggering increased levels of ambidexterity. Although it is speculative to infer a kind of causality between the changes in the performance contexts and the modifications regarding the ambidextrous level, case evidence hinted at this connection. Given that a further reflection on this issue would transform the descriptive character of the hypothesis generation to a mostly interpretative debate, the insights and implications are postponed to section 5.1, *Contributions to the Paradigm of Ambidextrous Organizations.*

While the discussion chapter continues to elaborate the correlation, cross-case evidence indicated to initially derive the subsequent proposition:

Proposition 7: Advancements regarding the organizational performance context positively correlate with enhancements in the level of ambidexterity.

4.2.4 Propositions with Regard to the Contextual Antecedents

The *Competing Values Framework* was utilized as an instrument to assess the most fundamental organizational changes. As already pointed out, the operationalization of the construct emerged iteratively during the analysis of the first cases, which resulted in the circumstance that the subsequently sent out questionnaires primarily provided insights into the nature of the construct in place.

The utilization of an ipsative rating scale forced informants to appreciate the dimensions of flexibility and control as well as the internal and external orientation as converse facets, i. e., as competing values. In line with Cameron and Quinn (2006), questionnaire results were utilized to illustrate the corresponding results by means of graphical illustrations. Functionally, the visualization of quantitative data was described by Tukey (1977) as an exceptionally meaningful tool for recognizing patterns. For this reason, quadrilateral polygons, indicating the configuration of competing values before and after the PE investment, portray the changes in the categorical elements.

The conducted analysis indicated in large part to disregard the emerging four quadrants of dominant orientations, i. e., clan, adhocracy, market, and hierarchy, but rather to concentrate on the two earlier mentioned continuums these dimensions refer to. Comparable to the previous constructs, the separation in majority and minority investments proved meaningful given that the former investment types were characterized by a considerable divergence whereas the latter investments appeared to be relatively stable. Table 6 provides the gathered interview and questionnaire evidence.

Propositions 8a and 8b

The buyout cases exhibited a relatively consistent pattern. On the one hand, the organizations became more externally oriented. On the other hand, control and stability became more dominant values in place of flexibility and discretion. In sum, the observed movement of the majority investments portrayed a conversion from clan-dominated toward market-dominated organizational values. Both directions can briefly be synopsized as follows: "Shared values and goals, cohesion, participativeness, individuality and a sense of 'we-ness' permeated clan-type firms" (Cameron & Quinn, 2006: 41). In contrast, "the core values that dominate market-type organizations are competitiveness and productivity" (Cameron & Quinn, 2006: 39). Whereas four of the five cases experienced this metamorphosis, *ConsumerBIMBO #5*, in which the former family shareholder retained a significant equity stake and his management position, was the only exception. The subsequent case descriptions emphasize these patterns. Given that the discovery was primarily contingent on the standardized questionnaire instrument, the descriptions of the individual cases progress more briefly than the explication of the previous constructs.

At *EngineeringMBO #1*, the dominant clan values (ex post: 29.33; ex ante: 17.83) were replaced by market values (ex post: 35.17; ex ante: 23.33). Therefore, a sound movement toward an intensified external orientation and a sound shift toward more control and stability were concluded. This incident can be briefly summarized with reference to an operations manager: "We rather came from the path that we were a family. This is primarily reasoned by the circumstance that

Table 6: Evidence and Classification of the Contextual Antecedents (1/3)

<table>
<tr><th rowspan="2">Case</th><th rowspan="2">Pattern Shift*</th><th rowspan="2">Interviews</th><th colspan="4">Questionnaires**</th></tr>
<tr><th>Graphical Illustration</th><th>Type</th><th>Difference</th><th>N***</th></tr>
<tr><td># 1</td><td>Internal →
External
Orientation:
+ +
Flexibility →
Control:
+ +</td><td>“Today, we have a CEO who is extremely systematic and dedicated to figures and who manages extremely competent. As a matter of fact, many controls and approval processes were introduced. Employees need to spend time with approval sheets, risk management tools, and so on.” (operations manager)

“Yes, I think that there are alternative values promoting social cohesion today. In the past, social cohesion was stronger […]. Today, social cohesion is generated by collective objectives and success. Performance undoubtedly comes to the fore.” (marketing manager)</td><td>
</td><td>Clan
Ad-hocracy
Market
Hie-rarchy</td><td>- 11.50
- 3.50
11.84
3.17</td><td>5/5</td></tr>
<tr><td># 2</td><td>Internal →
External
Orientation:
+
Flexibility →
Control:
+</td><td>“We face an enormous consolidation phase in [name of the industry] over the next 5 years. This means that we need to opt for growth; otherwise, we might be driven out of business. On the other hand, one of my objectives is to maintain our familial interpersonal relationships and cohesion.” (marketing manager)

“We would like to grow our business. This undertaking is made clear to the employees so that everybody commits himself. Prior to the transaction, such an endeavor would have been unimaginable.” (operations manager)</td><td>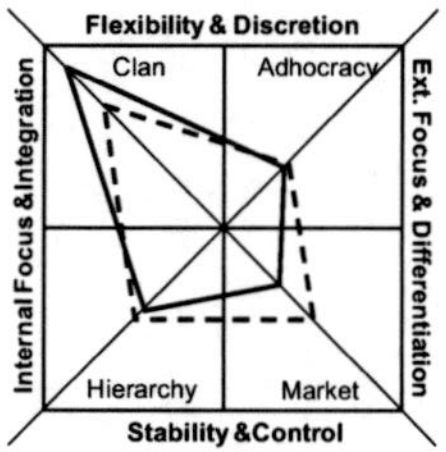
</td><td>Clan
Ad-hocracy
Market
Hie-rarchy</td><td>-9.44
0.28
7.50
1.67</td><td>3/4</td></tr>
<tr><td># 3</td><td>Internal →
External
Orientation:
+ +
Flexibility →
Control:
+ +</td><td>“The move to integrate brands […] did not succeed. Before, we had a strong, internally shared identity. Consequently, this culture was lost, and employees commenced to view each other as competitors.” (marketing manager)

“It was always the conduct at [name of the company] that there was a responsibility of the current generation to safeguard the company for the next generation. Simultaneously, there was a respectful behavior toward the achievements of earlier generations. This was over with the newly hired managers.” (operations manager)</td><td>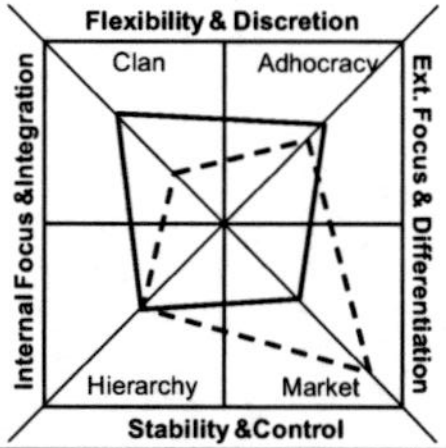
</td><td>Clan
Ad-hocracy
Market
Hie-rarchy</td><td>- 16.67
- 3.33
19.17
0.83</td><td>2/3</td></tr>
</table>

Table 6: Evidence and Classification of the Contextual Antecedents (2/3)

Case	Pattern Shift*	Interviews	Questionnaires**			
			Graphical Illustration	Type	Difference	N***
# 4	**Internal → External Orientation: + +** **Flexibility → Control: + +**	"Given that he [note: family shareholder] had a connecting personality, this trait is somehow missing today. [...] He was even acknowledged as a kind of father figure by several employees. He was the company and provided identification. [...] Today, this umbrella function to connect employees and to close ranks is missing." (marketing manager) "Emphases were altered. One of these was the internationalization - growing larger in size. This has become the primary guiding thought." (marketing manager)	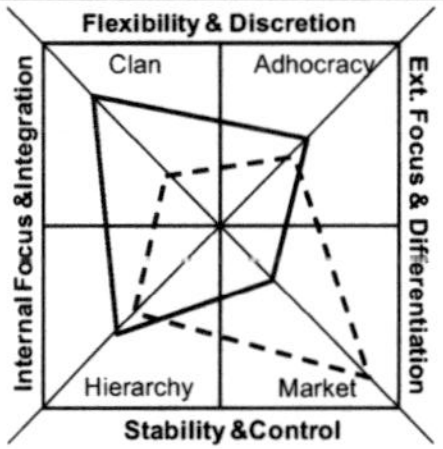	*Clan* *Ad-hocracy* *Market* *Hie-rarchy*	**- 19.53** **- 4.19** **27.92** **- 4.19**	4/6
# 5	**Internal → External Orientation: -** **Flexibility → Control: +**	"I have become acquainted with a quote by Max Planck, which I consider to be brilliant: 'People need science for discovery, but they need faith to act,' and for this they need people who are at the forefront. Therefore, I think that it is important for people to believe in somebody to whom they can hold on. This statement is relatively soft but appropriately describes the situation here." (strategy manager) "In principal, we have maintained the spirit that has ever dominated our way of doing things, but we have introduced the necessary structures to guide the transition from a small family-owned business toward an international company." (marketing manager)	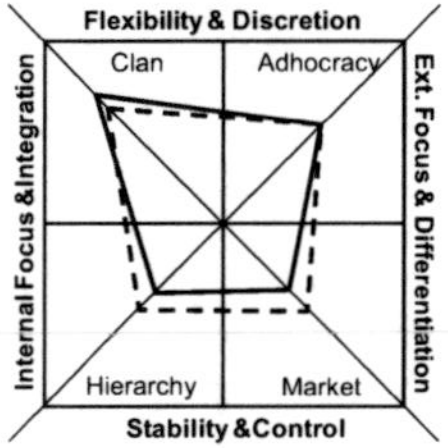	*Clan* *Ad-hocracy* *Market* *Hie-rarchy*	**- 3.75** **- 0.21** **5.42** **- 1.46**	4/4
# 6	**Internal → External Orientation: -** **Flexibility → Control: +**	"We were a relatively familial company in the early days. [...] Through the rapid growth, coupled with the entry of an investor, this identity partially fell by the wayside. More employees mean more structure, which again implies less familial behavior." (finance manager) "Decision-making was relatively unconstrained [in the past]. Employees were able to autonomously decide on small investments. Today, these properties look similar yet a bit less permissive." (operations manager)	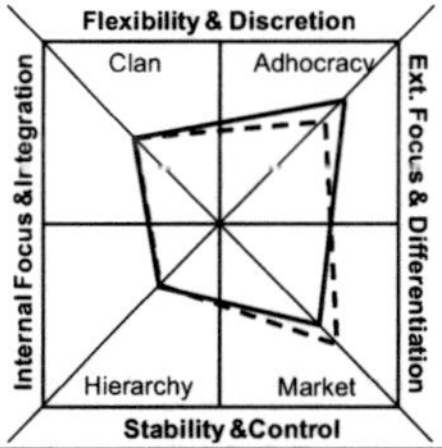	*Clan* *Ad-hocracy* *Market* *Hie-rarchy*	**- 0.56** **- 3.61** **5.00** **- 0.83**	3/3

Table 6: Evidence and Classification of the Contextual Antecedents (3/3)

Case	Pattern Shift*	Interviews	Questionnaires** Graphical Illustration	Type	Difference	N***
# 7	**Internal → External Orientation:** - **Flexibility → Control:** + +	"Today, there is a CFO and also a supervisory board. As a result, administration and documentation processes needed to be established; and as another result, the decision-making speed has clearly been downgraded." (strategy manager) "Since our company is substantially larger in size today, the readiness to assume risk decreased and was actively managed to do so. Themes such as organizational administration and guiding principles have evidently come to the fore." (finance manager)	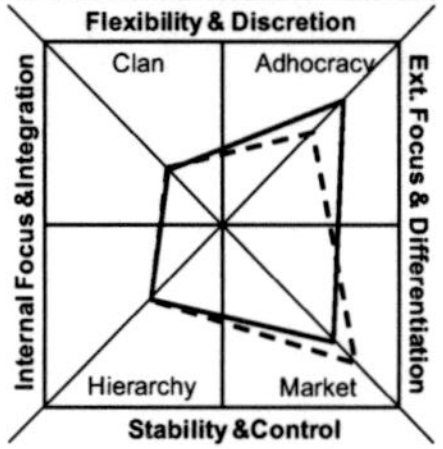	*Clan*	**1.04**	2/4
				Ad-hocracy	**- 6.88**	
				Market	**5.63**	
				Hie-rarchy	**0.21**	
# 8	**Internal → External Orientation:** - **Flexibility → Control:** +	"Division managers were able to engage in unconstrained decision-making [before the transaction]. Today, new top managers increasingly make their own decisions without involving division managers; rather, they [note: new top managers] rely on the introduction of guidelines." (operations manager) "In recent years, certain administrative levels were appended, especially in this year and the last one. This is correlated with the growth having occurred." (marketing manager)		*Clan*	**- 3.33**	5/5
				Ad-hocracy	**- 3.67**	
				Market	**5.50**	
				Hie-rarchy	**1.50**	

* The modification in the construct is subdivided into the two dimensions of the *CVF.* Given that modifications in each case merely progressed in two directions (from an internal to an external orientation and from flexibility to control), the two constructed pattern dimensions were designed to reflect this incident. Therefore, categorical transformations take on three appearances: no significant changes (-), fair changes (+), and sound changes (+ +). The pattern shift is based on a triangulation of interviews, questionnaires, and auxiliary sources.
** The *CVF* is illustrated by means of a graphical framework (cf. Cameron & Quinn, 2006), in which the solid polygons exemplify the situation before the PE investment. Correspondingly, the dashed polygons visualize the situation at the time when the research was conducted. The bold figures illustrate the temporal differences pertaining to each orientation (adhocracy, market, bureaucracy, and clan).
*** N signifies the number of validly returned questionnaires, e. g., 2/3 indicates that only two of three interviewed managers returned the questionnaires. Although considerable care was taken to collect all questionnaires after the verbal inquiry, certain interview partners were unwilling to fill out the survey.
Source: author's illustration

our previous CEO was a great role model. [...] The family sense has undoubtedly been on the decline, but if we behave more competitive is open to question." The interviewed managers consistently indicated that an immense formalization process altered organizational principles, and the company consequently turned into a more stable place. Concerning the internal/external dimension, a marketing manager reported that the organizational glue was based on "collective objectives and success" after the investment, which was winning in the market place.

The orientation of *ServicesMBO #2* remained stable with a dominating clan culture (ex post: 44.03; ex ante: 34.58) although the organization was subject to a sound transformation toward an increased external orientation as well as to a fair conversion toward stability, documented by intensified market values (ex post: 23.75; ex ante: 16.25). An operations manager substantiated that "a new philosophy which is much more focused on growth and organizational development" emerged in the organization. Whereas an amplified external orientation appeared to be the prevailing stimulus, the company was also described as a more controlled place after the transaction. For instance, a strategy manager mentioned that the improved procedural transparency was a result of an "elevated focus on planning." Nevertheless, the company was still characterized as a very flexible place, in which communication circulated boundaryless.

The gathered data at *EmergencyIBO #3* indicated that both relevant dimensions experienced a sound shift toward an enhanced external orientation and stability, respectively. The *CVF* summarized that the prevailing values characterized a clan atmosphere (ex post: 13.75; ex ante: 30.42) before the transaction, which hereafter turned into a market atmosphere (ex post: 39.58; ex ante: 20.42). Concerning the magnitude of the observed change, an operations manager maintained: "This was definitely a paradigm shift from a family business toward a plain truth, which was painful for many people. Humanity was suppressed, and many things were kept in perspective, considerably kept in perspective." The interviewed informants affirmed that the loss of the patriarch significantly changed the communication within the organization, which was described as relatively informal prior to the investment and as more hierarchical and formal after the transaction. Concerning the internal/external dimension, the informants consistently proposed that the atmosphere changed from an integrative place toward a reasonable aggressive place of interaction. This modification was again stimulated by the consolidation of the existing business units. As a result, a marketing manager expressed the thought that people commenced to "view each other as competitors."

According to case evidence, *ConsumerMBO #4* was portrayed by both a sound change toward elevated levels of external orientation and differentiation as well as toward stability and control, which resulted in the substitution of clan values for market ones. In this vein, the questionnaire data suggested that the dominant clan dimension (ex post: 14.44; ex ante: 33.97) was displaced by the market dimension (ex post: 41.67; ex ante: 13.75). Consistent with these findings, an operations manager reported that a sense of internal orientation was lost after the investment: "The sense of we-ness which was existent and this openness with each other [is missing today]. This was really a different situation back then." Instead, a marketing manager articulated that the organization promoted growth as a "guiding thought." Moreover, a financial manager mentioned that one could "clearly identify the company as a family business" before the transaction, which was not necessarily the case after the change of ownership. Summarizing, a marketing manager remarked, "I really think [...] that one is living in a microcosm in a family business. Opening up creates input from diverse parties. [...] Information from the world and markets provokes a certain kind of transformation."

As described in the beginning of this paragraph, the observed variance at *ConsumerBIMBO #5* was comparably lower compared to the remaining buyout cases. A fair shift of the flexibility/stability continuum in the direction of more stability and control was observable. However, the clan orientation (ex post: 31.46; ex ante: 35.21) remained to be the centrally framing scope. Explaining this sluggishness, a marketing manager pointed out that the "spirit" within the organization was not magnificently altered due to the new shareholder situation. According to an operations manager, "The target course has always been forward-facing, [delivering] good quality, providing confidence, remaining familial, keeping our feet on the ground. These elements are personified by [name of the family shareholder]." Despite this relatively stable development, the evidence also indicated that "necessary structures," verbalized by a marketing manager, were instituted to meet the new professional demands. These were reported to slow down actions and added complexity to organizational life. The former fact was also supported by a handed over organizational chart which underlined an amplified principle of formal control.

Consistent with the relatively unambiguous picture presented by the majority investment cases, the minority cases delivered an equally compelling description. Nonetheless, these cases were dominated by an adhocracy environment before the investment, which either remained in place or shifted toward a market orientation. Adhocracies, being based on the term "*ad hoc* – implying something temporary, specialized, and dynamic" (Cameron & Quinn, 2006: 43), already operate with regard to a high external orientation and thereby implicitly discriminate against significant changes in the former direction. The subsequent paragraph elaborates these thoughts and provides exemplary case evidence.

IndSpecialityMINORITY #6 was subject to a fair change toward more control and stability after the transaction. This move resulted in the replacement of the adhocracy type (ex ante: 32.78; ex post: 29.17) for the market setting (ex ante: 26.94; ex post: 31.94). A financial manager mentioned that there was historically a "laissez-faire structure," coordinated by a method described as "management by activism." The informant further pointed out that this behavior was partly replaced due to the requirements of the financial investor regarding transparent processes and planning figures; thus, there was some kind of "coercion toward more structure." Correspondingly, another interviewee reported that decision-making has always been unconstrained; however, it became a bit more formalized after the investment. Underlining the transition from adhocracy-dominated to market-dictated values, an operations manager pointed out that money was considered a more central issue: "With the entry of Private Equity, money happened to become a lot more important."

Similar to the previous case, *IndCommodityMINORITY #7* was submitted to a change concerning increased levels of stability and control. However, this shift emerged to be more powerful than in the previous case. Therefore, the transformation was characterized as sound. The questionnaire data indicated that the dominant orientation pertaining to adhocracy qualities (ex post: 26.25; ex ante: 33.13) were replaced by a market orientation (ex post: 37.92; ex ante: 32.29) when researched. In this sense, the internal/external continuum was not modified. To underline this incident, an internal document, describing the corporate culture, indicated a very externally oriented philosophy, in which "market leadership" and a management style that is "goal oriented and performance driven" have always constituted the guiding principles. Explicating the movement toward intensified levels of control and stability, two interviewed financial managers consistently remarked that the "readiness to assume risk decreased" and that elements pertaining to "administration and documentation processes" undoubtedly possessed higher organizational importance and attentiveness after the PE investment. The following quotation by a strategy manager was also interpreted to highlight this result: "Due to this gigantic financing sum, there are definitely different requirements and conditions to be met [...]. Today, there is the trend that entrepreneurship, which was based on bilateral conversations, fast decision-making, and autonomy, has been replaced. Today, decisions need to be safeguarded and corporate directives, such as investment decisions, need to be adhered to."

In line with the previous minority investment cases, the evidence collected at *EngineeringMINORITY #8* did not suggest a significant alteration along the internal/external dimension but a fair movement in the direction of stability and control; the adhocracy type (ex post: 27.50, ex ante: 31.17) continued to be the framing element, yet the market cluster (ex post: 27.00, ex ante: 21.50) evidently gained weight. All the informants mentioned that the company put an increased emphasis on bureaucratic activities since the ownership had changed from one

PE house to another one. A strategy manager explained this movement, "As soon as an enterprise grows by 20 percent over a quantity of years, the administration of this company needs to make a similar progress. [...] They [note: employees] must learn to define processes and to successfully implement the latter. This has commenced in [point in time when the second investor bought outstanding shares]." Concerning the internal/external continuum, a marketing manager pointed out that she did not observe any movements for the reason that the company has always been open to outside initiatives.

The examined cases gave rise to formally summarize the changes with the help of the following propositions:

> *Proposition 8a: In majority transactions, organizations promote elevated levels of stability in place of flexibility and encourage an intensified external focus rather than an internal orientation after an investment.*

> *Proposition 8b: In minority transactions, organizations are exposed to gradually ascending levels of control in place of flexibility after an investment.*

Proposition 9

It was interesting to observe that the five buyouts depicted certain differences regarding the changes in the corporate values, which were aggregated by *Proposition 8a.* In an earlier segment of this paper, the idea was introduced that management is a significant factor for inducing organizational change. This aspect reappeared in the researched cases. The replacement of top organizational personnel played an influential role, which mediated the magnitude of changes in the guiding values. Cases in which the CEO was replaced during the holding period (*EngineeringMBO #1*, *EmergencyIBO #3*, and *ConsumberMBO #4*) were associated with considerably higher fluctuations regarding modifications in the *CVF.*

The three above mentioned cases, which experienced a CEO replacement, were portrayed by a transformation from clan to market values. In contrast, the auxiliary two cases (*ServicesMBO #2* and *ConsumerBIMBO #5*) were found to maintain, although with a diminished intensity, their established dominant orientations. For instance, the shift toward a market culture at *ServicesMBO #2* relied on two dimensional transformations that were merely identified as having possessed a fair magnitude. Likewise, *ConsumerBIMBO #5* was merely classified by means of a fair oscillation regarding the flexibility/control dimension. Section 5.2, *Reflection on the Context and Process of Organizational Change*, deals with these findings in greater depth.

In sum, the case evidence provided substantial proof to derive the resultant proposition:

Proposition 9: Modifications in the composition of the top management team stimulate the conversion to more externally-oriented and controlled entities.

Proposition 10

Comparable to the derivation of *Proposition 7*, in which the relation between the transformation of the organizational context and the level of ambidexterity was considered, the final proposition analyzes the association between changes in the contextual antecedents and their effect on the fluctuation of the organizational context. Although this issue is intensely reflected in several later sections of this paper, the subsequent consideration introduces the basic picture that evolved.

Reverting to *Propositions 8a* and *8b*, cross-case patterns suggested inferring that an elevated degree of external orientation positively correlates with oscillations in the performance context. With regard to Table 2, an intensified external orientation usually triggered the performance context to develop positively across cases, except for *EmergencyIBO #3*. The second measurement continuum, i. e., flexibility versus stability, did not appear to have a decisive influence on the performance management or the social context. The transformation of the researched organizations that became increasingly externally oriented thus activated these entities to reconfigure their performance operations. A concentrated perception of the external environment and an alignment with the latter thus served as an initial benchmark of the own position. After having examined environmental reality, the resultant actions hereupon comprised the modification of performance standards. For instance, family conflicts (*ServicesMBO #2*) or the fierce calibration of the company regarding family goals (*ConsumerMBO #4*) were reported to have impeded the cognition of economic threats and opportunities. Once the companies overcame such internal obstacles, performance contexts were improved as a consequence.

In sum, there was compelling proof to infer the final proposition:

Proposition 10: An elevated degree of external orientation positively correlates with upper strata of organizational performance contexts.

5. Discussion

In general, the discussion is geared to the quality research guidelines of the *International Family Enterprise Research Academy* (IFERA, 2003): Theoretical consequences and potential shortcomings are discussed and subsequently connected to the research questions. Given that the derived results constitute an outcome of multifarious theoretical conceptions from the domain of FBes, PE, and the field of organization science, the design of this chapter permits broad freedom to select the most relevant themes.

Bem suggests that the discussion segment symbolizes "the bottom of the hourglass-shaped format and thus proceeds from specific matters [...] to more general concerns [...]. The sequence of topics is often the mirror image of the sequence in the introduction" (1987: 187). This recommendation was seized to thoroughly rationalize the subsequent structure adopted. Furthermore, the author states that one of the essential tasks in writing high quality discussions pertains to the selection of important themes, and researchers should focus on the positive advancements instead of getting lost in accounting for "every hiccup in the data" (1987: 188). This chapter consequently pays attention to certain important subjects. Concretely, the decision was made to comment on three central topics in reversed order compared to their derivation. Whereas the derivation of the research questions represented the dominant topic in chapter 2, *Family Businesses and Private Equity*, chapter 3, *Organizational Change, and Conceptual Model*, was generally subdivided into the theoretical foundation of organizational change and the consideration of the conceptual framework, i. e., the content of change. Drawing on Bem's (1987) recommendation, these three themes channel the discussion from specific to general issues, from a reflection on the utilized theory to a response to the two proposed research questions.

In section 5.1, *Contributions to the Paradigm of Ambidextrous Organizations*, the content of change is discussed. For this purpose, the research skeleton of ambidextrous organizations is enhanced by integrating the insights of this study, fostering the journey "from an emergent to a paradigmatic status" (Raisch and Birkinshaw, 2008: 403). Section 5.2, *Reflections on the Context and Process of*

Organizational Change, introduces some thoughts regarding the circumstance why and how categorical shifts took place; thereby, it connects the content of change to the process and context. Due to the natural complexity that the observed organizational changes need not necessarily have been induced by the PE investments, the discussion emphasizes that the observed variance can indeed be related to the investigated phenomenon. Therefore, the debate in this section bears an analogy to what Yin (2000) refers to as the analysis of "rival explanations," a process validating empirical impressions. In section 5.3, *Alterations in Performance and Intra-Organizational Energizers*, the "bottom of the hourglass-shaped format" (Bem, 1987: 187) synthesizes the former twofold debates while reverting to the research objective, which is to enhance our understanding of the organizational metamorphosis of FBes in the course of a PE investment. This part of the discussion eventually makes an attempt to rationalize the investigated transformations and thereby provides the basis for developing scientific and theoretical implications, which are presented in chapter 6, *Conclusion*. Each of the three following sections commences with a short, hypothetical dialogue in order to channel the reader's attentiveness to the dominant problems identified as well as to the solutions proposed by the insights that follow.

5.1 Contributions to the Paradigm of Ambidextrous Organizations

Practitioner: How do I ensure the survival of my company?

Academic: Liberate all resources in your company in order to make sure that you both exploit your current opportunities and simultaneously explore future prospect earnings.

Practitioner: How do I simultaneously integrate both directions?

Academic: Manage ambidextrously. Ignore artificial boundaries such as tradeoffs. In the past, academics were inclined to think that in certain periods you need to seed whereas in others you need to reap the fruits. Likewise, they thought that the coexistence of rigid bureaucracies and anarchic units integrates into meaningful structures. Contemporary scientific evidence, however, suggests that you need to build a context which stimulates both types of behavior. It is an enlightening concept combining many theoretical streams.

Practitioner: Why should I abandon to think in tradeoffs? What is the underlying reason to do so? Does this concept pertain to individual or collective behavior? How do I build a context that stimulates the former behavioral characteristics?

As indicated in the introductory paragraph of this chapter, the elements addressed in this section are supposed to enhance the paradigm of ambidextrous organizations by reverting to theoretical shortcomings. In consequence, the discussion progresses relatively isolated from the research questions of this paper, discriminating against the context from which the findings were derived. The elaborated insights from this section are, however, utilized in section 5.3, *Alterations in Performance and Intra-Organizational Energizers*, which eventually strives to integrate the considered elements into the discussion of the research questions.

Having followed Gibson and Birkinshaw's (2004) conceptualization of contextual ambidexterity, described by Simsek et al. (2009) as a harmonic interpretation of the concept, this study contributes to the research doctrine with regard to multiple dimensions and accordingly provides some answers to the fictional dialogue presented in the beginning of the section. In order to structure the following discussion, two central perspectives are considered. First, the study's theoretical implications, which follow for the field of ambidexterity, are briefly scrutinized. The focus of this debate pertains to the consideration of certain paradigmatic advancements inferred from this empirical inquiry. Second, attention is paid to the established propositions which reflect causal statements, i. e., *Proposition 7* and *Proposition 10.* In fact, this part of the discussion considers how the conversion of corporate values is mirrored up to an alteration in the performance management and social context. Likewise, the correlating patterns of the levels of the performance context and ambidexterity are discussed. This latter debate should deliver a better understanding of the antecedents of ambidexterity.

5.1.1 Consideration of Certain Theoretical Challenges

Many themes of the ambidextrous concept have meanwhile been subject to an intensified clarification, among them the heterogeneity in achieving exploration and exploitation regarding temporally sequential (Duncan, 1976), structurally separate (Tushman & O'Reilly, 1996), or structurally and temporally simultaneous (Gibson & Birkinshaw, 2004) conclusions to the problem. On this account, researchers do not call the existence of different paths to ambidexterity into question. Nonetheless, work in progress conceptualizations usually have certain deficiencies that deserve special attention to direct the development. The results presented in this research suggest addressing two issues, namely the logic of exploration and exploitation as well as the level of analysis, respectively. Both attributes are concisely discussed to confirm and advance existing thoughts on these themes.

Logic of Exploration and Exploitation

The academic community struggles to appreciate the interplay of exploration and exploitation as an orthogonal concept or as a continuous one (cf. subsection 3.2). Recently, most empirical studies utilized the orthogonal nature of the concept (see Beckman, 2006; Bierly & Daly, 2007; He & Wong, 2004; Jansen et al. 2006; Lavie & Rosenkopf, 2006; Lubatkin et al. 2006). Nevertheless, studies also analyze the phenomenon by reverting to a continuous logic (see Auh & Menguc, 2005; Sidhu et al. 2007; Uotila et al. 2009; Wadhwa & Kotha, 2006). Summarizing, Cao et al. conclude that "although there is broad agreement that organizational ambidexterity somehow relates to the simultaneous pursuit of exploratory and exploitative activities, there exists a lack of conceptual clarity regarding the extent to which ambidexterity concerns matching the magnitude of exploration and exploitation on a relative basis, or concerns the combined magnitude of both activities" (2009: 781). March's (1991) initial reasoning that both dimensions pertain to mutual tradeoffs is based on the insight that resources, stimulating either type of development, are scarce. According to him, organizations face mutually exclusive choices of consumption and utilization. This line of reasoning is all but attainable to reject, but the premises can be challenged. Upon this consideration, Gupta et al. (2006) posit three conclusions whether exploration and exploitation should be considered an orthogonal or a continuous concept. First, they propose that the scarcer the resources needed, the greater will be the likelihood that these emerge as mutually exclusive. Second, the scholars maintain that the choices are mutually exclusive within a single domain, which they see in an individual or an organizational subsystem. Third, they continue the previous argument by stating that the logic becomes orthogonal across different domains since the coexistence of various individuals or subsystems allows for an aggregation, which aligns explorative and exploitative domains. The three axioms are briefly considered in relation to the indication that ambidexterity represents an orthogonal phenomenon, which was implied by the results of this study (*Proposition 2*).

Concerning the first axiom, Gupta et al. raise the subsequent issue: "Although it is generally true that most resources are finite, this need not be so for all types of resources. Some resources, such as information and knowledge, may be infinite" (2006: 195). Most tangible assets might indeed be limited by physical constraints, yet, as the scholars suggest, certain intangible assets might be subject to an unlimited nature. Emphasizing this thought, Baum et al. (2000) maintain that exploration and exploitation related to organizational learning, in which the former is based on learning from other organizations and the latter is based on cultivating the experience from past occurrences, has an orthogonal character given that the attainable resources from learning seem endless. Along similar lines, Cao and colleagues (2009) differentiate between a balance dimension of ambidexterity (BD) and a combined dimension of ambidexterity (CD), describing the continuous or orthogonal nature, and they also maintain that the character of the considered resources plays a central role. They find that the BD of ambidexterity better explains companies' decisions that are limited by their resources whereas the CD of ambidexterity clarifies the development for institutions which possess a relatively unconstrained supply of resources. Furthermore, Cao et al. (2009) argue that resources can internally be leveraged from explorative to exploitative activities and vice versa, promoting a synergetic momentum effect of both elements. Converging with this line of reasoning, Taylor and Helfat (2009) show that organizational linkages, as an instrument to leverage resources, present important inputs for realizing ambidexterity. With reference to the findings presented in this research, the latter verdicts advocate that a potential explanation of the orthogonal phenomenon might be based on the circumstance that resources in the researched companies were not fully taken advantage of prior to the PE investment. In other words, the researched entities did not seem to be constrained by a general resource problem before the transaction, which discourages a continuous logic.

How were resource configurations of seemingly elevated quality reached after an investment? Given that the organizational context was partly found accountable for triggering modifications in the level of ambidexterity (*Proposition 7*), the focal point of scrutiny should be individuals as intermediaries of resource absorption and leverage as, for instance, demonstrated in Verona's (1999) agent based resource model. According to the scholar, agents are responsible for experimenting and managing resources and capabilities, such as in the area of technology or marketing. Following this logic, organizations need agents to manage the absorption of external, infinite resources and to administrate the internal leverage of resources and processes; both integral processes are defined as the origins of organizational learning (Huber, 1991). Expanding this thought, it appears that modified contexts thus indeed affect managerial behavior while stimulating altered decision-making as proposed by several studies (see Connor, 1992; Ghoshal & Bartlett, 1994; Gibson & Birkinshaw, 2004; Papadakis, 1998; Smith & Goddard, 2003). Therefore, it seems that organizational contexts, especially performance management systems, can be designed to encourage individuals to perform the above considered dual activities at higher levels. Although there are hypothetical maximums limiting the absorption and leverage of resources which forces to think in a continuous dimension, an orthogonal viewpoint seems to be a prevailing conceptualization concerning the individual stratum. Consistent with insights of Mom et al., this research's findings hint at the direction that "exploration and exploitation are not mutually exclusive at the manager level" (2007: 925). The former outcome can be identified as quite remarkable in relation to the second axiom raised by Gupta et al. (2006), which suggests that choices within single domains are generally mutually exclusive.

Finally, Gupta et al.'s (2006) third conclusion, considering the aggregation of different subsystems, seems to become reinforced by the findings of this study. The case evidence described the tendency that marketing and production departments diversely promoted explorative and exploitative activities (*Proposition 3*). Explorative advancements were primarily observed at the market end whereas exploitative advancements were predominantly examined at the product end when considering the two concepts along a company's product portfolio and its targeted markets (see Benner & Tushman, 2003; O'Reilly & Tushman, 2008). These activities synergistically combined at the organizational level, implying an orthogonal character of ambidexterity.

Summarizing the previous chain of arguments, Gupta et al. (2006) maintain that external resources might be infinite and that the possibility of absorbing these resources gives rise to an orthogonal perspective. From an internal or closed perspective, Cao et al. argue that "resources can often be effectively leveraged across both types of activities" (2009: 784), which implies the existence of internal mechanisms that excel the utilization of existent resources. Adhering to the results of this paper, managers from different organizational echelons seems to be an interfacing device enabling both processes. By doing so, the individual level is likely to proof as an organizational domain which can operate ambidextrously without being subject to continuous impediments (Mom et al. 2009, 2007). In conclusion, an ambidextrous logic that is stimulated by behavior does not necessarily seem to be restricted by static resource contingencies but rather rests on the insight that capabilities can be expanded and orchestrated by means of absorption and leverage.

Level of Analysis

Besides contributing to the debate how the combinatory nature of exploration and exploitation should be interpreted, the discussion above highlighted at least one further dimension of theoretical imperfection. In fact, the level of analysis deserves some attention to explain the interplay of different organizational echelons. Although this study reverted to Gibson and Birkinshaw's (2004) fundamental idea concerning organizational behavior as an instigating factor for inducing ambidexterity into organizations, the ambidextrous construct was applied distinctively in this paper. The scholars identify ambidexterity as a construct capturing a phenomenon at an individual level rather than at an organizational one. Precisely, they model exploration and exploitation as the individual characteristics of organizational members to simultaneously strive for alignment and adaptability in their task environment. Opposed to this categorization of Gibson and Birkinshaw (2004), ambidexterity was researched to relate to the organizational level in this inspection, but the organizational context was measured as a mean to stimulate individual commitment, which outlines a concern of multilevel organizational theory (cf. Klein et al. 1994; Kozlowski & Klein, 2000; Lindsey et al. 1995; Morgeson and Hofmann, 1999). Hence, it is not surprising that the combination of individual and organizational levels of analysis constitutes an unresolved issue in the theoretical debate of ambidextrous organizations (O'Reilly & Tushman, 2008; Raisch & Birkinshaw, 2008; Raisch et al. 2009; Simsek, 2009). Summarizing this theoretical deficiency, Raisch et al. state that a "tension relates to the question whether ambidexterity manifests itself at the *individual* or *organizational* level" (2009: 686).

Insights derived in this study seem to confirm the viewpoint that the individual echelon represents a decisive factor for the creation of organizational ambidexterity (*Proposition 7*), a finding that confirms recent studies (see Groysberg and Lee, 2009; Mom et al. 2009, 2007). The former empirical contributions emphasize Raisch and Birkinshaw's (2008) notion that "the level of analysis is vitally important, because choices about how to resolve the tension at one level of analysis are often resolved at the next level down" (2008: 396), which represents an issue that was also discussed with regard to complexity theory (see Anderson, 1999). For this relationship to work, individuals are subject to the premise that they can seize on explorative and exploitative actions (Raisch et al. 2009). Therefore, these individuals enjoy the capabilities to engage in paradoxical thinking (Smith & Tushman, 2005), obtain both a long-term and short-term perspective (O'Reilly & Tushman, 2004), and are capable of engaging in alignment and adaption activities (Gibson & Birkinshaw, 2004). Acknowledging these personal characteristics, organizational contexts were assumed to play a pivotal role in encouraging the former attributes. Through the positive relation between the intensity of the performance context and ambidexterity (*Proposition 7*), the association of the individual and organizational level of ambidexterity appears to be implicitly validated by the results of this paper. Although the accretion "implicit" deliberately hints at the circumstance that the relation only has a black box character, previously cited studies provide sufficient evidence to infer the proposed reasoning. Nevertheless, Mom et al. advocate that it remains highly "interesting to explicitly examine the relationship between managers' ambidextrous behavior and the firm's or business unit's level of ambidexterity and performance" (2009: 825).

5.1.2 Consideration of the Antecedents of Ambidexterity

To begin with, this research supports the idea that ambidexterity arises from the organizational context, which was implied by *Proposition 7*. The results therefore confirm the wide base of studies that attempt to find a behavioral rationalization of the emergence of ambidexterity (see Adler et al. 1999; Corso & Pelligrini, 2007; Gibson & Birkinshaw, 2004; Smith & Tushman, 2005). Gibson and Birkinshaw (2004) indicate that ambidexterity is contingent on both the existence of a sound social support and a demanding performance context, yet they only introduce initial arguments concerning the interplay of these constituents. The first paragraph thus elaborates this theoretical shortcoming. Moreover, the literature still lacks sufficient descriptions how to build such contexts. Performance contexts, especially the systems from which these evolve, do not appear arbitrarily though empirical works do not provide a sound explication of their origins. The results derived in this book are supposed to shed light on this theoretical deficit; for this purpose, it is elaborated in the second paragraph of this subsection.

Organizational Context

It was inferred that the positive development of performance contexts triggers elevated levels of ambidexterity (*Proposition 7*), a finding which demotes the social interrelations within institutions. In defense of the social context, however, *Proposition 5* indicates that an increase in an entity's performance system is constrained by the social context. The following discussion makes an attempt to clarify these findings.

An important theme that is elucidated by the findings of this empirical inquiry pertains to the pathway of building a high performance organizational context being the basis for superior levels of ambidextrous activities. With reference to Birkinshaw and Gibson (2004), there are different ways to design such a context. These can be demonstrated by means of two examples from restructuring activities at Renault and Oracle, which are summarized as follows: "Renault achieved it by building a performance context around its existing social support; Oracle built a performance context first, then looked for ways of building social support and trust across the organization" (2004: 52). As mentioned previously, the progress researched in this research evidently conforms to the strategy established by Renault. Precisely, the evidence illustrated that the elevation of performance contexts was predominantly based on a more ambitious target setting at the organization level, which was pushed down the organization to call for extended divisional and individual performance (*Proposition 6*).

As mentioned above, stable social relationships are found to build the basis on which performance contexts can be amplified. The cross-case findings therefore confirm the recognized incident that trustful relations are an integral part of organizing (e. g., Dirks & Ferrin, 2001; Ho & Weigelt, 2005; McEvily et al. 2003; Zaheer et al. 1998). More specifically, the insights of this study coincide with Dirks and Ferrin's (2001) contribution arguing that trust appears at two distinct levels in the academic literature. The scholars raise the issue that trust is almost exclusively researched as a main and direct effect for reaching certain outcomes, yet they argue that trust is a moderating theme as empirically verified by certain studies (see Dirks, 1999; O'Reilly and Anderson, 1980; Read, 1962). In other words, the authors "model suggests that trust provides the conditions under which certain outcomes, such as cooperation and higher performance, are likely to occur" (Dirks & Ferrin, 2001: 450). Trust can consequently be identified as the dominant characteristic of the social context that potentially also affected the second defined attribute, i. e., interpersonal and interdivisional support. Though it would be highly interesting to further research and explain the issues raised by *Proposition 5*, the proposition makes a case for expanding the existing literature streams on the issue. It appreciates a relatively stable social context as a necessary condition and an increased level of the performance context as a sufficient one to stimulate higher levels of ambidexterity.

Contextual Antecedents

The formed propositions imply that organizations experiencing a buyout put emphasis on elevated levels of stability in place of flexibility, and they encourage an intensified external focus in place of an internal orientation after an investment *(Proposition 8a)*. The increased tendency to organize based on market imperatives was interpreted to be a decisive stimulus for explaining the performance context's transition (*Proposition 10*). The subsequent discussion elaborates both underlying verdicts.

A growing body of literature in the field of strategic and marketing management analyzes the phenomenon of market orientation (*MO*) (see Connor 2007; Hult & Ketchen, 2001; Hult et al. 2005; Zhou et al. 2008). Slater and Narver (1999) early remarked that the notion of market orientation was underdeveloped, so they called for an elaborate substantiation. In response, Hult et al. (2005) summarize the literature streams pertaining to the utilized construal and report both a cultural approach and an intelligence one. The former refers to an organizational alignment with market principles whereas the latter draws on organizational systems facilitating the absorption of customers' needs.[28] Most

28 The interpretation of the concept in this study is in line with the cultural definition proposed

empirical studies analyzing the market orientation construct test the relationship with firm performance. These studies generally report that entities with market-oriented organizational setups perform significantly better in terms of organizational performance and effectiveness (see Hult and Ketchen, 2001; Kirca et al. 2005; Zhou et al. 2008; Zhou et al. 2005). The relation between an enhanced market-oriented culture and increased levels of performance, i. e., ambidexterity, seems also to be supported in this research. Nevertheless, Zhout et al. state that "simply assessing the direct link between MO and performance is not fruitful; rather, the key question must be what are the processes by which MO affects performance?" (2008: 985). In other words, the academic community calls for a more elaborate description of the internal processes moderating the former mentioned relationship (e. g., Gebhardt et al. 2006; Hult et al. 2005; Kirca et al. 2005).

The results presented in this book assist in identifying these internal processes. To be specific, an organizational market orientation was found to constitute the basis on which intensified performance contexts can develop (*Proposition 10*). In other words, the point made in this paper is that the modification of performance contexts requires a set of altered underlying principles and values guiding this transition. Having measured these basic values and principles of organizing with the help of the *CVF*, *Proposition 10* implies that a process of organizing which rests upon outside imperatives positively correlates with superior levels of performance contexts. Shifting attention to the social context, it seems noteworthy to articulate that the development of the latter, although becoming slightly negative (*Proposition 8a*), appears more stable in comparison to the performance context: Emphasizing external conditions instead of an internal integration, social contexts unsurprisingly possess weaker tendencies when the companies are subject to a PE investment. However, comparing the firm positive development of the performance contexts to the relatively moderate reduction in the social contexts, the latter can be interpreted to progress fairly steady: Once a tolerable social context has been built, it processes relatively stable and detached from changing organizational values. In this sense, social contexts were found to be less manipulable or controllable in comparison to performance contexts. Avoiding an over-interpretation of this behavior, such an analysis of an organization undoubtedly reminds one of the field's institutionalized dualism,which distinguishes rational, technical, manipulable organizations from natural, social, indeterminate ones (Scott, 2004).

Reverting to the introduced discussion of the market orientation concept, the findings of this study are in line with the literature claiming that values and

by Slater and Narver (1995) in order to achieve an integrative fit with the cultural imprints of the *CVF*.

principles are not alone sufficient for reaching certain outcomes; rather, authors propose that there is an additional need for processes and incentives which "operationalize" these basic organizational values (see Deshpande & Webster, 1989; Slater & Narver, 1995). Denison argues in this respect that values and principles "serve as the foundation for an organization's management system as well as the set of management practices and behaviors that exemplify and reinforce those basic principles" (1990: 2). The results derived in this empirical investigation confirm Denison's (1990) argument and additionally identify certain processes which mediate between market-oriented values and performance, thereby providing an answer to the earlier stated shortcoming.

5.2 Reflection on the Context and Process of Organizational Change

Academic: Can you please reflect on the reasons why you think that the company underwent the changes described?

Investment Manager: We encouraged them to do so, primarily through attempting to influence the company to finally adapt to our way of doing business. The family business history of the company constrained growth and profitability, and we had some conflicts to solve with the company and its management. Today, the company is really on track.

Manager: Let's drop the subject Private Equity, I'm tired of hearing that everything positive we do is accountable to them, yet we are blamed for all negative aspects. The truth is that I modified this company's strategy, and this move, with all its operational side effects, brought us to where we are now.

Political Regulator: In fact, a governmental incentive further liberalized the industry the company operates in. Naturally, some companies were driven out of the market, but the company under consideration took advantage and adapted to new environmental imperatives.

R&D Scientist: I have been working for 30 years in this company, and I have recognized many transformations. The background of my job is to conduct research on cells. This tells me that life with all its facets and cycles, potentially also organizational life, is determined by genetic codes and therefore moves beyond spheres such as childhood, adolescence, and maturity.

Academic: Who is right?

Chorus: I am!

With reference to the outline of change in previous chapters of this book, the case was made that the observed process of corporate transformation is contingent on the systemic perspective (Purser et al. 2005; Weick & Quinn, 1999; Weisbord,

1988). The hypothetical dialogue serves as an instrument to pragmatically illustrate the four derived doctrines, dialectic, teleology, evolution, and life cycle, respectively, in order to show the difficulty to segregate viewpoints. Yin suggests that high quality case studies are supposed to consider alternative perspectives "that most seriously challenge the design of the case study" (2003: 164). Deducing from this inference, critics might claim that the empirically derived propositions only have vague associations with the PE investment made. Replying to this legitimate claim, the derived propositions indicate that mere coincidence does not constitute a persuasive justification since the cases indicated differences relating to majority and minority investments. In other words, the null hypothesis stating that everything emerged randomly should have been properly rejected by what Yin (2000) refers to as a "craft rival," that is the multiple case design and the chosen replication strategy.

There is, however, a second set of rivals which the scholar describes as "real-life rivals," and he contends that these are often neglected by the academic community although they assist in creating scientifically convincing discussions. Real-life rivals are generally concerned with the analysis of the complex reality and attempt to identify further interventions which might have influenced the observations made. For this reason, Yin (2000) reports the subsequent six real-life rivals: direct rivals, commingled rival, implementation rival, rival theory, super rival, and societal rival. Five of these rivals can be ruled out, either because they have been implicitly addressed or due to the fact that they are not meaningful. For instance, societal rival holds social trends, instead of any particular intervention, accountable for changes in the researched object. Furthermore, direct rival and rival theory do not emerge feasibly given the circumstance that I already mentioned auxiliary explanations, precisely evolution or life cycle, which were assumed to operate irrespectively of the investment. Commingled rival, however, seems to represent an appropriate concept that requires more attention. Yin defines its role and claims "that another intervention of the same type, co-occurring with the targeted intervention, accounts for the observed results" (2000: 249). Acknowledging this point of view, certain evidence from the cases is utilized in the subsequent deliberation to corroborate the thesis that corporate transformation can indeed be associated with teleology and dialectic, which was discussed in a previous segment (cf. subsection 3.1.2). Nevertheless, life cycle and evolution seem to operate simultaneously, stimulating a "commingled" development.

Four Motors of Change Operating Through Periodic and Continuous Sequences

Fortunately, the informants usually did not communicate their observations in line with any stereotype the hypothetical constructed discussion might suggest.

Nevertheless, tendencies of this behavior were undeniably observable. CEOs possessed the natural tendency to emphasize their achievements and influence, which is a well-known character trait (Goel and Thakor, 2008; Hayward et al., 2004; Heaton, 2002; Malmendier & Tate, 2005; Staw et al. 1983). When PE companies installed new CEOs, these interviewed top executives spoke more positive about the development of the company under investigation. Besides, they maintained that the positive development can largely be attributed to them, an assertion proposing strong teleological stimuli. Most interviewed informants belonging to lower echelons of an organizational hierarchy substantiated that the new top management played an influential role pertaining to the modifications having occurred; however, they simultaneously raised concerns that the addition of a PE house accelerated initiatives which might have happened anyway sooner or later in the prospective life of the organizations. Furthermore, informants indicated that the changing business environment additionally triggered responses to ensure the economic survival of the researched companies. Lehman Brothers' filing for bankruptcy protection on September 15, 2008 resulted in environmental turbulences, to which informants generally constructed a relation. Similarly, general market trends were identified as an important impetus. For instance, a respondent from *EmergencyIBO #3* remarked that markets had reached peak long ago and corporate action was necessary to survive in competition.

Seizing the multiple reasons mentioned by the interviewed managers, the simultaneous operation of diverse change motors obviously formed a synergetic dynamic exceeding the sum of its parts; motors might have triggered each other, so each motor could have changed erratically in response to small changes in the other ones. With reference to Hayek (1972), the cognition of such interrelated phenomena can potentially be considered too complex for establishing a sophisticated comprehension of these dynamics. In this respect, Weick asks, "How can you tell which Van de Ven and Poole (1995) 'motor' is running when you watch a process?" (1999: 798). Nevertheless, certain patterns emerged throughout the analyzed cases, which assists in deriving some deeper awareness of the dynamics' "commingled behavior" (Yin, 2000). Attention is hence paid to three emerging themes, which, in sum, should provide a broad and thorough conceptualization: the interplay of dialectic and life cycle, the moderating role of teleology, and the framing characteristics of evolution. The section is finalized by an integration of the three dynamics into one model.

Interplay of dialectic and life cycle

Informants described an endless sequence of the following relationship: A PE investment required growth, which could only be handled by means of a transformation concerning new personnel, structures, and systems; in turn, this modification induced the necessity to embark on the growth strategy. According to Daft, "As organizations grow large and complex, they need more complex systems and procedures for guiding and controlling the organization" (2004: 319). Cross-linking this insight to the construct level of organizational antecedents, operationalized by the *CVF* (Cameron & Quinn, 2006), certain patterns seem to coincide. As demonstrated earlier, the buyout sample indicated a trend toward both an increased external orientation and stability (*Proposition 8a*). In minority investments, however, the observable trend merely pertained to augmented levels of stability (*Proposition 8b*). It is hence inferable that the dialectic motor is predominantly related to an increased external orientation while the life cycle motor facilitates an orientation toward augmented degrees of stability. This reasoning is explained in the following.

The interviewed top managers consistently argued that they did not feel constricted regarding coercive stimuli as long as monthly figures converged with the investors' expectations. For example, an informant from *EngineeringMINORITY #8* indicated that he did not necessarily feel constricted in his daily work although he had to devote more time to reporting, yet he knew, once covenants turned negative, there were disputes about the company to follow. With reference to Benson (1974), the previously mentioned situation seems to properly describe the phases between contradiction and praxis or, in the words of Bernstein (1971), the bridge between a reflective and active moment. Thus, it seems to be this particular moment when organizations decide to reconfigure their operations in line with the perturbation from their new environment, i. e., the financial investor. In this sense, the breach of financial contracts and the threat to do so serve as central pressure points causing organizational conversion. As a result, FBes start to adopt the operation logics from PE investors. In doing so, they seem to organize toward financial returns, which implies an enhanced external orientation. In formal terms, the thesis, affirming an internal orientation, gets replaced by the antithesis or results in the synthesis, both signifying an enhanced external orientation. This conversion is assumed to have an episodic character (cf. Weick & Quinn, 1999).

Life cycle models, on the other hand, facilitate an understanding along the flexibility/control continuum.[29] Informants consistently remarked that the investigated organizations became more inflexible over time, a process that was considered to have continuous roots (cf. Weick & Quinn, 1999). Quinn and Cameron (1983) provide a sound review of this circumstance by presenting the connection between the different phases of life cycles and the *CVF*. They utilize

29 Many contributions in the FB literature adhere to the life cycle image and suggest, for example, that FBes move beyond spheres of start-up, expansion/ formalization, and maturity (Gersick et al., 1997) or pioneer, growth, maturity, instability, and growth (Klein, 2010).

four stages – entrepreneurial, collectivity, formalization, and elaboration – and document an intensified movement toward control in place of flexibility when organizations become more mature. Likewise, they show that modifications in the internal/external dimension progress rather arbitrarily.

Integrating these forces from dialectic and life cycle deliberations, Greiner (1972) proposes a model in which times of evolution and revolution eventually regulate the movement between organizational states. The author posits that a life cycle motor is the dominant driver for organizational modifications progressing by an evolutionary spirit, but he maintains that episodes of dialectic are compelling to move beyond erudite stages, such as entrepreneurial, collectivity, formalization, and elaboration. In fact, Greiner's (1972) model of organizational change and development is identified by Van de Ven and Poole (1995) as a dual motor theory unifying dialectic and life cycle procedures. When being addressed with this thought, Greiner remarks that "life cycle explains the 'form' of the unitary stages, while the dialectics explain the underlying dynamics of movement" (Greiner, quoted in Van de Ven, 1992: 184). Applying this inspiration to the underlying phenomenon, it appears that the life cycle motor pertains to the readjusting process of the organizational character to the new orientation episodically induced by dialectic.

The symbiosis of the dialectic and life cycle paradigm seems to be the dominant driver behind organizational change as it properly explains observed changes. The rhythm of organizational change was described as a hybrid between an episodic, inertia determined, and equilibrium seeking paradigm versus a continuous, emergent, and self-organizing paradigm (cf. subsection 3.1.1). The interrelation of dialectic and life cycle images suitably creates such a perception of organizational change related to PE investments in FBes. The dialectic motor, operating through short-run adaptation, combines with the life cycle stimulus, seeking long-run adaptability, to manifest a primary rationalization of the observed modifications. By this means, the symbiosis of the dialectic and life cycle motor does not require auxiliary transformation doctrines, which is particularly compelling for explaining changes in the minority investments. Explicating this thought, the antithesis, i. e., the PE investor, is interpreted not to possess sufficient power to start operating in minority investments. Moreover, the thesis and the antithesis might not significantly vary for the reason that these entities were already aligned with external imperatives. Both explanations might have inhibited the dialectic motor to start operating. Accordingly, minority investment cases only show modifications concerning the flexibility/control continuum but remain stabilized concerning the internal/external continuum.

Mediating characteristic of teleology

Remaining in the exemplary world of continuous and periodic rhythms of organizational change (Weick & Quinn, 1999), managerial intervention was differentiated under both doctrines. In specific, the role of the change agent was identified as a "prime mover" (Kotter, 1996) in the periodic doctrine and as a redirector of change in the continuous dogma. Evidence from the investigated cases leads to accept both viewpoints since management acted as mediating force between dialectic and life cycle motors. As a matter of fact, teleology is assumed to merely constitute a secondary stimulus, which may possibly be absent while organizational conversion, stimulated by dialectic and life cycle, continues in isolation. Greiner's model falls short of deciphering teleology as a relevant force though he proposes that "management must be prepared to dismantle current structures before the revolutionary stage becomes too turbulent" (1972: 9). Such actions, indicating teleological initiatives, are explained in the remaining paragraph.

Functionally, the role of top management emerged to further accelerate corporate conversion or to impede what is on the way. When having considered the nature of teleology, two potential preconditions for an altered goal setting behavior of management were derived, namely the replacement of incumbent executives and the existence of novel pressures to meet cash flows. The analyzed case evidence clearly indicated that the replacement of management serves as a facilitating device of change (*Proposition 9*); such actions accelerated mechanisms which were already underway and simultaneously freed novel stimuli. Therefore, the results of this study generally reinforce academic contributions suggesting that top management plays a crucial role in the life of organizations (see Hambrick & Mason, 1984; Friedman & Saul, 1991; Zhang & Rajagopalan, 2004). An interesting example of this circumstance was observed at *EngineeringMBO #1* in which the organization was turned "upside down," verbalized by a marketing manager, after the CEO had been replaced. In contrast, in cases where the management remained in place, regardless of majority or minority investments, the forces impacting on both the external/internal and the flexibility/stability continuums did not set much variance free. This finding is backed by a relatively exhaustive literature stream which generally concludes that inside replacement of CEOs corresponds to a maintenance strategy whereas outside succession is associated with new administrative patterns and resource allocation activities (see Dalton & Kesner, 1983; Guest, 1962; Helmich & Brown, 1972; Lewin & Wolf, 1974). Simons, for example, exhibits that new top managers implement novel control systems, which are "important levers to manage both evolutionary and revolutionary change" (1994: 169). The statement reinforces that teleological stimuli mediate between evolutionary long-run adaptability, related to the life cycle motor, and revolutionary short-run adaption, which corresponds to the dialectic paradigm. Empirical insights from this research consequently underline both of Simons' (1994) empirical results. In addition, this study confirms attributes of upper echelon theory arguing that the ongoing socialization process inside organizations makes it difficult for long-tenured executives to escape the status quo (see Chaganti & Sambharya, 2006; Hambrick, 2007; Hambrick & Mason, 1984; Miller et al. 1998) because psychological barriers restrain the commitment to change (e.g., Finkelstein & Hambrick, 1990; March & March, 1977; Sutcliffe & Huber, 1998). Expressed differently, the mediating role of teleology to either accelerate or constrain the development of the symbiotic interplay of dialectic and life cycle seems to be theoretically and empirically in line with the wider managerial literature on top executive succession.

Framing behavior of evolution

If dialectic and life cycle motors seem to coordinate the continuums related to the external/internal orientation and flexibility/control, respectively, whose developments are either constrained or accelerated by teleology, where does evolution fit in? Case impressions indicated that this motor operates supplementary to, yet relatively independently of, the former ones. Evolution thus represents an element which continuously stimulates change. International rivalry, political (de)regulation, globalization of markets, shortened product life cycles, and rapid technology changes have created environments that are characterized as hypercompetitive (e.g., Bogner & Barr, 2000; D'Aveni, 1994; Hanssen-Bauer & Snow, 1996; Ilinitch et al. 1996; Volberda, 1996; Wiggins & Ruefli, 2005).[30] Hypercompetitive business environments initiate a competitive selection, which is the underlying principle the evolution motor adheres to. The dynamics of hypercompetitive business environments are thus illustrated in order to show how this motor contributed to the "commingled behavior" of change.

Literature falls short of describing a direct association between the evolutionary dynamics and the dimensions of the *CVF* as done by Quinn and Cameron (1983) regarding the life cycle doctrine, which makes it difficult to reflect the observed modifications. Nevertheless, the researched cases signified that an intensified external orientation also partly stemmed from a fiercer competition. For instance, the interviewed respondents consistently mentioned that the

30 While many scholars agree that the contemporary competitive landscape can be classified as hypercompetitive, McNamara et al. confront this doctrine and suggest that markets are "no more dynamic [...] than in the past" (2003: 261). Nevertheless, they argue that the perspective of hypercompetition facilitates a productive understanding in strategic management research since it draws attention to the managerial necessity to persistently benchmark organizational competences with market threats and opportunities.

business environment and the fight for margins required a continuous adaption. Deducing from this inference, evolution appears to stimulate a development which promotes an external orientation and hence coincides with the dialectic motor. On the contrary, evolution seems to induce an antithetic stimulation regarding the flexibility/control dimension compared to the dynamics triggered by the life cycle motor. Volberda (1996) properly provides a rationale why this occurrence might be expected. According to him, "[h]ypercompetition forces firms to move more quickly and boldly and to experiment in ways that do not conform to traditional administrative theory. Bureaucratic vertical forms severely hamper the ability to respond to accelerating competition. Flexible forms, in contrast, can respond to a wide variety of changes in the competitive environment" (1996: 359). As a matter of fact, Volberda (1996) proposes that flexibility in terms of management qualities and organizational design characteristics promotes survival in contemporary business settings.

Besides this direct impact on the symbiotic nature of dialectic and life cycles, evolution is conceptualized to also indirectly affect this relation by influencing teleology. Scholars usually state that the type of environment modifies the decision-making speed inside organizations given that high velocity surroundings are more complex to manage than stable contexts (e.g., Baum & Wolly, 2003; Bourgeois & Eisenhardt, 1988). For instance, an informant at *EngineeringMBO #1*, which was severely hit by the economic crisis following the insolvency of Lehman Brothers, indicated that the recession opened his eyes to expedite his plans regarding a new corporate setup. Such a statement is supportive of a recent publication of Nadkarni and Barr (2008). The scholars find that industry velocity levels influence the structure of managerial cognition concerning their analysis of environments.

Integration of perspectives

"Private Equity modified corporate development" was a claim that was often provided by informants during the interviews. The above conducted argumentation indicates that the statement proves meaningful and true, yet it merely mirrors a reality that is overly simplified. After having conceptualized the multi-layered elements of this effect, the interplay of diverse motors reveals complex dynamics, which are abstracted by Figure 12. The graphical illustration resumes the earlier discussion and visualizes how to think about the investment of PE houses in FBes. The first level symbolizes the interplay of dialectic and life cycle motors. Both stimuli are conceptualized to explain the novel orientation of underlying values. Triggered processes are mediated by teleological interference, which either accelerates or constrains level one dynamics. Evolution comprehensively frames the reactions of subordinate dynamisms. As a matter of fact, evolution is linked to influence both teleology and the development of competing values.

In the words of Yin (2000), such a construction of dynamics can indeed be classified as "commingled," indicating that the liberated variance is not fully projectable to the investment of a PE company. PE houses are rather identified as a catalyst of conversion in this research, which, however, strongly rejects the argument that observed changes are not traceable to the investment. In chemistry, catalysts serve the purpose to either accelerate or inhibit reaction rates by modifying the level of activation energy. In organizations, PE companies seem to serve as a positive catalyst and thus principally operate like in chemical processes for the reason that they seem to accelerate organizational change. Besides, it is arguable that the (partial) segregation of the established co-evolution of the company and the owning family explains transformations. In this respect, the family would symbolize a negative catalyst, an inhibitor of change. Independent of the debate whether FBes are implicitly constrained by their

Figure 12: Configuration of the Dynamics of Change

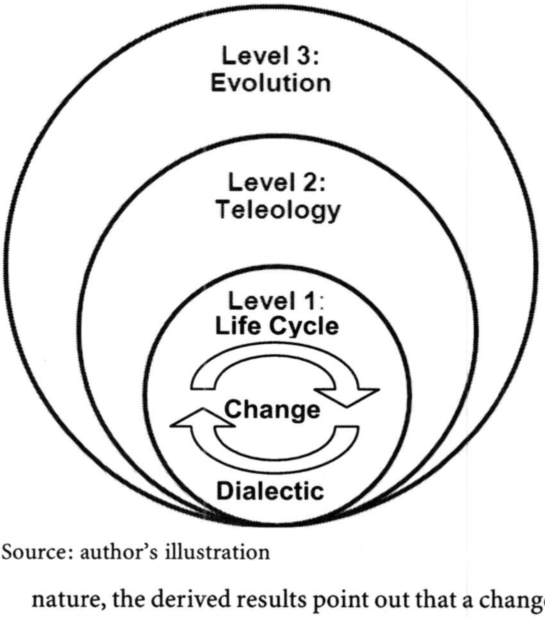

Source: author's illustration

nature, the derived results point out that a change of ownership triggers novel stimuli since it induces modifications and facilitates initiatives. This line of argumentation is revisited and further clarified in the following section.

5.3 Alterations in Performance and Intra-Organizational Energizers

Academic: I would like to understand the metamorphosis having occurred since your company has been financed with Private Equity.

Practitioner: Can you please state your question more precisely?

Academic: First, I have been inclined to think in terms such as organizational performance or outcome. How would you describe the dimensional shift reflecting those components?

Practitioner: It seems that we have improved regarding these elements. When considering performance to capture objects related to efficiency and innovative potential, we are doing a better job today.

Academic: This brings me to the second question. How would you explain this transformation? **Practitioner:** Realizing my limited potential as a designer or origin of this successful development, I cannot really tell you. However, what I can say is that we seemed to have created novel resources and capabilities as well as leveraged existing ones. I am curious to hear your analysis clarifying our journey.

Two research questions were derived for guiding the content of the empirical inquiry (cf. subsection 2.3). The first question considers the impact of PE investments on FBes with regard to their performance, which was defined by means of ambidexterity. The second question aims at explaining the variance in the performance variable. Both interrogations serve as reference points for the subsequent discussion, which is predominantly structured by means of O'Reilly and Tushman's (2008) insight that ambidexterity pertains to a dynamic capability, defined as "the organizational and strategic routines by which firms achieve new resource configurations" (Eisenhardt & Martin, 2000: 1107). In this sense, O'Reilly and Tushman (2008) posit that the processes to exploit and explore opportunities for orchestrating assets reflect the integral characteristics regarding a dynamic capability. Focus on organizational capabilities relies on the circumstance that these elements constitute the predominant source for establishing a competitive advantage (e.g., Collis, 1994; Conner & Prahalad, 1996; Ethiraj et al. 2005; Grant, 2005; O'Reilly & Tushman, 2008; Prahalad & Hamel, 1992; Teece et al. 1997; Vorhies & Morgan, 2005), which makes the concept particularly relevant.

As suggested above, the subsequent discussion attempts to answer the two derived research questions. Although the two remaining paragraphs portray an integrative inquiry of both previously clarified research targets, each question is, for convenience, discussed in a separate paragraph. To thoroughly answer both interrogations, the following argumentation implicitly or explicitly rejoins certain partial conclusions reached in the previous sections of this chapter. Since the discussion in the previous two sections progressed relatively independently of the FB literature, those generated insights are henceforth utilized for answering the research questions.

Organizational Performance

Insights indicate that PE financed FBes seem to experience a neutral to beneficial metamorphosis with the new shareholder regarding corporate performance (*Proposition 1a* and *1b*), which is achieved by a simultaneous intensification of explorative and exploitative activities (*Proposition 2*). In buyout scenarios, these entities primarily amplify their dynamic capabilities regarding product development competences and the exploration of new markets (*Proposition 3*).

When considering this argumentation, it appears that the first research question should have been sufficiently answered by the developed propositions. Nonetheless, a further concentration on this line of reasoning undoubtedly suggests paying attention to the FB literature measuring performance differences between family-owned and nonfamily-owned entities. Martinez et al. summarize this research area as "a controversial topic among economists and business scholars during the last two decades" (2007: 84), which is reasoned by the pluralism of theoretical positions and empirical findings. In other words, the question whether family influence eventually leads to a competitive advantage or disadvantage causes the analytical literature to "remain divided on the effect of family ownership or management on firm performance" (Lee, 2006: 106). Certain empirical studies report that FBes perform significantly better than their counterparts (see Anderson & Reeb, 2003; Lee, 2006; Martinez et al. 2007; McConaughy et al. 2001) whereas other studies document a negative or no significant correlation (see Chrisman et al. 2004; Holderness & Sheehan, 1988; Villalonga and Amit, 2006). Reviews of the extensive quantity of performance studies are provided by Miller and Le Breton-Miller (2005) or Zellweger and Astrachan (2008). Empirical studies that measure performance of FBes usually apply different methods, underlying definitions, as well as variables to encounter the phenomenon, "and this mix of 'apples and oranges' might account for the ambiguous findings" (Dyer, 2006: 254). The former quotation highlights the circumstance that attempts to make an empirical contribution to the field generally emerge to be difficult. Nevertheless, the character of this paper allows for the avoidance of several severe shortcomings the above cited studies typically have. Studying the transformation of entities which were identified as FBes before the transaction tolerates the interpretation of differences that are based on dynamic insights instead of static divergences stemming from artificial segregations of the organizational population. Moreover, the nature of the applied performance construct should be a more direct and advanced measure compared to, for instance, Tobin's Q (see Villalonga & Amit; 2006; Anderson & Reeb, 2003) or sales growth (see Chrisman et al. 2004).

Despite the generated propositions' first appeal, the findings do not imply that PE financed (former) FBes generally become better performers. With reference to Dyer's (2006) attempt to cluster the "family effect" on performance, this paper also illuminates different kinds of FBes; some entities already operated at considerably high levels of ambidexterity prior to the transaction whereas others did not. Therefore, these results support the viewpoint that the universe of FBes needs to be further subcategorized in order to account for the multiple configurations these entities call attention to (e.g., Westhead & Howorth, 2006). Although it is not inferable from the findings that FBes possess improved organizational capabilities after a PE investment on a general basis, findings yet substantiate the trend that the former develop positively. Do the findings of this study therefore imply that family influence and organizational performance are negatively correlated? At first glance, this connection cannot be denied for the sample of the studied entities. The quality to better exploit existing resources and to explore new elements thus signifies an improvement in the organizational dynamic capabilities, helping to achieve and sustain a competitive advantage. In fact, the results of this empirical inquiry rather seem to support the literature that interprets FBes as a restrained organizational form (see Fernandez & Nieto, 2005; Gallo & Sveen, 1991; Lansberg, 1988; Ward, 1997). Ward, for instance, remarks that "[f]or most family-owned businesses, the path to survival is one of stagnation" (1997: 329) for the reason that several family-specific issues, such as family conflicts, disparate goals, as well as entrepreneurial inflexibility, constrain the entities' development.

Besides the different initial situations that characterized the researched FBes in terms of the ambidextrous orientation, at least one further aspect should be evaluated when attempting to answer the performance puzzle. As indicated in the beginning of this paragraph, this study allows for an interpretation that is based on dynamic insights and hence requires an intensified consideration of the entities' history. The thesis accordingly emerges that the family roots should not only be considered negative, as preliminarily proposed above, but demand a more integral inspection. Collins and Porras' (1994) prominent book *Built to last: Successful habits of visionary companies*, in which the authors describe the peculiarities of a sample of the most admired global companies, among them 3M, Boeing, or Sony, documents that these companies' secret of success pertains to the yin and yang nature to preserve the dominating character and to simultaneously engage in the search for development.[31] Transferring this image to the

31 The yin and yang nature of stability and change can appropriately be verbalized as follows: "While it is important for organizations to change, it is also important to retain aspects of

underlying situation, the yin and yang nature of continuity and change manifests itself: Consistent with the interpretation of PE companies as catalysts of organizational change (cf. section 5.2), the positive development of FBes following a PE investment is therefore appreciated to be based on the mentioned symbiotic qualities. The family encouragement is acknowledged to provide stability and direction for safeguarding the (mostly) positive status quo prior to a PE investment. Nevertheless, the family dictated entities might have deficiencies in stipulating an organizational need for change and development, which is induced by a PE investor. Following this line of reasoning, a unidimensional interpretation of family effects as primarily negative falls short of appreciating the historical imprints this coevolution has generated for organizational life. For this reason, the previously verbalized negative correlation between family influence and organizational performance should be mitigated or at least be considered with caution. This viewpoint can more formally be explained by reverting to path dependence theory. Although the concept of path dependence has mostly been applied as an umbrella term for simply describing the notion that "history matters," Sydow et al review the concept and propose that the theory is based on "(1) singular historical events, (2) which may, under certain conditions, transform themselves into self-reinforcing dynamics, and (3) possibly end up in an organizational lock-in" (2009: 690). FBes are hence expected to sooner or later reach the state of an organizational lock-in with regard to their resources and capabilities (cf. Burgelmann, 2002; David, 1985). To escape these forces and to expand capabilities, organizations are required "to construe and integrate an exogenous perspective – that is, an activity that is not under the regime of path dependence. Such integration of an external lens – if you like – a 'second order observation' (von Foerster, 1991) enables knowledgeable agents to reflect practices in terms of path dependence and potentially opens a window for path-breaking activities" (Sydow et al. 2009: 702). Concretely, this external perspective would pertain to financial investors inducing impulses by means of teleology and dialectic.

In sum, the findings of this study suggest that (former) FBes experience a neutral to positive conversion of their dynamic capabilities when becoming confronted with a PE investment. At first, this metamorphosis implies a negative correlation between family influence and organizational performance. FBes are, however, a heterogeneous organizational class with varying peculiarities. In defense of the family effect, inferring a negative correlation between family influence and performance ignores the insight that the combination of a stable

their philosophies, learning, knowledge, systems and practices that contributed to their past success. In short, they need to change, but at the same time they need to maintain some of those stabilising element that served them well in the past and may preserve them in the future" (Burchell & Kolb, 2006: 33).

organizational continuity *and* the need for change is assumed to lead to enduring and successful organizations (Collins and Porras, 1994). The family influence should thus be interpreted to symbolize both a positive idiosyncrasy providing self-reinforcing stability as well as a negative quality inhibiting change. The subsequent paragraph discusses this verdict in greater depth.

Intra-organizational determinants

What are the determinants energizing the alteration in organizational performance, that is ambidexterity as a dynamic capability? How is the path-dependent FB history of the entity related to this conversion? These questions remained unsettled and should effectively be the starting point for finalizing the discussion.

Considering the first stated question in this paragraph, it appears meaningful to initially provide a theoretical reflection on the establishment of organizational capabilities. Concerning this issue, O'Reilly and Tushman remark the following: "Organizational capabilities are embedded in existing organizational routines, structures, and processes. More specifically, these routines are found in the way the organization operates, its structures, cultures, and mindset of senior leadership" (2008: 188). In this vein, the discussion in section 5.1, *Contributions to the Paradigm of Ambidextrous Organizations*, provides the basis for understanding the establishment of organizational capabilities as certain crucial conclusions were drawn that prove valuable to shed light on the relation. To be concrete, the discussion generated the notion that a moderately stable nature of social contexts is a necessary condition and an increased level of performance contexts is a sufficient one in order to expand and orchestrate organizational resources. Underlying values and principles along the internal/external and flexibility/stability dimensions were responsible for the modifications in the dualistic organizational context. Whereas changing values and principles appeared to provide the basis for altered performance contexts (*Proposition 10*), they possessed less power to modify social contexts. Based on these insights, the subsequent deliberation concentrates on certain peculiarities of FBes and reinforces the exemplified verdict that both the FB heritage and the addition of a PE investor should be considered influential for the examined transformation.

The notion was cautiously put forward in an earlier segment that the path-dependent history of FBes enabled these entities to have established solid social contexts (cf. subsection 5.1.2). The FB literature generally agrees that this entity class is characterized by decent levels of internal mutual trust (see Corbetto & Salvato, 2004; LaChapelle & Barnes, 1998; Jones, 1983; Steier, 2001; Sundaramurthy, 2008). Sundaramurthy theoretically illustrates that trust, once established in family firms, is maintained by a "sustaining cycle of trust" (2008: 92), caused by shifts from interpersonal to competence and finally to systems trust.

Thereby, the author mentions that interpersonal trust is usually formalized with the help of processes and structures and becomes institutionalized after all. Nicholson explicates and synopsizes that FBes "are able to generate unique advancements through their capacity to bind naturally diverse individuals together in a common enterprise and purpose" (2008: 114). In doing so, he reasons that this quality of FBes happens to form a beneficial component enabling these companies to "engage in processes and decisions that are much riskier for groups of decision makers who lack such ties" (2008: 114). Consistent with the results of this study, the creation of highly ambidextrous organizations partially builds on these social ties, which consequently reflects a positive characteristic that is stipulated by the FB heritage. Shifting attention to the performance context, almost nothing is known about this concept in the FB domain. Sharma (2004), for example, remains widely silent on these or related issues in her review of the FB literature, but the scholar calls for more research regarding investigations that explain the performance of FBes. Fortunately, a recent study conducted by Tsao et al. (2009) enhances our understanding of this theme. The scholars report that they could not find performance differences among their sample of 688 publicly listed enterprises regarding the circumstance whether these entities were family-controlled or not. However, FBes employing "high-performance work systems" are found to have a clearly superior performance compared to those scoring low in this domain. In consequence, their study indicates that the concept of "high-performance work systems" is a decisive intermediary variable for analyzing outcome differences in FBes. Connecting these findings of Tsao and colleagues (2009) to the arguments of this research, performance contexts played a similar role, i. e., they stimulated increased levels of organizational capabilities and effectiveness, respectively.

Underlying values and principles moving in an external orientation are found to be responsible for energizing high performance contexts (*Proposition 10*). Hence, it comes as no surprise that FBes are frequently described to be very internally oriented, encapsulating themselves from external environments and perspectives (see Cater & Schwab, 2008). The findings of this study support this viewpoint for the companies having experienced a buyout (*Proposition 8a*) but not necessarily for the companies having opted for a minority investment (*Proposition 8b*). Essentially, Zahra et al. provide the reasoning that "an internal orientation may evolve into inertia" (2004: 366) and "inhibit a family firm's ability to explore the innovative methods and practices introduced by its rivals" (2004: 366). Their findings consequently indicate that an external orientation of FBes emerges as a significant and powerful antecedent of entrepreneurship, which is substantiated by the results of this thesis.

Summarizing, FBes are generally characterized to possess sound social contexts, a facet that is found to endure to a high degree, though not entirely, when entering into a relationship with a PE investor. In contrast, performance contexts in FBes vary significantly (Tsao et al. 2009), giving rise to the circumstance that in certain cases suboptimal levels experience an ascending transformation after a PE investment. This study thus synthesizes that both social ties (e.g., Nicholson, 2008) and high performance work systems (Tsao et al. 2009) combine to explain performance differences, across the universe of business companies as well as within the population of FBes, by modifying the dynamic capabilities' composition. The FB literature falls short of explaining the emergence of such contextual setups. Insights, therefore, hint at the direction that the underlying cultural basis should be considered more extensively as a source of divergence, which is, for example, also articulated by Zellweger and Astrachanan (2008). An intensified external orientation might thus assist in building an improved performance context once solid social contexts have been established.

6. Conclusion

This chapter finalizes this work by means of focusing on certain decisive aspects. Huff provides some valuable guidance and proposes that a high quality closing chapter manages to pull the reader "back to the big picture with a conclusion so they will remember the broadest possible application" (1999: 92). In order to meet the reader's expectation to read something new, instead of a pure summary, she advises to "add some last thought" (1999: 92) enhancing the work's significance. The notion has been put forward in the introductory chapter that a relevant and rigorous knowledge generation can effectively be synthesized by addressing theoretical and practical spheres (cf. section 1.2). As a matter of fact, this chapter expands and summarizes the observations and discussed findings in relation to theoretical and practical applications.

Following this recommendation, section 6.1, *Scientific Implications*, deals with the inferences derived from the empirical findings and integrates these into the wider theoretical debate regarding FBes. In section 6.2, *Practical Implications*, attention is paid to certain consequences for investment managers and executives of FBes. Section 6.3, *Concluding Remarks and Future Research*, presents certain thoughts on the current status of the debate pertaining to PE investments in FBes and provides an outlook on future research perspectives in this area. Appreciating the circumstance that the derived results emerged through a combination of theoretical deliberations and methodical progressions, *Appendix C* critically debates these incidents.

6.1 Scientific Implications

The broadest possible application of the findings concerns three themes in the FB literature: heterogeneity, continuity, and change. Auxiliary issues, related to the advancement of the doctrine of ambidexterity or the viewpoint concerning the manifestation of organizational change, comprised essential constituents for answering and defending the research questions. These completed considerations, however, encourage utilizing the novel insights to reflect on elements of higher echelons. In consequence, the findings of this study contribute to the FB literature along the three themes mentioned above.

First, this study generally confirms academic contributions that FBes are indeed a very heterogeneous organizational class (see Birley, 2001; Dyer, 2006; Garcia-Alvarez & Lopez-Sintas, 2001; Sonfield & Lussier, 2004; Westhead & Howorth, 2006). In particular, findings corroborate Chrisman et al.'s (2005) declaration that performance and its antecedents should be considered an essential characteristic for understanding why FBes are potentially different from its counterparts. Moreover, a better comprehension regarding these aspects may also help to analyze intra-group variance. In this vein, heterogeneity transpired to be quite elemental between firms that experienced a buyout and entities that attracted minority financing, which essentially rested on differences of organizational behavior. To be concrete, the researched FBes that attained a minority investment already possessed specific attributes toward which the buyout group developed in the course of the transaction. These attributes pertained to an intensified external orientation, which served as the basis for improved performance contexts and eventually stipulated the composition of novel organizational dynamic capabilities. Therefore, this study supports the line of reasoning that family ownership, management, or supervisory participation are not sufficient for clarifying performance differences when dichotomizing the field into family-owned businesses and nonfamily-owned enterprises (e.g., Chrisman et al. 2005; Chua et al. 1999). In fact, a further exploration of FBes' heterogeneity, based on the proposed behavioral differences, should clearly enhance our understanding of the source of performance differences, both within the population of FBes as well as between the population of FBes and nonfamily-owned enterprises.

Second, this study enhances the literature pertaining to the sale of FBes in cases when generational succession does not constitute a feasible option. With regard to the importance and neglect of this topic by FB academics, Debicki et al. conclude that "selling out as an alternative to intrafamily succession has received almost no attention in the literature" (2009: 162). Along these lines, this study contributes to the very scarce literature considering the continuity of families and businesses as segregated systems. Drozdow remarks that the celebrated academic and practical doctrine of determining successful continuity on the basis of the enduring coevolution of both systems represents a "unidimensional, idealized state" (1998: 337). Hence, the scholar claims to finally break away from this inert dogma and to appreciate that continuity is not automatically terminated when the owning family withdraws from the business. Rather, "continuity should be defined as the preservation of one or more essential, unique core elements" (1998: 337). The "core elements" of continuity were identified in this study with regard to the established social context being an element of familiness (cf. Habbershon & Williams, 1999). Although not mentioned explicitly by the author, such an interpretation of FB continuity directs attention to the definitional approaches inasmuch as continuity changes its character from a components-of-involvement to an essence effect. When accepting the notion that key attributes of familiness can be preserved in organizations after these are acquired by external parties, at least one critical question develops in consequence: When should we stop speaking of a FB under this perspective?

Third, this thesis exhibits that FBes contracting with PE investors on a majority basis submit themselves to corporate renewal. It was assumed that FBes sooner or later reach a state of organizational lock-in, which requires external assistance, such as PE investors, for realizing a corporate transformation. Fresh initiatives, encouraged by either teleology or dialectic, were conceptualized to implement and accelerate conversion activities. In this respect, it is fair to say that inertial forces are not necessarily a dilemma that exclusively pertains to FBes, yet the literature agrees that this organizational species has strong tendencies to fall into competency traps. For instance, it is commonly proposed that "family firms become conservative and unwilling to take the risks associated with entrepreneurial activities" (Zahra, 2005: 23). Reasons for this behavior are multifold and pertain to the strong influence of the founder's values (Garcia-Alvarez & Lopez-Sintas, 2001), severe concerns of families to lose their wealth (Sharma et al. 1997), a lack of eagerness of following generations due to their financially secured situation when starting working in the business (Kets de Vries, 1993), or family wars and conflicts (Gordon & Nicholson, 2008), for example. Following the implicit call of papers by Hatum and Pettigrew (2004) or Dyer and Sanchez (1998), this study contributes to the issue of change in FBes and proposes explications concerning the subsequent themes: contextual dimensions, procedural issues, and as regard to content.

6.2 Practical Implications

A mutual dependence of FBes and PE companies was hypothesized in the introduction of this book. FBes were categorized to need financing for succession, growth, and special situations. Likewise, PE companies were classified to have a vital interest in investing in those entities given that formerly targeted deals, e.g., public-to-private transactions, secondary and tertiary buyouts, as well as corporate spinoffs, can be identified to become scarcer and more detrimental. The subsequent paragraphs briefly consider practical implications for both FBes and PE companies.

Implications for Family Businesses

When measuring the relationship's success to resiliently cope with environmental turbulences due to an augmented set of dynamic capabilities, FBes seem indeed to benefit from the partnership with PE companies. Therefore, FBes' shareholders considering handing over their companies to responsible buyers appear to find an appropriate successor to develop their life-work. Likewise, the sale of minority stakes to financial investors proves to be a feasible strategy under the above stated performance viewpoint although no substantial gains might be expected in these situations. A potential explanation is concerned with the incident that FBes qualifying for such investments already have the appropriate performance systems in place before an investment.

Findings of this type imply that FBes should make an active attempt to attract a small share of PE capital albeit the potentially higher costs of this financing source. Strategic management literature agrees that companies should "go where the action is" in order to benchmark with competition and to eventually create a competitive advantage.[32] By the same token, FBes should actively compete for the financial resources provided by PE houses. In other words, the meticulous quality requirements that PE investors utilize concerning the evaluation of potential investments appear to constitute a sound parameter to assess FBes' status quo. Once having contracted with a financial investor, the temporary time dimension to which each investment is subject to necessitates that organizational excellence becomes maintained. As a matter of fact, FBes should change their view on PE and consider this financing source as an instrument facilitating a race to the top. The attraction of a PE investor should thus ideally comprise an early option for FBes when they are in need of capital for either growth or the change of shareholders. Therefore, managers of FBes should resist the principle of least effort, which is the pecking order of finance prioritizing internal funds to debt and finally to equity (Myers & Majluf, 1984), but they should rather value the positive consequences a PE investment brings along and the positive signals it sends to the market.

Following the previous line of argumentation, one can ask whether it is really necessary to collaborate with a PE house for developing toward a more ambidextrous entity. Despite the finding that buyouts trigger an enhanced ambidextrous behavior and that FBes in minority participations maintain fairly moderate levels, this interrogation can clearly be denied; FBes are capable of working highly innovative and efficient without this partnership. Given that

32 Cluster theory indicates that the geographic location represents an important aspect to create a competitive advantage. According to Porter, "What happens *inside* companies is important, but clusters reveal that the immediate business environment *outside* companies plays a vital role as well" (1998: 78).

these organizational arrangements can also be achieved without PE cooperation, what can be learned for FBes? Focusing on the positive development of FBes after a PE investment, certain scholars simply advise to somehow mimic the operations of PE companies, i. e., to apply higher leverage ratios, to modify the governance mechanisms and operational activities, and to look for external experts, in order to accomplish a desired organizational transformation. However, if changing an organization was merely contingent on such comparatively naïve intervention procedures, the science of organizational development would have lost its legitimization. It consequently appears that a quantity of more subtle dynamics becomes liberated and induced by a PE investment. The anxiety concerning a possible failure of this partnership should not be overlooked in this context; it should rather be considered a crucial element in the transformation process, facilitating the dissolution of inertia, routines, and path dependence on the cusp of organizational life. Therefore, a sense of urgency and anxiety might constitute important attributes for the creation of change energy (cf. Cross et al. 2003; Jansen, 2004; Quinn and Dutton, 2005), which is implemented by a change of ownership.[33]

In sum, the complexity of corporate development makes it difficult to provide a blueprint how the situation of a PE investment and its effects can eventually be imitated. Nevertheless, managers of FBes should make an attempt to reconfigure their organizations by reverting to the hopefully valuable insights that this research delivers. They should ideally engage in trial and error processes to build contexts that promote performance but safeguard the interpersonal relationships as the latter are typically favorable in FBes. Thereby, they should experiment with increased levels of discipline and stretch by inducing more formalized and ambitious targets, by reconfiguring incentive system reflecting these objectives, as well as by devoting intensified levels of accountability to middle-level managers and lower-level employees in order to eventually encourage paradoxical activities with regard to exploration and exploitation. For establishing a foundation guiding these alterations, organizations need to behave more market-oriented and adapt its values and principles. Top managers can play a crucial role in this development as these agents should support the redirection of organizational values. In doing so, they need to create a sense of urgency to change existing conditions by replicating the required change energy.

33 Gersick (1994) as well as Ginsberg and Venkatraman (1995) both empirically verify that urgency represents a decisive catalyst for inducing organizational change. Kotter remarks, "When the urgency rate is not pumped up enough, the transformation process cannot succeed, and the long-term future of the organization is put in jeopardy" (2007: 98).

Implications for Private Equity Companies

Comparable to FBes, PE companies can also be identified to benefit from the mutual collaboration; the increased quality of portfolio companies following the holding period yields promising transactions for PE investors when financing buyouts. As a matter of fact, PE managers seem to have made a right move by focusing on the buyouts of FBes, if considered through the lenses of organizational performance, value creation, and potential returns. In contrast, PE companies seem to benefit less from taking minority positions.

When speaking of potential returns and benefits generated over the holding period of the investment, the associated concept of risk[34] should not be ignored. On this account, one should appreciate that investing in FBes is in general a more risky business model than accomplishing public-to-private deals and the like. The black box character of assets which are prone to significant information asymmetries and which have no available market price, such as FBes, is summarized by Capron and Shen: "[W]e argue that the lack of information on private targets limits the breadth of the acquirer's search and increases its risk of not evaluating properly the assets of private targets" (2007: 891). Considered with the help of real options, PE companies invest in an extensive and uncertain set of options when focusing on FBes (cf. Chen et al. 2011), which is particularly true for buyout scenarios. These are likely to payoff, as demonstrated by four of the five buyouts researched, but also incorporate the risk of becoming worthless. Minority stake financed FBes, in contrast, possess considerably less of these options given that such companies were classified to maintain systems and resource configurations that disallow for substantial advancements, eventually reducing the uncertainty in this kind of arrangements. In sum, the investment in FBes thus enhances the variety of potential targets and investment possibilities: Risky investments with exceptional returns seem realizable in the domain of buyouts whereas relatively conservative gains and risk levels appear achievable when taking minority positions.

Can PE managers effectively minimize these risk factors and increase the returns from investments in FBes? How can they do it? The results of this thesis suggest that PE houses can effectively decide on the strength of interventions as proposed by the different buyout cases. Willke (2005) formalizes intervention methods with regard to white, grey, and black box intervention, differentiating

34 In the following discussion, risk is defined as a deviation from an expected occurrence or future state. Therefore, the term risk essentially portrays the uncertainty that portfolio companies do not develop in accordance with expected scenarios. On this account, risk should not be confused with the circumstance that, from the perspective of an investor, equity and minority engagements are per se more uncertain than buyouts utilizing a large share of third party debt.

between the complexities of involvement in an ascending order. Whereas three buyouts relied on a white box or grey box intervention (*ServicesMBO #2*, *ConsumerMBO #4*, and *ConsumerBIMBO #5*), two cases (*EngineeringMBO #1* and *EmergencyIBO #3*) rather pertained to a black box intervention since the latter were characterized by intensive management changes, forced buy-and-build strategies, and reorganizations. Deducing from the bankruptcy of one of the investigated cases, increased intervention seems to exponentially augment the inherent risk but not necessarily the gains that come with it. Hence, PE companies are advised to employ conservative intervention techniques. In doing so, they should encourage that family members continue to hold equity stakes and management positions in the invested companies in order to make a strong case for preserving social contexts within such entities. Furthermore, they should advance managerial competence by establishing a dual structure of incumbent and new management as a mean to initiate corporate transformation, which was effectively demonstrated by one case (*ConsumerMBO #4*). In a similar vein, PE investors should be cautious with the enforcement of strategic changes, such as buy-and-build strategies or reorganizations. They should rather act as a sparring partner and leave the strategic choices to the discretion of their portfolio companies.

6.3 Concluding Remarks and Outlook on the Research Field

An argument that is often brought forward against PE investors pertains to the short-term maximization of corporate resources in place of a long-term optimization. But would such a behavior demonstrate a viable business model? Corporate finance literature substantiates that a firm's value is contingent on future generated cash flows; the exploitation of corporate assets during the holding period, while ignoring the exploration of future income, would thus constitute a contradictio in adjecto. Leaving the logically inconsistent accusation aside, the empirical insights elaborated in this contribution reject the understanding of the problem in terms of static tradeoffs but rather appreciates short-term and long-term development, instrumentalized as exploitation and exploration, as an orthogonal phenomenon that becomes amplified in buyouts and remains stable in minority investments. Thereby, this study synthesizes literature streams focusing on the operational gains of PE financed buyouts (see Amess, 2003, 2002; Bull, 1989; Harris et al. 2005; Lerner et al. 2008; Lichtenberg and Siegel, 1990; Ughetto, 2010) given that it illustrates that both efficiency gains and innovative advantages are realized.

Considering these issues in the research context of PE investments in FBes, the underlying results confirm and advance a set of studies. Concerning the scarcity of research results in the field of minority investments, this empirical investigation provides evidence in line with Achleitner et al. (2008a), who argue that a minority investment does not affect the development of an entity. According to the explanation in this research, there are neither new stimuli liberated by teleology nor by dialectic as a result of the investment. In other words, the management remained in place and did not face altered conditions which could have provoked administrative actions, and PE investors did not have sufficient power to come into conflict with their portfolio companies. In contrast, the buyout sample was subject to a relatively intense change. Scholes et al. argue that FBes "post-buyout emphasize improving efficiency and growth/expansion" (2009: 17), an assertion that reinforces the employed dualistic concept in this thesis as well as the results presented. Besides supporting the preceding notion, this investigation enhances the field by uncovering the impetus of the observed organizational metamorphosis. As indicated in the beginning of this paper, several scholars call for research efforts that uncover the effects that lead to increased performance in buyout scenarios. Among the scholars who deliver a contribution to this shortcoming, Wulf et al. (2010) reason that organizational resources and capabilities can be expanded in underperforming FBes by optimizing management systems, which they define with regard to the employed pay-to-performance sensitivity and the incentivization of middle management. The advancement of performance contexts, as elaborated in this paper, converges with the latter results. In a similar vein, the underlying findings reinforce results of Howorth et al. proposing that elements of familiness, "such as loyalty, long term commitment, and trust" (2008: 8), were preserved in their sample of studied MBOs in FBes. The scholars remarkably find evidence that companies which filed for bankruptcy after the transaction reported to have lost these elements of familiness. The authors' contribution thus highlights attributes which are comparable to this stuy's conceptualized path-dependent continuity of the social context.

Proposal for Future Research

Albert Schweitzer is quoted to have remarked, "As we acquire more knowledge, things do not become more comprehensible but more mysterious." Future research recommendations therefore usually propose refinements pertaining to methodical dimensions and also suggest a potential direction that is supposed to continue the line of reasoning concerning the contents. Both issues are separately considered in the subsequent paragraphs.

Outlook on methods

Future studies should make an attempt to circumvent methodical shortcomings recently discussed when replicating or refining the content of this study. The subsequent discussion briefly elaborates certain instruments and processes that are beneficial for realizing such an effort.

A large-scale, quantitative design seems desirable to verify and augment the propositions developed. Along these lines, further case studies might also be deployed to research the incidents in a pure deductive manner, opposing the theory building approach pursued in this book. Furthermore, it would be of immense interest to conduct a longitudinal design, instead of a cross-sectional one. By employing a longitudinal design, the observation of organizational change can make use of dynamic and process-oriented perspectives, improving the rather static insights originated. Ethnographic designs, such as a participant observation in the field[35] with an enhanced focus on the interpretation of human behavior and interaction, would potentially generate fertile insights, especially since this study has drawn on complex operationalized constructs. The search for knowledge, influenced and distorted by the informants' bounded ability to understand the things around them, would therefore be challenged by another character of social inquiry besides gathering data by means of interviews and questionnaires. As a beneficial side effect, the interrelations between the constructed building blocks would receive an additional clarification: A change from the doctrine to think in correlations of variables toward a paradigm celebrating process causality usually assists in elucidating results (e.g., Maxwell, 2004; Mohr, 1982; Pentland, 1999); it would consequently legitimize or abrogate the findings of this study. On this account, Raisch et al. document a shortage of longitudinal attempts in ambidexterity research and call for investigations "to address questions on the dynamic processes underlying organizational ambidexterity" (2009: 693). Finally, methodical refinement, potentially building on a longitudinal ethnographic study or a large scale quantitative observation, should more profoundly contemplate on the causation of change, which was differentiated between prescribed, deterministic and constructive, voluntaristic transformations. In doing so, the strength of each motor can be assessed more precisely to reject rival explanations, and the intervention methods of PE companies in inducing these motors can be more thoroughly analyzed. In order to reach this objective, quantitative studies should control for rival explanations. Likewise, longitudinal attempts should deploy supplementary resources on the

35 Fetterman states, "Participant observation characterizes most ethnographic research and is crucial to effective fieldwork. Participant observation combines participation in the lives of the people under study with maintenance a professional distance that allows adequate observation and recording of data" (2010: 37).

analysis of industries, general macroeconomic surroundings, the institutional environment, and the nature of the liaison of PE companies and FBes.

Outlook on contents

As documented in the literature review, academic papers related to the field of PE investments in FBes can be considered relatively scarce but of having certain momentum, implied by the amount of new research papers published over the last five years. Studies researching the phenomenon of PE investments in FBes are becoming more heterogeneous regarding their theoretical basis to structure the empirical discoveries. Hence, it seems that Wright et al.'s (2009) call to dismiss agency theory in favor of more theoretical diversity for examining private-to-private transactions has been anticipated and accepted by the academic community. Nevertheless, as proposed in the beginning of this section, certain studies are needed to further extend this theoretical foundation. The following thoughts consider certain pragmatic issues for advancing the research field of PE investments in FBes.

The academic community should strive for finding an agreed upon concept for avoiding incommensurability and incompatibility. On this account, scholars can further utilize the ambidextrous idea and integrate their research endeavors into the wider field of the organization science.[36] As a first step, it would be of considerable interest to conduct a representative study regarding the ambidextrous orientation of (former) FBes having been financed with PE capital, which can be achieved by means of quantitative surveying as suggested in the previous methodical proposal. As a second step, it would be very insightful to enrich the field by finding auxiliary explanations, besides replicating the perspective of contextual ambidexterity (see Gibson and Birkinshaw, 2004), to explicate the variances in performance. Considerations how altered corporate governance mechanisms influence the level of ambidexterity and inquiries on the role of the network component seem to be feasible, inferential issues. Likewise, the role of top management in modifying the ambidextrous setting requires an intensified clarification. For instance, Beckman (2006) illustrates that a heterogeneous composition of a top management team, measured in terms of professionals' diverse industry experience, is positively correlated with the setup of ambidexterity. Peretti and Negro (2006) moreover illustrate that the top management team structure, differentiated between "newcomers" and "old timers," positively affects the degree of ambidexterity. The findings of this study

36 The research community has already made initial steps to integrate the concept of organizational ambidexterity into the FB context. For instance, Frank et al. (2010) research the relationship of the top management family as an incubator for innovation. Furthermore, a quantity of work in process studies takes advantage of the ambidextrous concept.

seem to hint in the same direction but deserve elaborate analyses. In summary, it would be interesting to observe further factors that are responsible for influencing the organizational behavior of FBes in the course of a PE investment.

Finally, it should not be forgotten that the diffusion of knowledge from the research discipline regarding organizational change of FBes occurring in response to a PE investment can further assist in building an intensified understanding of FBes' idiosyncrasies as illustrated previously (cf. section 5.3). Themes such as FBes' heterogeneity, continuity, or change were explicated in this respect in the first section of this chapter (cf. section 6.1). In fact, it seems to be a pivotal strategy to further illuminate the distinctive nature of FBes by leaving familiar paths and paying attention to phases and events that severely threaten their existence, for example, PE investments.

Appendix A: Methods & Data

As revealed earlier, the character of this paper is empirical and accomplished by means of case studies. In order to exemplify this notion in more detail, this chapter is utilized to provide an overview of the instruments pursued for deriving the results presented in the following chapter. Along these lines, the derived research aim, the research questions, the presented discussion of organizational change, and the derived conceptual framework require a complementary research method for reasons of coherence. Case studies are introduced as the applied design in section I, *Research Method*. The rationale for this choice is discussed while considering central characteristics and implications being contingent on this selection. In section II, *Research Design*, further attention is paid to topics related to case selection, data collection, and data analysis. Eventually, section III, *Description of Data*, presents an overview of the investigated cases and collected evidence.

I. Research Method

Empirical research in the social sciences allows for drawing on several designs to systematically generate knowledge. Among the most prominent designs are experiments, case studies, questionnaires, and the analysis of archival information. Because all these methods have certain strengths and weaknesses, the selection of the most appropriate alternative should adhere to the deliberations implied by the research questions and the intention pursued (e.g., Marshal & Rossman, 2010; Maxwell, 2005). Besides, certain constraints, such as the possibility to control events or the circumstance that certain observations might have occurred in the past, represent auxiliary elements shaping the selection procedure for deriving the most convenient strategy (Yin, 2003). Having considered these pluralistic conditions, I decided to employ case studies in this investigation, which is motivated in the following.

The research questions, which aspire to uncover social dynamics, essentially obtain a "why" and "how" character (cf. subsection 2.3). The first research question analyzes how organizational performance is modified by a PE investment. The second research question attempts to consider why this aftermath occurs. In other words, the guiding research questions were deliberately designed to facilitate the comprehension of organizational dynamics by enhancing the findings of contemporary research. According to Yin (2003), experiments, history, and case studies represent research methods that are capable of treating such questions. The choice for a social experiment is unrealistic because no controlled laboratory studies regarding PE investments in FBes can be conducted. In a similar vein, history deals with the dead past, disallowing for direct observations or interviewing. In view of these issues, Yin posits that a "case study is preferred in examining contemporary events, but when the relevant behaviors cannot be manipulated" (2003: 7). An alternative guideline for the choice of case studies is provided by Dul and Hak (2008). The authors advise that case studies signify the most appropriate modus operandi when the subsequently deliberated conditions are met: First, the topic of investigation should be broad and highly complex. Second, there is not a lot of theory available; hence, the research field can be considered novel. Third, the context of the study is very important, prohibiting the segregation of the study's phenomenon from the surroundings in which it occurs. Comparable to Yin's (2003) recommendation, I identify these criteria to be fulfilled, which reaffirms the selection of case studies as the umbrella research strategy.

The term "research strategy," employed above, was not deliberately chosen. Early theorists propose that case studies rather symbolize a "way of organizing social data" (Goode & Hatt, 1952: 331) than a research method. Although methodical advancements have occurred meanwhile, it is still contestable whether case studies represent a sophisticated method (e.g., Lamnek, 2005; Punch, 2006; Stake, 1994). The reason pertains to the incident that this method does not necessarily follow severe guidelines but offers multiple ways for reaching results. Therefore, it is imperative to profoundly describe the characteristics of case studies, a progression to which the following paragraphs are dedicated to. Based on this clarification, the application of case studies is discussed in relation to auxiliary thoughts and conceptions of this empirical work in order to illustrate the methodical fit between this thesis' segments.

Definition, Characteristics, and Conformance of Case Studies

Literature provides numerous descriptions and definitions concerning case studies. Hence, a definition is introduced first to indicate how case studies were appreciated in this paper. Contingent on this definition, the nature of case studies is clarified by reverting to an initial categorization. This attempt should further substantiate why case studies appeared to be the most appropriate research technique. Finally, case studies are discussed with regard to auxiliary issues and themes contemplated on in this thesis.

Definition

On the one hand, the case study method has an extensive history: Being first applied in the beginning of the 20th century by the University of Chicago, it was rediscovered in the 1960s (Tellis, 1997), experienced a crisis in the 1970s (Yin, 1981), and received a new wave of attention in the 2000s (Siggelkow, 2007). On the other hand, case studies represent research strategies for several disciplines, such as psychology, sociology, political sciences, social work, as well as business studies and economics (e. g., Dul & Hak, 2008). These multifaceted properties give rise to the notion that a general accepted definition of a case study is difficult to consummate. Gerring refers to this obstacle as a "definitional morass" (2007: 17).

In general, scholars widely agree with Yin's suggestion that "a case study is an empirical inquiry that investigates a contemporary phenomenon within its real-life context" (2003: 13). In this respect, Punch maintains that case studies aim to "preserve and understand the wholeness and unity of a case" (2006: 144); therefore, case studies obtain a holistic focus. Concretizing the former definition with respect to this research, the phenomenon corresponds to the PE investment in a FB, which cannot be simulated or controlled but necessitates real-life investigations in the actual contexts. Although this classification assists in defining the term, it inadequately conveys information about the uniqueness of case studies in relation to other methods. Yin states that the

> case study inquiry copes with the technically distinctive situation in which there will be many more variables of interest than data points, and as one result relies on multiple sources of evidence, with data needing to converge in a triangulating fashion, and as another result benefits from the prior development of theoretical propositions to guide data collection and analysis. (2003: 13 – 14)

In essence, the scholar's argumentation indicates that the character of case studies is very flexible, especially with regard to design considerations. The following paragraph highlights certain categorization attempts to structure a quantity of these elements and to indicate the progression opted for in this paper.

Characteristics

Case studies usually allow for a multiple number of designs and realizations. De facto, critics often see a lack of rigor concerned with case studies (e. g., Meredith, 2002). For instance, Stuart et al. (2002) report evidence that a high number of conducted case studies in operations and supply chain management do not comprehensively discuss the applied case method and its design. Scholars, however, strongly argue that the lack of scientific rigor does not rely in the method's nature but in a deceptive application and ignorance (e.g., Eisenhardt & Graebner, 2007; Hamel et al., 1993; Lee, 1989; Meredith, 2002). Eisenhardt notes in this respect that "confusion surrounds the distinction among qualitative data, inductive logic, and case study research" (1989a: 532). Case study research is neither per se qualitative, nor inductive, but can materialize in variable combinations of the former elements. Eisenhardt and Graebner remark that a case study is often associated with qualitative research "simply because it relies significantly on qualitative data" (2007: 28), yet it might incorporate auxiliary data as well. In consequence, literature defines several types of the case study approach.

Yin (2003) fragments case study methods regarding the following dimensions: exploratory, descriptive, or explanatory. He posits that exploratory case studies are characterized as inductive progressions, whereas the deductive component gains increasing eminence in descriptive and explanatory approaches, respectively. Explanatory techniques can be considered to generate dynamic knowledge, instead of static insights, as the impetus of discovery is facilitated by questions directed to the procedural mechanisms in place, i.e., "how" and "why." Although Yin (2003) remains widely silent whether pure deductive case study designs represent feasible research strategies, Dul and Hak (2008) differentiate between case studies on a continuum ranging from explorative, to theory-building, and finally to theory-testing research, suggesting that such designs might be pursued; nonetheless, Gerring proclaims that such a modus operandi is not the "case study's strong suit" (2007: 42). Considering both categorizations, it seems evident that the case study method in this research can be illustrated as explanatory (cf. Yin, 2003) or proposition-building (cf. Dul and Hak, 2008). Such a technique draws on known concepts and makes an attempt to highlight their relations, which reinforces the implied logic that the progression in this empirical study is neither completely inductive nor entirely deductive. It is rather theory driven with the objective to extend existing theory and to describe real-life phenomena (cf. Lee et al. 1999). Figure 13 visualizes the emphasized categorization.

Figure 13: Differentiation of Case Studies' Characteristics

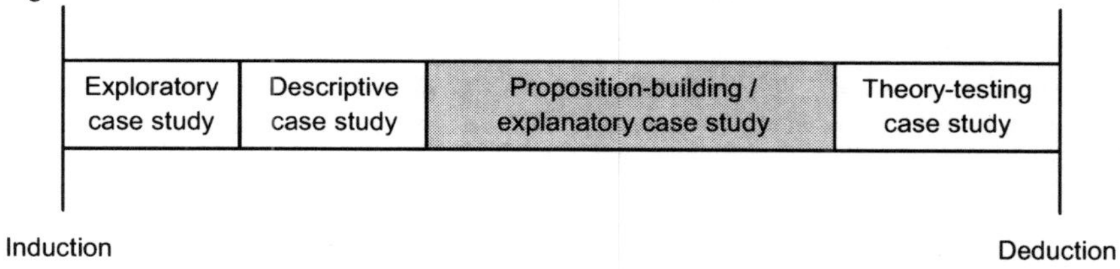

Source: author's illustration

The chosen form of case research has advantages over pure inductive approaches, being usually qualitative in nature, or deductive ones, being usually quantitative in nature. Opposed to Dyer and Wilkins (1991), who criticize this "paradoxical" and "hybrid" form of case studies regarding the capability to generate both rich descriptions while adhering to rigorous constructs, I relied on Eisenhardt's reply that "good storytelling is an essential first step, but good theory is fundamentally the result of rigorous methodology" (1991: 627). Along these lines, Weick (1999) suggests that theorizing is supposed to manage tradeoffs. For instance, he maintains that thought trials *and* induction, theory building *and* testing, as well as continuity *and* novelty embody complementary qualities researchers should strive for. In fact, these paradoxical qualities were adhered to in this inquiry so that an inductive progression was eventually pursued, which comprised certain deductive elements that assisted in having a clear research focus (cf. Mintzberg, 1979). Substantiating this choice, Wolcott (1982) exhibits that it represents an unattainable desire to approach any research without some idea of what one is looking for. He continues that the mere claim of researchers to do so constitutes an unreliable attitude. In a similar vein, Miles and Huberman posit "that better research happens when you make your framework – and associated choices of research questions, cases, sampling, and instrumentation – explicit, rather than claiming inductive 'purity'" (1994: 23). Given that a research stream pertaining to PE investments in FBes has already been established (cf. *Appendix B*), the progression to exploit established knowledge for the underlying investigation was, as a matter of fact, a logical inference. Components signifying deductive elements in this paper include the review of the relevant literature, the construction of guiding research questions, the composition of a conceptual framework, as well as the selection of particular cases, respectively. It should therefore be apparent that methodical considerations do not exclusively pertain to this chapter, but the overall construction of this paper was streamlined in order to incorporate the ideas presented in the underlying part.

Summarizing the preceding discussion, case studies were identified to represent the most appropriate method for answering the research questions. The explanatory or proposition-building nature of the case study method utilized in this paper was dependent on an interdenominational arrangement of induction and deduction (cf. Miles & Huberman, 1994), balancing storytelling and the adherence to theoretical verdicts (cf. Eisenhardt, 1991) as well as continuity and novelty (cf. Weick, 1999).

Conformance

Edmonson and McManus stress the point that a consistent fit of elements in a research project is "a critical [...] input to high-quality field research" (2007: 1177), which underlines Daft's (1995) recommendation to correlate chapters with each other. To substantiate this issue, the employment of case studies is exemplarily highlighted with regard to two themes that emerged earlier, explicitly the rigor and relevance debate (cf. section 1.2) and the consideration of the means and ends of empiricism in the underlying part.

With reference to Vermeulen (2007, 2005), an attempt was made in this paper to handle the paradox of rigor and relevance. Case studies facilitate relevant empirical descriptions, i.e., storytelling, and simultaneously tolerate the exploitation and refinement of rigorous theory. Accordingly, the method represented a suitable device for conducting research in the "Pasteur's Quadrant" of the social sciences (cf. Tushman & O'Reilly, 2007; Stokes, 1997). To this effect, it was argued that the character of this investigation represented "problem-driven work" (Davis & Marquis, 2005), which was progressed by means of empirical observations, theoretical abstractions, and model refinement (cf. Chatman & Flynn, 2006). The case study method, especially the explanatory (Yin, 2003) or proposition-building (Dul & Hak, 2008) type selected, combines these virtues and forms a complementary research technique.

In addition, it should be recognized that case study research harmonizes with Gergen's (2002) positions on empirical research: Case studies represent an "alternative to 'mainstream' or positivist research methods" (Gibbert et al. 2008: 1473), escaping imperatives of natural science inquiries (e.g., Daft & Lewin, 1990; McKelvey, 1997; Mir & Watson, 2001). Along these lines, Lee (1991) deliberately reminds us of the circumstance that approaches relying on an exceeding dimension of interpretation, such as case studies, do not signify second-rate quality research methods in terms of rigor. Likewise, it should be recalled that the case study method produces relevant outcomes, which was pointed out previously. This issue becomes reinforced as the method properly conforms to three central achievements of empirical research described by Gergen (2002). First, the method facilitates the derivation of detailed and magnificent descriptions of real-life phenomena without segregating the phenomenon from its context. The symbiotic character of phenomenon and context is usually considered important given that early theorists maintain that field methods "should always include qualitative research to describe and illuminate the context and conditions under which research is conducted" (Cook & Campbell, 1979: 93). Detailed and magnificent insights were corroborated with the help of the utilization of diverse data, which were collected from multiple sources and which were qualitative or quantitative in nature. Therefore, the method adheres to Van Maanen's early argument that "qualitative methodology and quantitative methodology are not mutually exclusive" (1979: 520). Second, case study research is described to deliver captivating insights (see Bartunek et al. 2006), fulfilling Sutton and Staw's criterion that organizational theory should be "particularly interesting" (1995: 49). Due to the concrete disposition of the results derived from case study research, these are sometimes able to stimulate political or societal discussions. Third, the chosen explanatory, proposition-building type strengthens the method's capability to make predictions of complex social phenomena for the benefit of societal application.

II. Research Design

Due to the "characteristic flexibility" (Gerring, 2007) of case studies, this section thoroughly specifies the applied procedures and is separated into three subsections. First, the background of the selection of cases is provided; hence, the corresponding subsection illustrates the research setting. Second, the techniques employed to gather field data are highlighted. Third, the analysis of data and the supplementary research strategy are described.

In order to critically assess these three subsections, reliability and considerations relating to construct, internal, and external validity are deliberated alongside. In fact, I made use of these four elements to overcome certain concerns regarding methodical rigor in case study research (cf. March et al. 1991; Miles, 1979; Yin, 1981). Yin defines construct validity as the establishment of "correct operational measures" (2003: 34), internal validity as "causal relationships" (2003: 34), external validity in relation to how a "study's findings can be generalized" (2003: 34), and reliability as the ability to comprehend the "operations of a study" (2003: 34). While I utilized Bacharach's (1989) and Whetten's (1989) suggestions and parameters to guide the construction of the conceptual model, Yin's (2003) quality criteria were adhered to in this chapter. Although Numagani asks whether those "criteria are really necessary" (1998: 2) and contends "that reliability/replicability and external validity are irrelevant not only for case study, but for any method of management studies" (1998: 2), it seems arguable that a consideration of these measures results in elevated levels of transparency, facilitating an improved communication with the reader of this book. Noticeably, a recent study conducted by Gibbert and colleagues (2008) adopts Yin's (2003) measures and evaluates 159 case studies from ten influential academic management journals. The authors report that the investigated papers emphasize external validity considerations at the expense of internal and construct validity, which repeatedly experience neglect. Moreover, they discover that the case studies that are published in the top three journals of their sample, consisting of the *Academy of Management Journal*, *Administrative Science Quarterly*, and *Strategic Management Journal*, are methodically more rigorous because these studies employ concrete measures to meet the entire quaternary quality criteria. Eventually, Gibbert et al. (2008) testify that the four elements represent the exclusive devices made use of in the reviewed studies. This leads to the inference that the construction of this paper, by reflection on the four issues, should have resulted in a reasonable rigorous empirical discovery.

1. Research Setting

Case study research represents a frequently criticized method in the field of the social sciences, and the technique has historically been encountered with skepticism. According to Punch, this attitude "is usually based on the generalizability criticism, and is expressed by the condescending remark 'that's only a case study'" (2006: 147). Contemporary methodologists, however, challenge this allegation and provide techniques facilitating the advancement from a "research strategy" (Goode & Hatt, 1952) toward an elaborate method. The advancements in case study methods primarily comprise the evolution of designs regarding the technique of case selection. As a matter of fact, the case selection procedure is critically assessed at first in order to clarify the approach followed in this thesis. Hereupon, a second paragraph describes the application of the derived implications and hence exemplifies how cases were practically selected.

Discussion of Methodical Issues Related to Case Selection

Case selection comprises deliberations concerning the issue whether to conduct a single-design or to rely on a multiple-case design. Furthermore, the unit of analysis deserves certain attention to clarify the examination's scope. Both issues are addressed in the following paragraphs.

Single-case vs. multiple-case designs

Traditionally, case study research consisted of exploratory studies that made use of single-case studies (Yin, 2003). Single-case studies are usually associated with rich descriptions (e.g., Dyer & Wilkins, 1991; Siggelkow, 2007), yet they are imperfect for building theoretical knowledge (e.g., Eisenhardt, 1989a). Although Kennedy (1976) and Flyvbjerg (2006) show how one can generalize from single-case evidence,[37] the academic community posits that multiple-case methods are superior for attaining sound levels of generalizability.

In order to differentiate between single and multiple-case designs, Stake (1994) distinguishes between three types and proposes that case studies might be intrinsic, instrumental, or collective. Whereas intrinsic case studies are utilized to build an understanding of an element's dynamics, instrumental approaches are described to refine or build theory. Collective case studies advance the character of instrumental proceedings and broaden the scope of investigations regarding the inclusion of several cases. This method is termed comparative case study by Dul and Hak (2008). Correspondingly, Yin (2003) refers to the coverage of more than one case as a multiple-case design, which was the design applied and term respected in this analysis. Single-case designs are advocated to be used in situations when the phenomenon of investigation is unique, rare, representative, or revelatory, but multiple-case designs usually provide increased levels of robustness when drawing conclusions (e.g., Herriot & Firestone, 1983). Adhering to the conceptualization of a multiple-case design, external validity was eventually strengthened, which in turn corroborated the findings of this thesis.

In line with the decision to accomplish a multiple-case design, a related choice pertained to the question how many case studies one should conduct. Eisenhardt posits, "Finally, while there is no ideal number of cases, a number between 4 and 10 cases usually works well" (1989a: 545). She denotes that it might be difficult to generate externally valid theory with a quantity fewer than four cases, yet she also proposes that double digit scenarios result in too much complexity. From a theoretical viewpoint, scholars recommend to stop adding cases when marginal observations only deliver little new insights, and Gerring (2007) notes that discretionary and judgmental choice should set the boundaries for the former consideration. Having seized these suggestions, I conducted eight individual cases, which fulfilled the prior debated scientific requirements.

Unit of analysis

Yin (2003) proclaims that the selection of a single or multiple-case design goes along with the choice for the unit of analysis. The scholar distinguishes between holistic and embedded designs; the latter designs contain more than one unit of

37 Flyvbjerg (2006) considers Galileo's experiment of gravity, in which the scientist tested the velocity of falling elements in relation to their weight, and demonstrates that one experiment might provide compelling evidence to assume generalizability: Galileo rejected Aristotelian laws that weight is correlated with fall velocity and simultaneously suggested that no interdependence between height and fall velocity subsists. According to Flyvbjerg (2006), the same logic from an experiment is trajectory to case studies.

analysis. With regard to the research objective and the conceptual framework, this paper adopted a holistic focus. The unit of analysis was the organization itself.

The decision to conduct a holistic design with the organization as the observable dimension followed previous segments of this paper and was especially inspired by the derived constructs (cf. subsection 3.2). Gupta et al. (2006), for instance, argue that the organizational level is most likely to signify the latitude of exploration and exploitation as it represents the stratum upon which most researchers position their unit of analysis. Likewise, scholars researching organizational contexts, as the term already reveals, typically identify the organizational level as the appropriate unit (see Howard-Grenville, 2005; Zellmer-Bruhn & Gibson, 2006). For instance, Mowday and Sutton emphasize that an organizational context pertains to the "stimuli and phenomena that surround and thus exist in the environment external to the individual" (1993: 198), which highlights the organizational level. In conclusion, the research objective, corresponding research questions, and preliminary theoretical considerations incontrovertibly confirmed the selection of a holistic design with the organizational level as the observable unit.

Application of the Methodical Issues Discussed

In line with previous thoughts, the subsequent paragraphs explain how the case selection was executed. Finally, a short paragraph concludes the research setting.

Case selection

How should the appropriate cases be selected? With reference to Flyvbjerg (2006), the rationale for sampling in case study research converges with the modus operandi of experiments; thus, sampling does not conform to the logic of surveys striving for generalizability in terms of samples and populations. Rather, external validity should be appreciated as a form of an analytical generalization, instead of a statistical one (Yin, 2003). Cases should, according to this logic, be selected in a way that "they are particularly suitable for illuminating and extending relationships and logic of constructs" (Eisenhardt & Graebner, 2007: 27). In other words, a sampling logic in case research would be clearly misplaced because "a case study would have to cover both the phenomenon of interest and its context, yielding a large number of potentially relevant variables" (Yin, 2003: 48). In accordance with this awareness, Seawright and Gerring (2008) propose several strategies for selecting cases. The scholars summarize that a case selection can focus on typical, diverse, extreme, deviant, influential, most similar, as well as most different cases. These strategies reveal two broad patterns that Yin (2003) describes as replications pertaining to literal and theoretical dimensions. Literal replication means that cases should predict similar results, and theoretical replication implies that results might differ but for predictable reasons. The formalized disposition supports auxiliary suggestions from scholars who advise to select cases based on variance, which corresponds to structures of theoretical replications, or consistency, which symbolizes literal scopes (see Bennett & Elman, 2006; Flyvbjerg, 2006).

I employed literal and theoretical replications to select the relevant cases. Mature FBes can principally be subject to two divergent transaction types, which were identified as minority and majority transactions (e. g., Kaserer et al. 2007). In consequence, I utilized minority investments and the various types of buyouts as the mean and changes in the derived constructs as the end to differentiate between literal and theoretical replications. In practical terms, I first addressed buyouts as they were expected to convey sufficient insights regarding the content of organizational change: Increased observable variance in these entities, compared to minority investments, enabled to shape and operationalize the relevant constructs. The established evidence and preliminary insights gathered from the initial set of cases were then utilized to look for similar or deviating phenomena within the buyout group. Hereupon, the outcomes from the buyout cases were challenged by further replications with the help of the investigating minority investments. The latter cases naturally represented a set of theoretical replications given that "contrasting results," yet for "predictable reasons," were anticipated. Predictable reasons effectively pertained to the type of the investment because dialectic and teleological motors were expected to start operating with distinctive energy in both scenarios.

Additional selection criteria

Case studies usually do not impose additional selection principles, and even papers considered to possess outstanding quality, such as Ferlie et al.'s (2005) contribution which won the best article award by the *Academy of Management Journal*, remain regularly silent on the utilization of supplementary principles constraining the assortment of cases. In contrast, I decided to implement two additional selection criteria that limited the universe of potential cases since they were necessary for drawing legitimate evaluations. The selected cases needed to be identified as FBes before the investment. In a similar vein, the investors needed to be clearly identified as PE companies. The underlying definitions and techniques utilized for identification were explained in earlier segments of this paper (cf. chapter 2). These approaches, however, were not sufficient for answering the research intention. Therefore, it is purposeful to revisit Whetten's (1989) parameters, which were employed to structure the conceptual framework (cf. section 3.2). In the former discussion, the fourth set of interrogations, pertaining to "who," "where," and "when," was postponed when having considered the conceptual framework's building blocks and its relationships. Whetten notes that these "temporal and contextual factors set the boundaries of generalizability, and as such constitute the range of the theory" (1989: 492). Therefore, I intentionally controlled for the dimensions of time and space. With regard to the circumstance that organizations do neither necessarily change their character revolutionary nor essentially evolutionary (Weick & Quinn, 1999), setting an appropriate time frame for the conducted observation was a difficult challenge. Pragmatically, the included cases had to fulfill the requirement that the investment of a PE investor was at least one year but no longer than five years ago. Having set this timeframe, it was assumed that change processes were already initiated and that the most significant corporate conversion should have been completed when having investigated the case. This timeframe was also chosen with reference to the literature on buyouts which usually reports holding times of financial investors in the range from five to seven years (e. g., Kaplan & Strömberg, 2009). The second constraint, namely the geographical scope, obligated to exclusively focus the inquiry on German organizations. This procedure followed the research intention to investigate PE investments in German FBes.

Summary
Both design considerations advised by Yin (2003), i. e., the alternative of conducting a single case study or a multiple design and the adoption of a holistic or embedded progression, were thoroughly scrutinized. I constructed the case research as a holistic, multiple-case design in order to achieve a methodical fit with the research objective and prior theoretical deliberations (cf. Edmonson and McManus, 2007). The applied multiple-case design made use of theoretical and literal replications to draw robust conclusions from the field. In doing so, it strengthened the robustness criterion of external validity (cf. Herriott & Firestone, 1983). An overview of the researched cases is provided in section III, *Description of Data.*

2. Data Sources and Data Collection

Following the choice of the research setting, this subsection concerns the data sources and collection attempts, and it constitutes the second critical design element in this study. Comparable to the degrees of freedom in designing the case selection, case studies legitimize the employment of diverse collection techniques to generate results. Gephart summarizes this thought by implying that a qualitative procedure "often involves fieldwork, and the word 'work' is important here. There are no algorithms for producing it" (2004: 461).

Although case studies might be subject to a lack of a standardized data collection, particularly in comparison with deductive, statistical inspections, methodologists agree that a meticulously conducted data collection in case study research has the potential to encourage elevated levels of reliability and construct validity (e. g., Dul & Hak, 2008; Gibbert et al., 2008; Miles and Huberman, 1994; Yin, 2003). Both quality criteria serve as reference points in this subsection. Attention is first paid to the reliability criterion; the corresponding segment outlines certain measures taken advantage of when having designed the data collection. Hereupon, the next segment describes the actual practice of inquiry, which was the interview procedure and questionnaire outline. The final part of the subsection eventually illustrates how the derived constructs were operationalized.

Discussion of Methodical Issues Related to Case Evidence

The subsequent paragraphs discuss construct validity and reliability issues which have emerged in the data collection process. Thereby, the first paragraph presents the included sources of evidence, and the second paragraph considers how the transparency of thoughts and documentation principles should have augmented reliability.

Sources of evidence

Scholars point out that research in the organization science is frequently confronted with a "problem of unobservables" (Godfrey & Hill, 1995: 513), implying that empirical investigations draw on insufficient construct descriptions. Boyd et al. (2004) substantiate this observation given that they examined articles from the *Academy of Management*, *Administrative Science Quarterly*, and *Strategic Management Journal* with the intention to decipher the applied construct measurement. The authors conclude that "many academic researchers ignore or are unaware that their measures often do not fully or accurately capture the constructs of interest" (2004: 240).

To avoid this liability, methodologists suggest utilizing multiple sources of evidence in case research. Whereas interviews and questionnaires were employed as the primary instruments to collect evidence, most cases depended on the insertion of additional information. Supplementary evidence included newspaper articles illuminating the cases' contexts, annual reports and further reports accessible, impressions gathered at site inspections, or internal documents (cf. Yin 2003). For instance, I recognized an ancestral portrait gallery at one company when visiting the site. Having addressed the issue to the secretary taking me through the company, she described how former family managers have always provided a reference point for employees, which has created a family-like place to work. In another case, I received an internal document concerning the informant's view on the firm's performance following the PE investment.

The consideration of such multidimensional evidence usually assists in describing constructs with elevated precision (cf. Yin, 2003). Therefore, the employed triangulation of evidence was achieved through the incorporation of multiple data sources and combinatorial collection formats. The triangulation pursued in this paper hence followed Jick's notion that "'within-method' triangulation essentially involves cross-checking for internal consistency" (1979: 603). "Within-methods" relating to interviews, questionnaires, and desk research were in fact exploited to establish a convergence of inquiry and to reach an effective orchestration at the case level. The unification of qualitative and quantitative insights from interviews and questionnaires was described as "a new style of social research" (Sieber, 1973: 1335) by early scholars and is regarded as highly synergistic by the contemporary academic community (e.g., Eisenhardt & Graebner, 2007; Punch, 2004; Ragin, 1987). Firestone (1987) proposes that the incorporation of quantitative data helps to convince skeptical readers with the help of hard facts. Furthermore, he states that the inclusion of quantitative data facilitates the cross-case comparability due to the employment of identical concepts. Moreover, Sieber (1973) accentuates that quantitative data help to prevent fallacies since researchers are confronted with another perspective, which inhibits premature judgments.

In sum, I strived for the incorporation of multiple lines of evidence in order to establish an advanced degree of construct validity; this procedure attempted to synthesize deductive and inductive elements, which was described as the strength of case study research in the previous subsection.

Transparency

Punch (2006) makes the distinction between reliability and "dependability" (Lincoln & Guba, 1985) concerning quantitative and qualitative research, respectively. In quantitative research, reliability is primarily concerned with the consistency over time and internal consistency. In qualitative research, "dependability" has a similar nature but puts emphasis on the process, rather than on the results, of consistency. The decisive task of a researcher is thus to account for all aspects of the subjective perspective from which the research evolves. Yin denotes that in case study research the "general way of approaching the reliability problem is to make as many steps as operational as possible and to conduct research if someone were always looking over your shoulder" (2003: 38), which reinforces the idea to celebrate processes over outcomes.

Given the fact that qualitative research should follow systematic principles (e.g., Glaser & Strauss, 1967; Mayring, 2010; Miles & Hubermann, 1994), transparency was appreciated as a crucial merit throughout the research process.[38] Therefore, I followed standard advices to build case study databases in order to enhance levels of reliability/dependability in case research. Case study databases primarily consisted of interview protocols, filled in questionnaires, and certain field notes (cf. Levine, 1985). The transcription procedure, defined as a "fundamental component of rigor in qualitative research" (Poland, 1995: 290), is elaborated in a further part of this chapter. Besides, it should be appreciated that aspects of reliability/dependability do not exclusively concern data collection procedures or documentation practices but already commenced at earlier stages of this book and also continue in subsequent sections. Most passages of this book, up to the chapter exhibiting the results, were utilized to promote high transparency levels by exemplifying underlying thoughts, concepts, and beliefs.

Discussion of the Data Selection Procedure

Singleton and Straits (1999) stress that the quality of data collection in the social sciences is contingent on three parameters: sampling, resources, and content. The three parameters are subsequently addressed. Sampling and resources are deliberated at first. Given that content is rather independent of the remaining two issues and also to a higher extent under the researcher's control, the element is discussed in more detail and includes the description how interviews and questionnaires were conducted.

Sampling

In principal, I adhered to Sekaran (2003) for choosing appropriate informants in the studied organizations by means of non-probability sampling. This procedure was necessary to avoid sample selection biases caused by access restrictions (cf. Manksi, 1989; Winship & Mare, 1992). Whereas probabilistic sampling attempts to create samples with the aim of achieving representativity, which usually demands that every element of the target population should have the same probability to be in the selected sample (e.g., Schnell et al. 1995), non-

38 Sutton's (1997) makes a provocative appeal in his essay *The virtues of closet qualitative research* to conceal the basis of data in qualitative research. Sutton describes four situations in which such a progression seems feasible: "These are: (1) when weak qualitative data lead to good insights; (2) when describing the qualitative research reduces the quality of the writing; (3) when an outlet does not publish 'empirical' papers, and (4) when writing for an audience that remains biased against qualitative research" (1997: 99). Given that none of these situations appeared to be extraordinarily relevant, this study discusses the foundation of the utilized data.

probabilistic sampling relies on divergent objectives conflicting with representativity (e.g., Glaser & Strauss, 1967).

The selection of informants thus followed a purposive sampling strategy, which is "confined to specific types of people who can provide the necessary information, either because they are the only ones who have it, or conform to some criteria set by the researcher" (Sekaran, 2003: 277). Purposive sampling comprised two generic conditions. All informants had to belong to the examined company before the financial investment occurred so that these informants were able to properly describe the organizational development. In certain cases, managers, particularly finance and accounting professionals, did not accurately fulfill this criterion as they got employed simultaneous with or some weeks after the PE investment. Nevertheless, these persons were also able to describe the modifications which took place during their tenure. According to Eisenhardt and Graebner, "A key approach is using numerous and highly knowledgeable informants who view the focal phenomenon from diverse perspectives. These informants can include organizational actors from different hierarchical levels, functional areas, groups, and geographies" (2007: 28). In line with this notion, I additionally made the determination to rely on respondents who varied in terms of hierarchy and managerial function. I thereby increased the variance in perspectives while I have effectively bypassed the practical limitation to access a restricted quantity of informants in each case.

Identified organizational members provided the case evidence: They were interviewed, asked to fill out the questionnaire, as well as invited to provide additional information in form of archival records and documents. Comparable to the presentation of cases, a concrete overview of the interviewed respondents is provided in this part.

Resources

This study had to make certain compromises with regard to the resources dedicated to the empirical inquiry. In short, the basic economic problem of scarce resources and infinite wants (e.g., Sloman, 2007) naturally affected the data collection in specific ways.

Scarce resources and the cost of investigations disallowed for the collection of evidence with multiple researchers, which could have hypothetically reduced cognitive biases and erroneous conclusions (cf. Singleton & Straits, 1999). Another tradeoff can be identified with regard to the dimension of time: The chosen design in this paper was cross-sectional although researchers proclaim that longitudinal attempts are typically preferred to cross-sectional progressions when investigating organizational change (see Avital, 2000; George & Jones, 2000; Lindell & Drexler, 1979; Pettigrew, 1990; Romanelli & Tushman, 1986; Zaheer, 1999). This incident is especially true for case studies (Leonard-Barton,

1990). The latter shortcoming, however, was beyond my control since investigated companies bore the costs of this research through the provision of valuable time, and this time was eventually limited. I discuss the shortcomings of sampling and resources in more detail in the limitations part (cf. *Appendix D*).

Content

In the following paragraphs, I elaborate the third component to which Singleton and Straits (1999) refer to as content. Having indicated that interviews and accompanying questionnaires represented the main sources of evidence, both techniques require an intensified clarification in order to conform to the purpose of achieving a robust fit through the spheres of this paper (cf. Edmonson & McManus, 2007).

Interviews

Most architectural text books about case study research methods which were primarily adhered to in this study remain widely silent on the employment of specific interview techniques for collecting data. The academic community generally classifies interview methods along the degree of structure and report techniques that range from unstructured, to semi-structured, and to structured interviews (see Minichiello et al. 1990). In addition, Mayring (2002) points out that interviews might be further distinguished into open or closed approaches, which describes the degrees of freedom in the respondent's answers. Consequently, an open discussion combined with certain closed and structured questions was assumed to deliver the most viable results. Unstructured, open-ended questions allowed for gaining insight into the respondent's key opinion on the researched matter and thus facilitated the description of significant concepts. Structured questions were then utilized to collect in-depth information about critical constructs.

Furthermore, I employed auxiliary elements and techniques besides the degree of structure and the degree of freedom. In a preceding segment of this section, I stated that the level of analysis in this paper pertained to the organizational level, but organizational members were utilized as raters of the constructs. This represents the standard procedure to observe organizations (e.g., Pfeffer, 2004; Simon, 2007) and was feasible as respondents were assumed to be most familiar with the attributes of their organizations regarding changes in the contextual antecedents, the organizational context, and the level of ambidexterity. Nonetheless, the existence of multiple perspectives between the informants on the researched matters introduced an additional level of complexity.

In order to explore this obstacle, Kozlowski and Klein (2000) decode different construct characteristics. The authors distinguish between three types of constructs which have different properties: global, shared, and configural constructs. Global properties pertain to "relatively objective, descriptive, easily observable characteristics" (2000: 45) illustrating a proximity to objectivistic perspectives since a definite description of a phenomenon seems attainable. Opposed to global unit constructs, shared and configural unit constructs originate at the individual level, yet they are reinforced at the unit level. Shared constructs are assumed to "emerge as a consensual, collective aspect as the unit as a whole" (2000: 45). Shared unity constructs thus embody isomorphic observations. Configural properties, however, "capture the variability or pattern of individual characteristics, constructs, or responses across the members of a unit" (2000: 45). In theory, the clear cut differentiation between shared and configural constructs is meaningful although Kozlowski and Klein (2000) propose that the differentiation is difficult to maintain in empirical research, and consequently it finds only limited application. In fact, I expected that all researched constructs possessed a hybrid nature of shared consensus and configural diversity. Nevertheless, the presentation of evidence naturally needed to adhere to a holistic perspective, which is why constructs were functionally reported as shared unit constructs in the results (cf. section 5.2). This procedure was facilitated by the subsequently proposed interview technique.

Because interviewing portrays a mean to "understand other persons' constructions of reality" (Jones, 1985: 46), it should seem apparent that interviewing had to incorporate systemic principles for resolving the impediment of subjectivity. I applied the circular interviewing technique developed by Selvini Palazzoli et al. (1980) in order to partially resolve this obstacle (cf. Penn, 1983). Due to the fact that scholars propose miscellaneous approaches under the umbrella term of "circular interviewing," such as interventive interviewing (see Tomm, 1987) or systemic interviewing (see Rothermel & Feierfeil, 1990), I made use of Pfeffer's (2004) description and definition in this paper.[39] The author stresses that one of the foremost virtues in utilizing circular questions pertains to the rejection of objective descriptions, which coincide with global unit constructs (cf. Kozlowski and Klein, 2000). However, the achievements of circular interviewing advance this conjecture. Whereas standard interview methods merely allow for researching configural constructs, which emerge from the diversity of respondents' perspectives, the circular interviewing technique generates insights concerning shared unit level constructs. This effect is stimulated by the utilization of reciprocal observations cross-linking evidence.[40]

39 Pfeffer remarks, "Das zirkuläre Fragen versucht nicht, Informationen über (scheinbar) beobachterunabhängige Phänomene zu erheben. Statt dessen werden im Interview Beobachtungen beobachtet, im speziellen die Art und Weise, wie Interviewpartner unterscheiden und bezeichnen. (2004: 66)"

40 According to Pfeffer, "Eine der wesentlichen Leistungen des zirkulären Fragens besteht genau darin, die Idee einer vereinheitlichten, konsensuell zu teilenden Weltsicht, die Idee der

Circular interviewing was primarily adopted in the interview process with regard to its basic attribute, i. e., the request to make presumptions about other organizational members' beliefs concerning discussed aspects (cf. Pfeffer, 2004). Whereas this attribute represents the most fundamental element in the interviewing method, Selvini Palazzoli and colleagues (1980) mention two further factors embodying the postures of each interview: hypothesizing and neutrality. Neutrality refers to the researcher's tendency to conceal his viewpoint on researched incidents, which is coupled with the avoidance to oppress particular opinions (Pfeffer, 2004). Open questions were employed, as identified in the beginning of this subsection, in order to tolerate ambivalence in the respondents' answers. Hypothesizing is described as a central element in the circular interviewing process since it reduces complexity and assists in structuring an interview. In line with this notion, structured questions were utilized to shape the understanding of occurrences, constructs, and the interrelations between those elements. Besides circularity, hypothesizing, and neutrality, Pfeffer (2004) identifies four additional attributes researchers are supposed to comply with: strategic proceedings, self responsibility, respect for interviewees, and curiousness. The interview process could be considered strategic forasmuch that I intended to eventually answer the research question with the help of the discovery of within-case and cross-case evidence. Self-responsibility pertains to the necessity to clearly identify oneself as an interviewer. Obeying to this issue, I introduced myself before each interview and outlined the background of the interview even though I did not meticulously disclose the investigation's attempt for the benefit of reducing a priori influence. I had the feeling that respondents showed a tendency to be more accessible after the expectations of the interview were articulated. Likewise, I expressed gratitude to the interviewees for their provided time and opinions before and after the dialogue. Thus, I attempted to assure that respondents felt comfortable during and after the process, which reinforced the principles of respect for interviewees. Eventually, the final posture, to be exact curiousness, naturally constituted a framing element that has initiated the inauguration of this paper.

Questionnaires. Lamnek (2005) describes questionnaires as a quantitative interviewing method, which corresponds to my perspective in this investigation. Given that data collection, analysis, and conclusion drawing should follow iterative principles in case study research, questionnaires were designed in re-

'als gemeinsam angeschauten Welt' zu unterlaufen. [...] Aber damit nicht genug. [...] Man müsste davor resignieren, dass endlos viele Beobachter jeweils ihre eigenen, untereinander unverbundenen Beobachtungen machen. Doch die im zirkulären Fragen gemachten Aufforderungen zur Beobachtung beinhalten auch die Aufforderung zur Beobachtung andere Beobachter. Da diese Beobachtung des anderen als Beobachter nicht nur in eine Richtung geht, sondern wechselseitig stattfindet, werden die Beobachtungen verschiedener Beobachter rekursiv miteinander vernetzt und erhalten dadurch Stabilität" (2004: 75).

sponse to early gathered insights for improving construct descriptions (cf. Miles & Huberman, 1994). In this matter, I adhered to Jauch et al. (1980), who provide the rationale to design questionnaires in response to an initial saturation of themes when the first waves of case analysis are accomplished. The scholars recommend that "[i]nvestigators using questionnaires can compare their findings with those generated from a structured content analysis of cases" (1980: 522). Inferring from this notion, I created the questionnaires iteratively once evidence from the opening interviews indicated suitable operationalizations of constructs. The questionnaires thus harmonized with auxiliary data, which resulted in an effective triangulation (cf. Miles, 1990). Such a proceeding necessitated to contact former interviewees with the request to fill out the questionnaire whereas remaining interviewees were asked to complete the questionnaire directly after the verbal inquiry. This process was to the best advantage for the reason that it epitomized the most effective manner of triangulation: Cross-case patterns were thus subject to an intensified attention through the questionnaires' deductive component. The utilization of questionnaires and the described iterative embedding of the former hence respected the notion that "perception without conception is blind; conception without perception is empty" (Weick, 1999: 803).

Operationalization of Contructs

The developed constructs have not been operationalized up to this stage. Therefore, falsifiable elements, such as measurements issues, and the utility of the employed variables are analyzed subsequently. The constructs' operationalization was the basis for all questionnaires filled out. Furthermore, the operationalized variables were also employed in the majority of the conducted interviews, which, driven by iterative mechanics, progressively adopted the following descriptions.

Ambidexterity

Having indicated in the former chapter that the concept of ambidexterity is subject to multidimensional operationalizations, I decided to employ the operationalization of Lubatkin et al. (2006). The authors extend He and Wong's (2004) operationalization of exploration and exploitation relying on product design differences by incorporating Benner and Tushman's (2003) dimensions regarding the market side of innovations to form twelve items capturing the nature of exploration and exploitation. As a result, exploration and exploitation were researched to indicate alterations pertaining to each company's current technological/product path, and the concepts were employed to investigate changes in the customer/market segment the researched companies operated in.

This choice was contingent on a dominating characteristic that facilitated the convergence of Lubatkin et al.'s (2006) measure with the empirical background of the underlying study: the nature of the investigated entities. Lubatkin et al. (2006) deliberately research the ambidextrous orientation in SMEs whereas the usual proceeding of most empirical articles is to focus on MNEs (see Adler et al. 1999; Birkinshaw & Gibson, 2004; Jansen et al., 2005; Mom et al. 2009). Although SMEs do not virtually correspond to FBes (e.g., Wimmer, 2009), all studied FBes in this research could be classified as SMEs.

In conclusion, I made use of He and Wong's (2004) argument that most firms in my sample did not focus on breakthrough innovations, which was contingent on the industrial environment the organizations operated in. As a matter of fact, a pure operationalization regarding the radicalness of innovation (see Bierly & Chakrabarti, 1996) or patents (see Katila & Ahuja, 2002) did not provide meaningful instruments. Benson and Tushman (2003), however, stress that organizational adaptation is highly correlated with technological innovation, and they advise to include an innovation proxy for this reason. Lubatkin et al. (2006) manage to combine the more conservative focus on product design differences of He and Wong (2004) with the enrichment of Benner and Tushman's (2003) orientation pertaining to the market side of innovations, which should have validated the utility of the variable. Table 7 visualizes the operationalization.

With regard to the questionnaires, I utilized a 5-point Likert scale for capturing the items' variation. Respondents were asked to rate their organization regarding the situation when filled out and the situation before the PE investment was accomplished.

Table 7: Operationalization of Ambidexterity

Exploration	Exploitation
The organization…	
(a) …looks for novel technological ideas by thinking "outside the box."	(a) …commits to improve quality and lower cost.
(b) …bases its success on its ability to explore new technologies.	(b) …continuously improves the reliability of its products and services.
(c) …creates products or services that are innovative to the firm.	(c) …increases the levels of automation in its operations.
(d) …looks for creative ways to satisfy its customers' needs.	(d) …constantly surveys existing customers' satisfaction.
(e) …aggressively ventures into new market segments.	(e) …fine-tunes what it offers to keep its current customers satisfied.
(f) …actively targets new customer groups.	(f) …penetrates more deeply into its existing customer base.

Source: author's illustration; items adapted from Lubatkin et al. (2006)

Organizational context

While many descriptions subsist to measure ambidexterity, empirical instruments for operationalizing the organizational context can be considered rather scarce. As already indicated in preceding parts (cf. subsection 3.2), I employed Birkinshaw and Gibson's (2004) operationalization to encapsulate the nature of the construct given that this classification was found to be meaningful during the initial waves of interviews. The scholars suggest that an organizational context can essentially be segregated into two variables, namely a performance management context and a social context. The measurement of the performance management context consisted of six items which have captured the nature of discipline and stretch (cf. Ghoshal and Bartlett, 1994). Likewise, social contexts, conforming to Ghoshal and Bartlett's (1994) components of trust and support, were assessed by the employment of further six items proposed by Birkinshaw and Gibson (2004). Table 8 visualizes the operationationalization.

Comparable to the construct of ambidexterity, scaling was contingent on the employment of a 5-point Likert scale. Informants were requested to distinguish between the situation before the PE investment and the setting when filled out.

Table 8: Operationalization of the Organizational Context

Performance Context	Social Context
The organization encourages processes to…	
(a) …to set challenging/aggressive goals.	(a) …devote considerable effort to developing subordinates.
(b) …issue creative challenges to their people, instead of narrowly defining tasks.	(b) …push decisions down to the lowest appropriate level.
(c) …make a point of stretching their people.	(c) …have access to the information one needs to make good decisions.
(d) …use business goals and performance measures to run the business.	(d) …quickly replicate best practices across organizational boundaries.
(e) …hold people accountable for their performance.	(e) …treat failure in a good effort as a learning opportunity, not as something to be ashamed of.
(f) …reward hard work through incentive compensation.	(f) …are willing and able to take prudent risks.

Source: author's illustration; items adapted from Birkinshaw and Gibson (2004)

Contextual antecedents

In the early stages of the research process, this construct was the least defined element. The derivation of an appropriate operationalization thus followed inductive patterns and a non-linear process (cf. Daft, 1973). The construct had to be multidimensional, yet not overwhelmingly exhaustive, but parsimonious and sufficient (cf. Bacharach, 1989) in order to balance concreteness and abstractness. Hence, the search for a suitable operationalization needed to account for attributes of an organizational context, the unique characteristics of FBes, and certain established studies on basal organizational changes following a PE investment. In other words, construct dimensions such as falsifiability, related to the logical adequacy, and utility, related to the explanatory potential, were both reinforced by the search progression (cf. Bacharach, 1989).

The measurement scheme that best combined all dimensions was the Competing Values Framework (CVF) (see Quinn & Rohrbaugh, 1983). Cameron and Quinn (2006) developed the Organizational Culture Assessment Instrument (OCAI) on the basis of the CVF. The OCAI achieves solid results in terms of reliability (Yeung et al. 1991) as well as validity (Cameron & Freeman, 1991), and it relies on similar assessment dichotomies utilized by psychologists (see Mitroff & Kilmann, 1978; Myers & Briggs, 1962). The instrument evaluates six categories and differentiates between four dominant organizational orientations: clan, adhocracy, market, and hierarchy.[41] The underlying categories are coordinated along the competing dimensions of external orientation and internal integration as well as flexibility and stability. These two competing continuums effectively reflected interview statements which indicated that organizations opened up to external stimuli and that administration procedures were emphasized. A change in these two dimensions was hence interpreted to signify the most fundamental level to classify an entity. Table 9 visualizes the operationationalization.

In line with the suggestion of Cameron and Quinn (2006), I utilized an ipsative scale for measurement. This scale forced respondents to identify tradeoffs.

41 Although the *Competing Values Framework* is utilized to identify organizational culture by Cameron and Quinn (2006), as denoted by the term *Organizational Culture Assessment Instrument*, this study rather employs the *CVF* as a tool to categorize the manifold variance that is induced by a PE investment. Thereby, the six items, i. e., the dominant characteristics, organizational leadership, management of employees, organizational glue, strategic emphases, and criteria of success, measuring the two dimensions internal/ external orientation and flexibility/ stability delivered a highly parsimonious and substantially comprehensive description of organizational life, which does not necessarily need to be termed culture. In line with Smircich, the argument in this empirical inquiry thus pertains to the viewpoint that "culture is not a variable at all, but is a root metaphor for conceptualizing organization" (1983: 342). The observed changes along these two continuums hence portrayed a frame of the evolving picture, which was expanded by the performance and social processes as well as the outcome of exploration and exploitation.

Table 9: Operationalization of the Contextual Antecedents

Measurement Dimension	Measurement Item*
Dominant Characteristics	A. The organization is a very pleasant place. It is like an extended family. People seem to share a lot of themselves. B. The organization is a very dynamic entrepreneurial place. People are willing to stick their necks out and take risks. C. The organization is very results oriented. A major concern is with getting the job done. People are very competitive and achievement oriented. D. The organization is a very controlled and structured place. Formal procedures generally govern what people do.
Organizational Leadership	A. The leadership in the organization is generally considered to exemplify mentoring, facilitating, or nurturing. B. The leadership in the organization is generally considered to exemplify entrepreneurship, innovating, or risk-taking. C. The leadership in the organization is generally considered to exemplify no-nonsense, aggressive, results-oriented focus. D. The leadership in the organization is generally considered to exemplify coordinating, organizing, or smooth-running efficiency.
Management of Employees	A. The management style in the organization is characterized by teamwork, consensus, and participation. B. The management style in the organization is characterized by individual risk-taking, innovation, freedom, and uniqueness. C. The management style in the organization is characterized by hard-driving competitiveness, high demands, and achievement. D. The management style in the organization is characterized by security of employment, conformity, predictability, and stability in relationships continued.
Organizational Glue	A. The glue that holds the organization together is loyalty and mutual trust. Commitment to this organization is high. B. The glue that holds the organization together is commitment to innovation and development. There is an emphasis on being the cutting-edge. C. The glue that holds the organization together is emphasis on achievement and goal accomplishment. Aggressiveness and winning are common themes. D. The glue that holds the organization together is formal rules and policies. Maintaining a smooth-running organization is important.
Strategic Emphasis	A. The organization emphasizes human development. High trust, openness, and participation persist. B. The organization emphasizes acquiring new resources and creating new challenges. Trying new things and prospecting for opportunities are valued. C. The organization emphasizes competitive actions and achievement. Hitting stretch targets and winning in the marketplace are dominant. D. The organization emphasizes permanence and stability. Efficiency, control and smooth operations are important.

(Continued)

Criteria of Success	A. The organization defines success on the basis of the development of human resources, teamwork, employee commitment, and concern for people. B. The organization defines success on the basis of having the most unique and newest products. It is a product leader and innovator. C. The organization defines success on the basis of winning in the market place and outpacing the competition. Competitive market leadership is key. D. The organization defines success on the basis of efficiency. Dependable delivery, smooth scheduling, and low-cost production are critical.

* The statements signify the subsequent orientations: clan (A), adhocracy (B), market (C), hierarchy (D).
Source: author's illustration; items adapted from Cameron and Quinn (2006)

3. Data Analysis

The former subsection revealed that data collection and analysis represented interdependent modes; this facet is more thoroughly explained in the following paragraphs. A profound clarification hence considers the actual analytical steps that were conducted. Miles posits that the "most serious and central difficulty in the use of qualitative data is that methods of analysis are not well formulated" (1979: 591). He further describes the within-case analysis as "intuitive, primitive, and unmanageable" (1979: 597) as well as the cross-case synthesis as "even less formulated than within-site analysis" (1979: 599). The belief that the analysis of qualitative data is more difficult than the analysis of quantitative data might be true; however, his notion might also be outdated for the reason that the research community has made extensive progressions in the systematic data analysis since then. To account for the condition that conducted analyses took place on two divergent, yet interlinked, dimensions, the subsequent discussion is differentiated between the amplitudes of the aggregated case level and the individual echelon.

Case Analysis

In general, I geared to Eisenhardt's (1989a) iterative chronology for building evidence from cases and thus followed her advice of getting started, selecting cases, crafting instruments, entering the field, analyzing data, shaping hypotheses, enfolding literature, as well as reaching closure. According to her, case analysis is primarily a description of each case, which is afterwards checked for similarities and differences in comparison with auxiliary cases. Although this progression represents a feasible strategy to capture the within-case evidence, it raises certain concerns regarding the functionalities to provide a cross-case comparability as the individual dynamics of each case can hardly be compared with each other. In this respect, it is crucial to apprehend the fine nuances distinguishing the scholar's suggestion from the progression opted for in this thesis. Categorizing the hybrid nature of case studies on a continuum along the degree of pre-structuring as done earlier in this segment, this paper would potentially be located on a spot typified by augmented deductive elements in comparison to Eisenhardt's (1989a) method given that she, for example, advises to employ grounded theory analysis (see Glaser & Strauss, 1967).

To discuss the diverging logics, the case analysis was conceptualized to embrace three mutual levels. The macro stratum considered Yin's (2003) advice to rely on theoretical propositions. This technique was reinforced at the meso tier by having followed pattern matching progressions (cf. Trochim, 1989). At the micro, operational level, the analytic strategy was energized through procedures of data reduction, data display, and conclusion drawing (cf. Miles & Huberman, 1994).

Macro stratum

Yin (2003) describes several strategies for structuring empirical case analyses, among them the utilization of theoretical propositions and the development of case descriptions. The development of a case description corresponds to the procedure Eisenhardt (1989a) recommends, but it is less preferable for explanatory, multiple-case techniques (Yin, 2003). In fact, the general analytic strategy decided on was the employment of theoretical propositions, which Yin identifies as the "most preferred strategy" (2003: 111); this strategy reinforces the fundamental objectives and design characteristics of this thesis, for example, the establishment of a conceptual framework, the case selection, and the data collection. Thereby, the dominant theoretical proposition followed was the insight that organizational behavior has an effect on the level of ambidexterity (cf. subsection 3.2). Precisely, alterations in the setup of organizational contexts, induced by a new orchestration of antecedents, were thus expected to explain potential modifications in the ambidextrous orientation an organization upheld.

Meso stratum

The utilization of a macro analytic strategy that has followed theoretical propositions required that constructs needed to be measured and identified before correlations could have been assumed. Likewise, the final quality criterion identified, internal validity, demanded a sound procedure regarding this analytical step. To meet this quality imperative, I principally employed the concept of pattern matching (cf. Campbell & Fiske, 1959; Einhorn & Hogarth, 1986; Trochim, 1985).

In general, pattern matching can be described as a useful mechanism for utilizing theory in outcome evaluations. Trochim states that "firm knowledge of pattern matching principles will guide the researcher in developing better theory and integrating that theory in the research process" (1989: 356). The idea behind this technique can be identified as "an attempt to link two patterns where one is a theoretical pattern and the other is an observed or operational one" (Trochim, 1989: 356). In this paper, the theoretical patterns gained attention in the conceptual model whereas the observed patterns were discovered in the empirical part. The author emphasizes that pattern matching represents an effective device to create internally valid knowledge as the procedure leads to the creation of theoretical compelling interrelations.

Noticeably, the employment of the circular interviewing method, which relies on hypothesizing as a main element (Pfeffer, 2004; Selvini Palazzoli et al. 1980), benefited from pattern matching and, in turn, also encouraged its use. As a result, the application of pattern matching limited fallacies of erroneous within-case constructions and strengthened the "repeatable regularities" (Kaplan, 1964) of cross-case comparability.

Micro stratum.

My viewpoint on data analysis followed the principles of Miles and Huberman (1994), whose work is generally recommended by the academic community for conducting case study analysis. Miles and Huberman "define *analysis* as consisting of three concurrent flows of activity: data reduction, data display, and conclusion drawing/verification" (1994: 10), which is visualized in the subsequent figure.

Figure 14: Interactive Model of Data Analysis

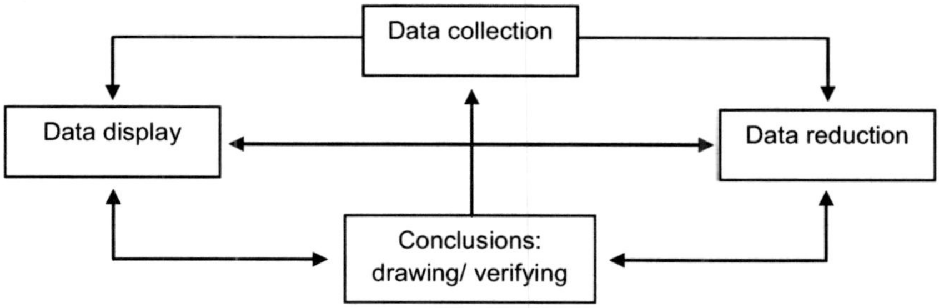

Source: adapted from Miles and Huberman (1994)

The scholars posit that their interpretation of data analysis has analogous hallmarks compared to quantitative analysis. In quantitative analysis, data is first reduced to demonstrate its univariate dimension, such as means, medians, and standard deviations. The multivariate setting, generally in the form of regressions, emulates data display. Conclusion drawing is usually associated with the discussion of significance levels and robustness checks.

In qualitative research, data reduction consists of the continuous process of simplifying and focusing the collected data, representing the first analytical step. To be precise, data reduction intentionally commenced with the collection of certain evidence. The earliest form of data reduction therefore already pertained to the selection of deliberately asked questions during the interview and the chosen questionnaire design. Hereupon, data were displayed in order to account for humans' cognitive limitations to process a large amount of information. Diverse matrices, all described by Miles & Huberman (1994), were employed to accomplish the display of data. For instance, "checklist matrices" were made use of to identify the most appropriate operationalizations for the questionnaire design. "Explanatory effects matrix" helped to construct within-case dynamics and "conceptually ordered displays" facilitated cross-case investigations. Finally, the third analytic process was the Gemini configuration of drawing and verifying conclusions. The separation illustrates the iterative nature of the modus operandi: Preliminary insights stimulated new tactics with regard to the collection and reduction of data and also affected the display of established data. This process was finalized when all relevant themes appeared to be saturated.

Interview Analysis

The analysis of interviews principally reflected the logic considered above and generated the primary evidence for further analysis. In essence, the examination of interviews adhered to qualitative content analysis. In contrast to supplementary analytical procedures from interpretative and hermeneutic schools, qualitative content analysis is a systematic procedure that explores material by utilizing established theoretical verdicts (e.g., Mayring, 2010; 2002), imitating the logic of the macro and meso stratum of the chosen form of case analysis. Mayring (2010, 2002) subdivides the method into three analytical procedures, which can either be applied independently or jointly: aggregation, explication, and structuring. Aggregation has similar qualities compared to open coding practices (see Glaser, 1978; Strauss and Corbin, 1998), in which the material is constantly reduced to attain an abstractive overview. Explication is based on intensified levels of interpretation and utilizes additional contextual elements explaining the investigated material. Structuring has parallels with axial coding (see Glaser, 1978; Strauss and Corbin, 1998) as it makes an attempt to filter certain content from the material based on specified criteria.

Structuring best describes the modus operandi opted for in this paper.

Mayring (2010) defines four dimensions to structure material: form, content, typology, and scale. The applied technique primarily adhered to content structuring. Structuring based on content attempts to extract and summarize passages pertaining to specified criteria.[42] The former technique was accomplished with the help of specialized software (cf. Lewins & Silver, 2007). In particular, ATLAS.ti was employed since the program was established on the basis of qualitative content analysis. Structuring by content is carried into effect by means of several steps. It starts with the determination of the content dimensions and its specifications, continues with the coding procedure of the material, and is finalized by summarizing the sources of information (Mayring, 2010). The determination of the content dimension was naturally in line with the derived three building blocks relating to contextual antecedents, organizational context, and ambidexterity (cf. subsection 3.2). Thereby, it harmonized with Trochim's (1989) concept of pattern matching, which symbolized the meso stratum of the applied case analysis. The scholar maintains that "[q]ualitative research could usefully utilize pattern matching as a rubric for categorizing data" (1989: 365) to systematically channel data and focus on particular research themes. In order to attain optimized descriptions and an augmented internal validity, the operationalization of the main dimensions was derived after a screening of the initially gathered material. Specifications of codes were thus geared to the operationalization presented in *Appendix C*. Hereupon, the material was coded and subsequently summarized by means of Mayring's (2010) procedure of aggregation. This conclusive progression acted on the highlighted micro operation of case analysis.

The analyzed material consisted of interview protocols. Poland (1995) indicates that the possibilities of transcribing interviews appear innumerable, and he criticizes that most researchers do not properly describe how they have processed this assignment. In a similar vein, Kvale remarks that the "transcript is a bastard, a hybrid between an oral discourse unfolding over time, face to face, in a lived situation – where what is said is addressed to a specific listener present – and a written text created for a general, distant, public" (1996: 280). Moreover, he stresses that to "*[t]rans*cribe means to *trans*form" (1996: 280). In the light of this insight, interview protocols represented a condensation of recorded conversations.[43] The reduction of certain parts of the original content followed the

42 With reference to Mayring, "Ziel inhaltlicher Strukturierung ist es, bestimmte Themen, Inhalte, Aspekte aus dem Material herauszufiltern und zusammenzufassen. Welche Inhalte aus dem Material extrahiert werden sollen, wird durch theoriegeleitet entwickelte Kategorien und (sofern notwendig) Unterkategorien bezeichnet" (2010: 85).

43 In certain cases informants neglected the utilization of a tape recorder in order to conceal their opinion on critical issues. Buzzwords and catchphrases have been noted during the

proposed principles of Mayring (2002). The steps essentially replicated what Mayring (2002) refers to as a summarizing and a selective protocol: Due to the analytical focus on content and a considerable amount of irrelevant interview passages, the interview protocols consisted of grammatically paraphrased statements, which, although being paraphrased, emulated the dynamic conversation. Liebhold and Trinczek (2009) require that such reduction processes have to be completed by the researcher her/himself to ensure an understanding of the verbalized content. In essence, the scholars see an improvement in working with a reduced material when the focus is based on content dimensions.

In conclusion, the applied interview analysis was embedded in the general analytical process regarding the examination of cases. Accordingly, I identified Mayring's (2010) systematic procedure of content-based structuring as the appropriate technique to reflect the three dimensions of case analysis, which was the utilization of theoretical propositions (cf. Yin, 2003), Trochim's (1989, 1985) conceptualization of pattern matching, as well as Miles and Huberman's (1994) trinary process of data collection, reduction, and conclusion drawing.

Questionnaire Analysis

Despite of its quantitative nature, the analysis of questionnaires does not necessarily require advanced statistical methods. This incident was exemplified by several case studies published in high quality journals (see Brown & Eisenhardt, 1997; Eisenhardt, 1989b; Jaspers & Van den Enden, 2006; Kaplan & Duchon, 1988) and theoretically validated by methodologist (see Jauch et al. 1980; Larsson, 1993; Yin & Heald, 1975). Tukey (1977), for instance, stresses that the act of visualizing data usually represents the most effective way to generate meaning and to interpret information. The exact progression of the questionnaire analysis is revisited in the result segment (cf. section 4.2).

III. Description of Data

Because case studies fundamentally represent a binary symbiosis of each case's context and the researched phenomenon, attention is first paid to the surrounding conditions from which the findings of this thesis arose. The section is subdivided into two segments. The first subsection comprises an initial presentation of the companies under consideration including the interviewed informants. The second subsection describes the context of the investigated

interview. The interview was reconstructed after the inquiry with as much precision as possible.

phenomena, which concerns the background of the examined FBes, the invested PE companies, as well as the motivation of the transaction. Both segments make use of definitions and delineations described earlier (cf. chapter 2).

Owing to the circumstance that I ensured confidentiality to both the researched companies and the informants, the following subsections rely on anonymized data. As a result, comprehensive descriptions of cases were relinquished to guarantee that the researched companies remain concealed. As another result, I frequently portray data intervals in the following tables instead of providing the specific corresponding figures. I believe that the procedure to employ anomynized data enhanced this paper in terms of quality; for instance, the provision of confidentiality encouraged organizations to participate in the research. It is a common phenomenon that the PE industry does not operate transparently and even refuses guidelines to improve this behavior (e.g., Robbins, 2009). A rejection of studies concerning the development of their portfolio companies should thus be apprehended as a natural component of such a behavior. Furthermore, confidential agreements facilitated ingenuous discussions so I had the impression that interviewees were less inclined to show behavior of socially desirable responding. After I declared to the respondents that their answers are rendered anonymous and simultaneously solicited them to provide the most accurate and appropriate answers, respondents verbally approved of this request. Finally, the non-disclosure agreement of interview data was in line with the principles of the systemic interviewing process, promoting a respectful treatment of interviewees (cf. Pfeffer, 2004).

1. Cases and Informants

As described above, this subsection introduces the researched organizations and provides insights into the characteristics of the interviewed informants. Hence, it is supposed to outline a first overview before issues such as the family influence, the characteristics of PE investors, and the background of the transaction are elaborated.

Cases' characteristics

To begin with, Table 10 provides a brief overview of the investigated companies. Categorizations were derived by means of desk research and interview data. I decided to use pseudonyms for each case. The latter should help the reader to become familiar with each case, facilitating the identification of individual cases. Pseudonyms were assigned on the basis of the cases' characteristics; the determination was stimulated by the classification of industries and the type of transaction having occurred. Each pseudonym has a suffix reflecting the consecutive numbering.

Table 10: Overview of Cases

Case	Industry	Revenue*	Employees*	Informants	Pseudonym
# 1	Engineering	51 - 100	101 - 500	5	EngineeringMBO #1
# 2	Services	1 - 50	0 - 100	4	ServicesMBO #2
# 3	Not to be disclosed	Not to be disclosed	Not to be disclosed	3	EmergencyIBO #3
# 4	Consumer Goods	1 - 50	0 - 100	6	ConsumerMBO #4
# 5	Consumer Goods	51 - 100	101 - 500	4	ConsumerBIMBO #5
# 6	Industrial Goods	1 - 50	0 - 100	3	IndSpecialityMINORITY #6
# 7	Industrial Goods	>101	> 501	4	IndCommodityMINORITY #7
# 8	Engineering	51 - 100	101 - 500	5	EngineeringMINORITY #8

* Both figures pertain to the fiscal year prior to the investment. Revenue figures are denominated in € Mio.
Source: author's illustration

As pointed out earlier, eight cases were conducted in total. Companies were from manufacturing and engineering industries (*EngineeringMBO #1* and *EngineeringMINORITY #8*), operated in the market of consumer goods (*ConsumerMBO #4* and *ConsumerBIMBO #5*), and manufactured industrial goods (*IndSpecialityMINORITY #6* and *IndCommodityMINORITY #7*). Whereas these companies manufactured physical goods, *ServicesMBO #2* specialized in the provision of services and trading activities. As documented by the revenue figures, three companies generated revenues up to €50 million in the year prior to the transaction, three companies reported revenues between €51 and €100 million, and one company showed more than €101 million in total sales. The three companies of the sample with the lowest revenue figures employed up to 100 employees before the transaction. The three companies with sales between €51 and €100 million reported employment figures from 101 to 500. Finally, the remaining company employed more than 501 people. In line with the definition of the Institut für Mittelstandsforschung (IfM) Bonn, these figures substantiate earlier thoughts, remarked in the operationalization of ambidexterity (cf. *Appendix C*), that the researched FBes converged in size with SMEs.[44]

---

44 The IfM Bonn defines SMEs on the basis of annual revenue and employees. The institute distinguishes between two types of SMEs on the former basis. Small sized enterprises employ up to 9 individuals with annual revenues lower than €1 million. Medium sized enterprises employ between 10 and 499 individuals and generate annual revenues in the range from €1 to €50 million. Companies exceeding these artificially defined boundaries usually do not

Informants' characteristics

In total, 34 informants were interviewed and asked to fill out the questionnaires. The informants in every case varied from three interviewees (*EmergencyIBO #3* and *IndSpecialityMINORITY #6*) to six respondents (*ConsumerMBO #4*). Table 11 portrays auxiliary information regarding the informants' characteristics. Two criteria were discussed to select informants via purposive sampling. These principles are discussed in the following.

Table 11: Outline of Informants

Case	Seniority*	Function**	Level of Hierarchy***
# 1	(A) >20	(A) Strategy	(A) Top-Level
	(B) 6 – 10	(B) Operations	(B) Top-Level
	(C) >20	(C) Operations	(C) Middle-Level
	(D) >20	(D) Marketing	(D) Lower-Level
	(E) >20	(E) Marketing	(E) Lower-Level
# 2	(A) >20	(A) Strategy	(A) Top-Level
	(B) 6 – 10	(B) Marketing	(B) Top-Level
	(C) 6 – 10	(C) Operations	(C) Lower-Level
	(D) 11 – 15	(D) Operations	(D) Lower-Level
# 3	(A) >20	(A) Strategy	(A) Top-Level
	(B) >20	(B) Operations	(B) Middle-Level
	(C) 11 – 15	(C) Marketing	(C) Middle-Level
# 4	(A) 0 – 5	(A) Strategy	(A) Top-Level
	(B) 0 – 5	(B) Marketing	(B) Top-Level
	(C) 16 – 20	(C) Finance	(C) Middle-Level
	(D) 11 – 15	(D) Marketing	(D) Lower-Level
	(E) 11 – 15	(E) Operations	(E) Lower-Level
	(F) 11 – 15	(F) Operations	(F) Lower-Level
# 5	(A) 11 – 15	(A) Strategy	(A) Top-Level
	(B) 0 – 5	(B) Finance	(B) Top-Level
	(C) >20	(C) Marketing	(C) Lower-Level
	(D) >20	(D) Operations	(D) Lower-Level
# 6	(A) 11 – 15	(A) Strategy	(A) Top-Level
	(B) 0 – 5	(B) Finance	(B) Lower-Level
	(C) 11 – 15	(C) Operations	(C) Lower-Level
# 7	(A) 0 – 5	(A) Finance	(A) Top-Level
	(B) 6 – 10	(B) Strategy	(B) Middle-Level
	(C) 0 – 5	(C) Strategy	(C) Middle-Level
	(D) 6 – 10	(D) Finance	(D) Lower-Level

rank among SMEs anymore. According to the IfM, 99.7 % of German companies can be considered to fall within the cluster of SMEs.

(Continued)

# 8	(A) 6 – 10 (B) 16 – 20 (C) >20 (D) >20 (E) >20	(A) Strategy (B) Marketing (C) Marketing (D) Operations (E) Operations	(A) Top-Level (B) Middle-Level (C) Lower-Level (D) Lower-Level (E) Lower-Level

* Seniority emerged as the difference in years between the organizational entry and the time the data collection was conducted.
** Functions pertain to management positions in the field of strategy, marketing, operations, as well as finance and accounting (cf. Heizer and Render, 2004).
*** With reference to Ireland et al. (1987), top-level managers were defined as the chief executive officers and immediate subordinates, i. e., the "Geschäftsführung." Middle-level managers were defined as those who had at least one level of supervisors under their authority and were no more than two levels below top management. Lower-level managers pertained to organizational members that reported to middle-level or top managers.
Source: author's illustration

The first criterion refers to the column seniority, which displays the period the informants worked in the organization under consideration. Given that it was considered a necessary prerequisite that the informants were employed in the company before the transaction, the distribution was dominated by agents who had a long-term employment relationship.

As can be derived from Table 11, 6 informants (18 %) worked less than 5 years in the researched companies, 6 respondents (18 %) between 6 and 10 years, 8 informants (24 %) between 11 and 15 years, 2 interviewees (6 %) between 16 and 20 years, as well as 12 respondents (35 %) for more than 20 years. The maturity of the company under investigation naturally set the boundary for each case.

The second criterion was twofold. On the one hand, the criterion required a certain level of diversity regarding the informants' administrative functions. On the other hand, it necessitated that informants worked at different organizational levels. Administrative functions were classified in terms of four broad management domains: strategy, operations, marketing, as well as finance and accounting. This classification represents a frequently utilized subdivision of managerial functions. According to Heizer and Render, "Operations, marketing, and finance/accounting are the three functions basic to all organizations" (2004: 19). This typology, however, falls short of including non-operational, strategic management. Nag et al. see in the area of strategic management a complementary function to these fields, yet they indicate that it is less "'specifics-oriented,' 'detail-oriented,' and 'operational'" (2007: 949). Referring to this viewpoint, strategic managers were distinguished from operational managers, who were active in marketing, operations, or finance and accounting. The differentiation of the entire sample suggests that 9 informants (26 %) held positions with a strategic accentuation whereas 25 respondents (74 %) can be considered to have worked in operational functions. In the latter, 9 informants (26 %) worked in marketing, 11 informants (32 %) worked in operations and related activities, and 5 informants (15 %) were employed in professions best described by the field of financial management.[45] Pugh et al.'s (1968) concept of centralization served as the backbone to categorize the hierarchical level each informant belonged to. For this purpose, Pugh and colleagues (1968) distinguish between six levels of responsibility that comprise an organizational hierarchy: above the chief executive, the whole organization, all workflow activities, workflow subunit, supervisory positions, and operating functions. I merged sequential levels, for example operating and supervisory levels, to derive a more appropriate tripartite classification. In line with Ireland et al. (1987), informants were thus differentiated between top-level, middle-level, and lower-level managers. Overall, the sample consisted of 12 top-level managers (35 %), 7 middle-level managers (21 %), and 15 lower-level managers (44 %), suggesting a relatively balanced selection.

2. Contextual Background

Cases were selected with the help of theoretical and literal replications. In addition, three auxiliary elements were controlled for. First, the researched organization needed to be identified as a FB before the investment. Second, the investor had to belong to the craft of PE. Third, the investment type had to be a majority or minority investment. The following paragraphs discuss these dimensions embedding the observed phenomena. To begin with, a brief description of the family influence is provided. Hereupon, the characteristics of PE investors are identified. Finally, a paragraph presents the nature of the transaction and the corresponding motivation.

Characteristics of Family Businesses

Table 12 illustrates the power aspects of the F-PEC scale (cf. Astrachan et al. 2002), that is Klein's (2000) SFI, which was described to symbolize the components-of-involvement element in Wimmer's (2009) definition utilized (cf. subsection 2.1.1). In order to verify differences before and after the investment, the table displays both states. For determining the family influence with an advanced precision, a subjective classification of the researched cases, with reference to Gimeno et al.'s (2010) typology, was derived. The scholars classify the subsequent six types of "mental models," which summarize the dimensions

45 Figures in parentheses denote relative proportions related to the total number of respondents.

of both the family and the business complexity: captain, patriarch, family team, professional family, enterprise, and family investment group.[46] The identification of these patterns of involvement offered valuable evidence related to the question how the family shaped the companies under consideration. The categorization assisted in describing the origins of the essence approach, reinforcing Wimmer's (2009) definition stating that family ownership, management, or board control are not alone sufficient elements for making an enterprise a FB.

Table 12: Overview of Family Influence

Case	Period	Ownership*	Management*	Supervisory Board*	Typology**
# 1	ex ante	76 – 100 %	0 %	0 %	Family Investment Group
	ex post	*0 %*	*0 %*	*0 %*	*Loss of Family Identification*
# 2	ex ante	76 – 100 %	0 %	n/a	Captain
	ex post	*0 %*	*0 %*	*n/a*	*Loss of Family Identification*
# 3	ex ante	51 – 75 %	0 %	26 – 50 %	Patriarch
	ex post	*0 %*	*0 %*	*0 %*	*Loss of Family Identification*
# 4	ex ante	76 – 100 %	26 – 50 %	26 – 50 %	Captain
	ex post	*0 %*	*0 %*	*0 %*	*Loss of Family Identification*
# 5	ex ante	76 – 100 %***	76 – 100 %***	n/a	Captain
	ex post	*1 – 25 %****	*26 – 50 %****	*1 – 25 %****	*Captain*
# 6	ex ante	51 – 75 %	76 – 100 %	n/a	Captain
	ex post	*51 – 75 %*	*76 – 100 %*	*0 %*	*Captain*
# 7	ex ante	76 – 100 %	76 – 100 %	0 %	Captain
	ex post	*76 – 100 %*	*26 – 50 %*	*0 %*	*Captain*

46 Captain: "KMU vom Unternehmensgründer geführt;" patriarch: "von einer Führungsperson zusammengehaltene Unternehmen und Familien;" family team: "Großfamilie mit Kleinunternehmen;" professional family: "wenige Familienmitglieder leiten professionell ein komplexes Unternehmen;" enterprise: "weitverzweigte Familie führt komplexes Unternehmen;" family investment group: "Familie mit unterschiedlichen Komplexitätsniveaus investieren zusammen" (Gimeno et al. 2010: 86).

(Continued)

# 8	ex ante	51 – 75 %	0 %	26 – 50 %	Enterprise
	ex post	*51 – 75 %*	*0 %*	*26 – 50 %*	*Enterprise*

* Ownership, management, and supervisory involvement of family members reflect Klein's (2000) SFI typology.
** The corresponding FB is categorized with regard to Gimeno et al.'s (2010) typology.
*** "Ex ante" figures pertain to three separately owning families whereas "ex post" figures show the influence of one offspring of the former families.
Source: author's illustration

Table 12 illustrates that the sample of the cases fulfilled the necessary conditions for being a FB. For example, Klein (2000) posits that a SFI sum of at least one serves as an appropriate threshold level in order to classify an entity as a FB. The cases researched in this study fulfilled this criterion. The majority investments, i. e., cases one to five, were typically influenced by the owning families through the ownership dimension approaching 100 percent. Except for *ConsumerMBO #4* and *ConsumerBIMBO #5*, family members did not hold operative management functions prior to or after the investment. They rather asserted their influence formally with the help of supervisory boards (*EmergencyIBO #3*), devoted their power to persons of trust to control the companies via supervisory participation (*EngineeringMBO #1*), or informally monitored the management and operations (*ServicesMBO #2*). The minority investments revealed different arrangements. At *IndSpecialityMINORITY #6* and *IndCommodityMINORITY #7*, members of the owning families possessed as much as 100 percent of the equity and also served as CEOs. As a result, there were no active family members in the corresponding supervisory boards. At *EngineeringMINORITY #8*, family ownership fluctuated around 50 percent before and after the investment, and the supervisory board involvement of the family was in the range between 26 and 50 percent.

Considering the typology of Gimeno et al. (2010), the conducted classification revealed that the captain pattern was the prevailing "mental model" of the investigated FBes prior to the PE investment. In fact, five cases were effectively typified by this kind of family influence. The auxiliary companies were controlled by a family investment group (*EngineeringMBO #1*), a patriarch (*EmergencyIBO #3*), or an enterprise model (*EngineeringMINORTIY #8*). These involvement characteristics suitably reinforce the cases' dispositions in terms of generational continuity forasmuch as most researched entities were operated by the first or second generation; Gimeno et al. (2010) propose that the captain model presents the dominating orientation of FBes relating to an organizational life span from 10 to 30 years.

Private Equity companies

In addition to the characterization of the researched FBes, the corresponding PE houses were classified by means of Achleitner et al.'s (2008a) typology introduced in an earlier segment of this paper (cf. subsection 2.2.1). Moreover, the legal structure of the investors was reflected. Data obtained from PE houses' websites and press releases that exhibited information about the companies' assets under management, targeted geographical foci, employed holding periods, and investment attitudes allowed for a relatively unambiguous categorization between "moderate" and "classical" financial investors (cf. Achleitner et al. 2008a).

Table 13: Characteristics of Private Equity Companies

Investor	Structure*	Classification**	Evidence***
A	PE fund	Classical PE company	"We are a leading European private equity company. [...] We manage more than €2 billion assets under management and focus on transactions with a volume of at least €100 million." (company website)
B	LPE company	Moderate PE company	"We buy, develop, and sell majority interests in small to medium-sized enterprises. [...] Potential companies should be favorably priced while possessing extraordinary growth prospects. [...] We do not stick to predefined holding periods but decide to sell portfolio companies when a value enhancement has been realized." (annual report)
C	PE fund	Classical PE company	"We invest in small to medium-sized enterprises and focus on German family businesses. Due to our thorough track record, we consider ourselves as experienced professionals enabling us to actively dedicate strategic advice to our portfolio companies. Thereby, we strive to add value to our investments." (company website)
D	PE fund	Classical PE company	"Our company concentrates on investing in cutting-edge global companies and on developing them thereafter." (company website)
E	PE fund	Moderate PE company	"Our company is a national champion in providing financing solutions to small to medium-sized companies. We conceptualize ourselves to be a long-term oriented investor providing capital for entrepreneurs. [...] We collectively attempt to increase the value of our portfolio companies. Our investment philosophy inhibits to determine holding periods prior to the investment." (company website)

(Continued)

F	PE fund	Moderate PE company	"We are a leading capital provider in German speaking Europe. Our unique selling position is the long-term orientation and our commitment to invest in family businesses, targeting both majority and minority positions. [...] We value cooperation, trust, and responsibility." (company website)

* The legal structure is assigned on the differentiation regarding PE funds and Listed Private Equity (LPE) companies.
** PE companies are differentiated between moderate and classical PE companies with reference to Achleitner et al. (2008a).
*** Original wording and figures were paraphrased and slightly modified to conceal the investor under consideration.
Source: author's illustration

Table 13 indicates that six PE companies invested in the eight examined cases. Financial investors *D* and *E* thus each held two investments. Except for investor *B* which possessed a permanent capital basis through public listing, the remaining PE companies were legally structured as investment funds.

The categorization of the vehicles by means of Achleitner et al.'s (2008a) typology revealed that three investors were associated with moderate investment doctrines whereas the remaining three PE houses employed business models that reminded one of classical investors, promoting a balanced design. To be concrete, moderate PE companies showed tendencies to especially focus on German FBes as they have adapted their business model toward this organizational species. These investors communicated that they did not have pre-specified holding periods but rather decided to exist their investments when long-term value enhancements have been realized. Moreover, they described their investment style as collaborative and signalized their aim to establish good relationships with the incumbent management and the shareholders. Finally, these PE companies verbalized their experience in dealing with FBes as they had established a thorough track record with regard to financing themes such as succession or growth. In contrast, classical financial investors rather emphasized their intention to invest in cutting-edge global companies with the intention to resell these within a projected time frame.

Transaction characteristics

The employed replication strategy suggested differentiating between minority investments, in which the family retained to be in charge of the business, and majority investments, in which the family either sold their entire stake or preserved a minority position. In accordance with the typology of PE investments presented by Kaserer et al. (2007), majority investments are further subcategorized (cf. subsection 2.2.1). Table 14 exemplifies this categorization and also considers auxiliary insights, such as the holding period or the sale rationale, in order to deliver descriptions of elevated precision.

EngineeringMINORITY #8 was a special issue: It represented the only case in which an equity stake was sold from one investor to the next one, usually referred to as a secondary investment (e.g., Manchot, 2010). The remaining cases embodied primary commitments, indicating that these researched organizations have never been in contact with PE prior to the transaction. Rationally, *EngineeringMINORITY #8* was included in the sample to obtain evidence regarding the fact whether an organization responds to changing investors. In this respect, evidence was established on the long-term symbiosis between FBes and PE companies.

The categorization of the five buyouts comprised three MBOs (*EngineeringMBO #1*, *ServicesMBO #2*, and *ConsumerMBO #4*), one BIMBO (*ConsumerBIMBO #5*), and one IBO (*EmergencyIBO #3*). The minority investments were not further subclassified. The family, by definition, retained a stake in the latter category, and financial investors held stakes from 0 to 25 percent (*IndCommodityMINORITY #7*) as well as from 26 to 50 percent (*IndSpecialityMINORITY #6* and *EngineeringMINORITY #8*) when having realized these transactions. Table 14 portrays that seven investments were typified by holding periods ranging from 2.6 to 5 years; only one investment (*IndCommodityMINORITY #7*) was younger than 2.5 years when researched. This circumstance indicates that most of the investments were conducted in the exceptionally successful years of PE during 2006 and 2007. Some of the researched organizations were thus already approaching the exit phase. Attention was also paid to the rationale of the families to resign from company ownership. Informants, especially members from the strategic top management, were asked concerning the underlying motives of the family to sell their stakes in the business. As proposed by table 14, several potential reasons were identified during the analytical process. Motives were multidimensional in certain cases, but a solitary motivation prevailed in most cases. In sum, the reasons pertained to the old age of family owners (*EmergencyIBO #3*, *ConsumerMBO #4*, and *ConsumerBIMBO #5*), the opportunity to cash out (*ConsumerBIMBO #5*), conflicts between owning families (*ServicesMBO #2*), strategic reasons (*EngineeringMBO #1*), financing needs (*IndSpecialityMINORITY #6* and *IndCommodityMINORITY #7*), as well as the replacement of auxiliary shareholders (*ConsumerBIMBO #5*, *IndSpecialityMINORITY #6*, and *EngineeringMINORITY #8*). The communicated reasons of the buyout sample were, in consequence, predominantly motivated by personal and family related considerations, except for *EngineeringMBO #1*. The latter company was divested given that the enterprise did not any longer fit in the strategic profile in the course of the reorientation of the whole group. This circumstance can be explained with regard to the "mental model" of the family under consideration. As suggested previously, *EngineeringMBO #1* was operated by a family investment group, indicating a less stringent relation between the family and the company (cf. Gimeno et al. 2010). This book hence reinforces certain established evidence concerning the reasons of families to sell their businesses. For example, Klöckner (2009) demonstrates in his study of buyouts in German FBes that the shareholder's age, the opportunity to cash out, and financing problems represented the predominant drivers of families to sell their businesses. Opposed to the buyout sample, the minority investments were also characterized by motivations concerning the shareholder situation, yet the business played a more dominant role in these transactions. To be precise, growth financing and the replacement of auxiliary shareholders represented important stimuli. These findings are, for instance, in line with Achleitner et al. (2008a), who discover that the motivation to sell minority stakes is primarily contingent on the above described two reasons.

Having identified the reasons that energized the sale process, the issue emerged why owners of FBes opted for the utilization of PE capital. As described above, the most important theme in the buyout sample was succession. The natural source of handing over a FB in Germany is usually the sale of the company to the next generation.[47] For instance, Kirby and Lee (1996) show empirical evidence that the offspring of families represent the prevailing choice when handing over the company. However, certain impediments can be identified that inhibit such a tradition even when the process has already commenced (see De Massis et al. 2009). In this study, succession was impeded due to the following reasons: The owning family was not blessed with an offspring (*EmergencyIBO #3*); potential successors were too young to take over the company (*ConsumerMBO #4*); the owning families could not agree on the internal succession (*ServicesMBO #2*); the family offspring lacked the financial strength to buyout the remaining shareholders (*ConsumerBIMBO #5*). Due to the inability to manage an internal succession, external choices usually come to the fore. In general, shareholders have the possibilities to either sell their businesses to strategic investors, to the public via IPOs, or to financial investors. In this respect, PE companies were considered an appropriate solution to financing constraints when owners wanted to hand over their companies to internal management (*ServicesMBO #2*) or families' offspring for buying out auxiliary family shareholders (*ConsumerBIMBO #5*). In the three remaining buyout cases, PE companies were primarily

47 A study conducted by PricewaterhouseCoopers (2008) presents evidence that owners of FBes would select the subsequent options when considering the sale of their company: 73 percent of owners prefer selling to the next generation, 23 percent consider selling to the incumbent management, 20 percent reflect on selling to a strategic acquirer, and merely 13 percent would opt for a private equity investors (multiple answers were possible).

Table 14: Overview of Transaction Characteristics (1/2)

Case	Transaction	Stake of Investor	Holding Period*	Reason to Sell**	Reason to Sell to PE**	Interview Evidence**
# 1	MBO	76 -100%	2.6 - 5	• Strategic reasons: shareholder decided to divest the company as it did not fit anymore in the strategic profile.	• Strategic investors did not offer a satisfiable purchasing price. • A PE investor paid a reasonable price and was assumed to be the best solution for the near future.	"To date, this industry has never really made him [note: former family shareholder] happy. […] He was just not satisfied with the poor profits which were generated." (strategy manager)
# 2	MBO	76 - 100%	2.6 - 5	• Conflicts between the two owning families: no consensus about the company's prospective development.	• Family succession was not possible due to the conflictive situation. • Incumbent management lacked the financial strength to exclusively realize the transaction.	"[…] new business areas were supposed to be developed, but no real consensus between the owning families could be reached. […] There had to be a change of ownership to further develop the company. [Name of the company] qualified for a MBO […]." (strategy manager)
# 3	IBO	51 - 75%	2.6 - 5	• Succession: old age and unwillingness of the family shareholder to further take responsibility.	• No family successor: no offspring. • Difficult market situation discriminated against strategic buyers. • PE was expected to bring capital and expertise.	"He [note: former family shareholder] realized that markets were becoming more turbulent; he felt incapable to keep up with the pace and wanted to transfer the company into experienced hands. A financial investor was assumed to possess financial strength and expertise to further internationalize the company." (strategy manager)
# 4	MBO	76 - 100%	2.6 - 5	• Succession: old age and motivation of the family shareholder to cash out and retire with the money.	• No family successor: The only son was too young. • Family shareholder wanted to maximize the sale price and PE offered the highest bid.	"There was no regulated succession planning. [Name of the family shareholder] had a son who was still relatively young at this point in time […]. Then, there was a point in time when he [note: family shareholder] wanted to convert the risky amount of his personal wealth into secured assets as a form of retirement arrangement." (marketing manager)

Table 14: Overview of Transaction Characteristics (2/2)

Case	Transaction	Stake of Investor	Holding Period*	Reason to Sell**	Reason to Sell to PE**	Interview Evidence**
# 5	BIMBO	76 - 100%	2.6 - 5	• Succession: old age of the family shareholder and a strategic disagreement between families. • Replacement of shareholders.	• Family successor lacked the financial strength for buying out remaining partners. • Succession and replacement could easily be resolved with the help of a financial investor.	"The company was controlled by three families. One of these partners was the chief executive officer, but he was approaching retirement. Another partner walked away and appointed me as his successor in the board in [year]. The third was my father who was also a shareholder and approaching retirement. These three had different visions compared to me." (strategy manager)
# 6	Minority investment	26 - 50%	2.6 - 5	• Growth financing. • Replacement of shareholders.	• Leverage ratios should remain stable. • PE capital simultaneously allowed for both growth and replacement financing.	"Two decisive circumstances were accomplished: financing the establishment of a new site and getting rid of two shareholders." (strategy manager)
# 7	Minority investment	0 - 25%	0 - 2.5	• Growth financing.	• Financial institutions provided debt financing but also required new equity capital for realizing corporate investments.	"The reason was growth financing. The company has grown extraordinarily, yet certain realizable projects were still in progress. [...] Banks, which were supposed to finance these steps, required to also include further equity." (finance manager)
# 8	Minority investment (secondary)	26 - 50%	2.6 - 5	• Invested PE house wanted to divest its shares.	• Strategic buyers were only interested in a controlling stake, which was not up for debate.	"These [note: strategic investors] were only interested in acquiring the entire company, and the family was not willing to resign." (strategy manager)

* The holding period signifies the time difference in years between the investment in the FB and the point in time when the company was researched.

** The categories briefly discuss the reasons why the company under consideration was sold, especially why no trade sale or IPO was realized. Interview evidence is provided to underline the presented reasons. The interview extracts shown in this table and in the following ones were translated to my best knowledge and belief.

Source: author's illustration

chosen because they paid a reasonable price (*EngineeringMBO #1*, *EmergencyIBO #3*, and *ConsumerMBO #4*). In contrast, the dominant theme in the minority investment cases was growth financing. Respondents from *IndSpecialityMINORITY #6* indicated that a PE investor was included in order to maintain moderate leverage ratios. Similarly, informants from *IndCommodityMINORITY #7* proposed that additional equity capital was required to meet certain obligations from banks which have contributed to financing the growth project via debt. Informants from the secondary investment case, *EngineeringMINORITY #8*, indicated that the sale of the minority shares to another PE investor constituted a choice without any serious alternatives given that the family was not willing and able to repurchase the divested shares.

Appendix B: Literature Review

Having made the distinction between minority and majority investments with regard to Kaserer et al. (2007), the following literature review is structured accordingly; literature concerning minority investments is reviewed first, which is followed by the literature review concerning buyouts.

Minority Investments

The literature on PE investments in FBes is dominated by the buyout theme, so it considerably discriminates against minority investments (Achleitner et al., 2008a). Nevertheless, certain studies have recently advanced the field. Achleitner et al. (2008a) investigate the experience of German FBes with minority PE capital and document a relatively high level of satisfaction among the interviewed owners. Furthermore, they report that the financing alternative positively affected the capital structure and aspects of professionalization in the examined companies. In addition to their main findings, they gathered evidence indicating that PE houses' investments substantially differ in terms of intervention and capital costs. In a further paper, Achleitner et al. (2008b) analyze the situations leading to a minority investment. They report that owners of FBes can be differentiated into the subsequent four categories: "smart-money seekers," "balanced rationalists," "desperate needers," as well as "family bulkheads." As the pseudonyms suggest, each group has specific demands pertaining to the potential investor being contingent on personal characteristics and the conditions the company operates in. Prym (2010) researches aspects of the value generation hypothesis and the role of FBes' objectives in the context of a PE investment. He concludes that FBes utilize PE as a mean to realize monetary and non-monetary objectives, and he confirms that these instruments enhance value as an end to this relationship. On this account, Prym (2010) maintains that the relationship between FBes and PE companies brings about a beneficial result when both systems synergistically enforce their objectives. The study therefore seems to confirm two typologies presented by Achleitner et al. (2008b), explicitly "smart-money seekers" and "balanced rationalist," given that these groups attempt to add value to their companies by attracting financial investors.

Majority Investments

The literature on buyouts of FBes can be classified as more advanced and multifarious. Klöckner (2009) remarks that theoretical and empirical contributions can principally be divided into two streams: The first stream examines occurrences prior to a transaction, and the second one concentrates on phenomena after an investment. The following review is structured in accordance with this insight.

Ex ante research

Scholars conducting research in the domain of PE investments in FBes prior to the completion of a transaction draw attention to issues such as the investment criteria of PE companies, the deliberations of families to sell their companies, and the dynamics of the transaction process. Upton and Petty (2000) argue that PE houses identify certain "deal killers" inhibiting investments. These pertain to the quality of the management, non-existing expanding possibilities, weak financial strength, and the absence of a suitable exit strategy. In a similar vein, Huydts (1992) illustrates that PE houses look for FBes which are prone to generate above-average value in the near future. Moreover, he reasons that investors are driven by a motivation to identify undervalued targets, implying a certain degree of opportunism. Switching perspectives, FBes consider the utilization of PE when they require financing for growth, intend to replace owners, and need capital in turnaround situations (e. g., Reimers, 2004). With reference to earlier thoughts, Poech and colleagues (2005) remind us of the psychological barriers between families and PE houses, which constitutes a decisive phenomenon regardless of the investment type. They point out that owners fear the loss of authority and a clash of organizational cultures. In addition, owners of FBes were found to perceive the investment as a sign of personal weakness. The finding that owners identify organizational cultures as incompatible represents an argument implicitly pursued throughout this research. Similarly, Seet et al. (2010) identify certain institutional contradictions between FBes and PE companies with regard to finance, knowledge, and empathy. A study conducted by PricewaterhouseCoopers (2007) substantiates these mentioned barriers but also presents the finding that owners of FBes are becoming more accessible for PE capital. The study further highlights the qualities FBes' owners consider important when selecting an investor. These pertain to the investment horizon, the investor's reputation, and a trustful relationship in early phases of encounter. Such findings channel the review to the sale process and the interaction of both systems, respectively. Knowledge regarding the sale process has primarily been created by scholars of *The Centre for Private Equity Research* of Nottingham University. Howorth et al. (2004) research the deal negotiations between FBes and MBO/MBI teams from the standpoint of the principal agent framework. They document the existence of an information asymmetry between the negotiation sides, naturally enabling one party to have superior information, though the results of their study indicate that "[g]ood relationships and trust between the vendor and MBO/MBI team mitigated information asymmetries" (2004: 509). Scholes et al. (2007) as well as Scholes et al. (2008) further scrutinize the sale process and focus on the mutually agreed sale prices. Insights suggest that mutually agreed sale prices have a lower chance of being realized when PE companies are in contact with the MBO or MBI team in the beginning of the transaction process.

Ex post research

Academic papers on the development of FBes after a PE investment can be considered to have emerged in equal dimensions regarding quantity although they appear less coherent compared to the research analyzing phenomena before the transaction. Early insights of Forst (1992) indicate that PE interventions modify FBes in the course of the investment with regard to structure and internal processes. In this light, Howorth and colleagues (2008) document that former FBes in the United Kingdom (UK), sold via MBOs, become more professional after the transaction, yet these entities preserve aspects of familiness. In fact, the scholars propose that a conversion from family to managerial ideologies does not capture the essence of the observed alterations in the companies; in other words, such an explanation is insufficient for explaining the substance of the metamorphosis. The authors conclude that the ambiguity regarding professionalism and familiness represents a phenomenon which is not fully understood and therefore deserves more academic attention. Comparable to Howorth et al. (2008), Wulf et al. study buyouts in FBes and report that FBes having "deficiencies in organizational structures and management systems [...] can expect the most value" (2010: 25) from a PE investment. Besides, they find that FBes have shortcomings in networking with other companies, which becomes improved after the buyout. Klöckner (2009) introduces the term of an "economization" of FBes in his study and maintains that the former, besides a professionalization and the prevention of agency conflicts, explains a conversion related to governance, managerial control, and financial praxis. Comparable to Klöckner (2009), Hehn (2011) documents changes in the corporate governance structures of family-owned enterprises when these are acquired by financial investors. Buttignon et al. (2005) examine the financial performance of accomplished majority investments in Italian FBes and document mixed findings, which were derived from a sample of 21 FBes. In essence, they find that "PE intervention causes discontinuity in the life of a firm, generating a shift in performance trends: from good to bad and vice versa" (2005: 1). Achleitner et al. (2010) scrutinize the case of the buyout of *Messer Griesheim* and discover that the company was restructured under PE ownership, which was facilitated by the employment of improved monitoring devices, external advice, and powerful managerial incentives. They contend that organizational change emerging in private-to-private transactions constitutes a field that deserves additional attention in order to create a better awareness of the dynamics in place. Scholes et al. (2009) research the strategic orientation of FBes following an MBO. Their results indicate that implemented strategies aim at promoting efficiency and growth after a buyout. The alteration of the strategic accentuation emerges as particularly significant when founders held a management position before the buyouts, when no managers with equity stakes were employed pre-buyout, and when both the PE house and the management were involved in planning the succession.

Appendix C: Limitations

"In fact, there are no perfect studies" (Hunter & Schmidt, 2005: 18). The authors develop their argument that the idea of a perfect study is a myth; all studies suffer from measurement errors, biases, or sampling constraints so that no study "can provide an optimal basis" (2005: 18) for the generation of knowledge. In order to evaluate the quality of the generated knowledge in this research, it seems necessary to reflect the components on which the former is established. Hoerster (2010) states that knowledge is contingent on three axioms: belief, truth, and justification. The author maintains that believing in certain circumstances represents the basal requirement for knowledge. If we do not believe in a circumstance under consideration, we can never establish a bridge leading to the higher good of knowledge. Believing in a particular circumstance necessitates that it is true, which therefore represents the second supposition of knowledge. For categorizing any incident as true, it needs to be justified. The justification procedure finalizes the conditions tolerating the utilization of the term knowledge.[48] With reference to Hoerster (2010), the axiom of truth is based on an evaluator's contemporary view on incidents whereas justification is constrained by the temporal conditions under which it was generated. This line of argumentation converges with previous thoughts on contextualism rejecting the image of an infallibly or absolute knowledge, and it therefore suggests that three levels of observations should be analyzed for evaluating the quality of knowledge generated in this study.

48 According to Hoerster, "Wir haben nun drei Voraussetzungen oder Bedingungen dafür kennengelernt, dass eine Person P einen Sachverhalt s weiß: 1. P muss s glauben; 2. s muss wahr sein; 3. P muss in ihrem Glauben an s gerechtfertigt sein. Jede dieser drei Bedingungen scheint für Wissen notwendig zu sein, und alle drei Bedingungen zusammen scheinen jedenfalls im Normalfall auch für Wissen hinreichend zu sein" (2010: 15).

Three Levels of Knowledge Generation

The reader of this paper naturally bases her/his beliefs, perception of truth, and instruments of justification on different foundations compared to me. My construction of knowledge, grounded in interviews or questionnaires, thus represents an important level, which needs to be assessed regarding the tripartite dimensions. Finally, the informants' observations signify a third level of knowledge construction. Expressed differently, phenomena themselves are constructed and transmitted by diverse parties all generating their idiosyncratic knowledge. Reichenbach explains, "Since our experience is very limited in time and place, much of our information comes from other sources" (2001: 231). In accordance with this declaration, the three different levels are briefly considered in the subsequent paragraphs.

Reader's perspective

Although a limitations part in scientific papers is dominated by a consideration of the attributes of truth and justification concerning the above identified second and third level, short attention is initially paid to the perspective of the reader.

The introduction discussed the notion that writing is both a process of knowledge creation and communication (see Gilbert, 2008). In the following debate, writing was primarily interpreted as an instrument of knowledge creation since the question how the communication reaches its audience was considered to be beyond the editor's discretion. I hence undertook several efforts to make my viewpoints and thought processes transparent (cf. section 1.3) in order to meet certain imperatives facilitating a decent communication, thereby providing a guideline how knowledge was derived. Consequently, the reader of this book should have the opportunity to understand adopted justification elements.

Nonetheless, it should be apparent that my truth does not necessarily conform to the viewpoint of truth that the reader of this book might have. The reader is consequently required to certify conditions based on her/his personal perceptions, i. e., she/he might know a set of falsifying cases or she/he might have evidence that all informants manipulated evidence to set me on the wrong track. As a matter of fact, it is essentially up to the reader's judgement to accredit or discredit the legitimacy of this contribution.

My perspective

This level is primarily concerned with the employed scientific method and case design. Accordingly, the issue of truth, considered in terms of alternative perceptions, constitutes the debate's prevalent attribute. The collected and analyzed evidence only contains a small fraction of data compared with what would have been theoretically possible in a world without boundaries and constraints. Due to this natural deficiency, issues concerning the research setting, data collection, and analytical process appear to be a thoughtful guideline for reflection.

Although having followed a careful replication logic (cf. Yin, 2003), the selection of cases could have severely affected the researched matters because it might have suffered from two important selection biases. It is possible that companies only participated in the study when they felt positive about the topic; such a behavior is closely related to a self-selection bias (see Winship & Mare, 1992). I indeed came across such a behavior when I contacted several companies and asked for their participation. The survivorship bias is closely related to this shortcoming and describes the phenomenon that researched cases, by definition, communicate a positively framed development since negative examples have already been driven out of the market (cf. Brown et al. 1992). In order to account for the latter bias, I attempted to include "bad investment" cases; except for the informants from *EmergencyIBO #3,* the addressed companies, however, typically rejected their participation.

The data collection could also have been biased, which can be evaluated with regard to two themes. The first theme considers the utilization of theoretically guided questions. Such a procedure could have resulted in incomplete perceptions of the phenomena studied. This shortcoming constitutes a general tradeoff in the social sciences. Miles and Huberman posit that a multiple case study "is looking forward to cross-case comparison, which requires some standardization of instruments" (1994: 35), representing the line of argumentation I followed when having decided on the degree of pre-instrumentalization. Another issue of this study deals with the cross-sectional character of the gathered data. Given that longitudinal perspectives prevail over cross-sectional ones for researching organizations and change (e.g., Avital, 2000; George & Jones, 2000; Lindell & Drexler, 1979; Pettigrew, 1990; Romanelli & Tushman, 1986; Zaheer, 1999), the concept of time can be considered imperfect in this empirical inquiry. Pettigrew et al. explicate this issue as follows: "The only way to reveal the relationship between multiple levels of context in the interaction field is to have a time series sufficiently long to show how firm, sector, and economic levels of context interact to energize change processes" (2001: 699). An inclusive longitudinal study on the topic is naturally limited by the researcher's ignorance that a PE investment will occur, which prohibits the investigation of the target company before the PE investment. Furthermore, constraints arising from the search for companies which are willing to accept longitudinal observations additionally discourage such proceedings. In order to partially circumvent this empirical shortcoming, I attempted to reflect and integrate theoretical issues regarding the change process in general and its time dimension in particular (cf. section 3.1 and section 5.2).

Whereas the research setting and data collection followed relatively prescribed principles, the analysis and "dance of interpretation" (Miller & Crabtree, 1999) are often described as an art, instead of a rigorous scientific procedure, which is particularly true for qualitative research (e.g., Chambliss & Schutt, 2006). As a matter of fact, interpretation might be subject to an enormous amount of fallacies, which are grounded on cognitive biases. Kahnemann and Tversky (1972) define a cognitive bias as a distortion in the human mind that leads to ambiguous perceptions, illogical conclusion drawing, or imprecise judgments. Given the quantity and complexity of biases described by the psychological literature (see Gilovich et al. 2002), the subsequent consideration merely discusses some preeminent examples. In line with the earlier mentioned application of pre-instrumentalization, the analysis and interpretation might have suffered from a confirmation bias, defined as the tendency to interpret evidence in support of earlier expectations (e.g., Plous, 1993). An effective triangulation of the evidence should have minimized this fallacy. On the same account, clustering illusion, denoting the tendency to see patterns where actually none exist (e.g., Gilovich, 1991), and illusory correlation, signifying the predisposition to spuriously infer relationships (e.g., Plous, 1993), might have influenced the generation of this study's results. The utilization of Trochim's (1989) concept of pattern matching and Yin's (2003) proposed research strategy to rely on established theoretical propositions should have reduced, although not eliminated, these distortions.

Informants' perspective

From my perspective, this level essentially deals with the quality of justification with regard to the gathered evidence; it considers the question why collected data, which justified my creation of knowledge, could have potentially included fallacies.

In essence, the cognitive biases that affected my perception could also have been operative in the minds of the informants when they have constructed knowledge of the things around them. Auxiliary relevant issues, besides these cognitive distortions, are memory errors because informants were asked to reconstruct the different organizational states between two points in time. Schacter (2001) summarizes the most common memory failures in his book *The seven sins of memory*, which are shortly discussed. "Transience" deals with the effect that the human mind has a tendency to better remember recent events than things back in the past. "Absent-mindedness" describes the deficiency to remember specific incidents when there is no deliberate attention paid to the observed phenomenon. "Blocking" is based on the idea that numerous recollections might interfere and thus oppose each other when the human mind attempts to dissolve them. Schacter (2001) summarizes these three "sins" as deficiencies to recall information. In contrast, the subsequent four themes are based on the insight that the reported recollections do not reflect the actual events having occurred. "Misattribution" illustrates the fallacy that respondents might report correct information, which is, however, derived from false contexts. "Suggestibility" exemplifies the distortion that auxiliary information is spuriously merged with the actual occurrence. Similar to suggestibility, "bias" is defined as the tendency to value retrospective happenings in relation to current worldviews or perspectives. Finally, "persistence" illustrates the problem that informants might be exposed to an overkill of information, which makes it difficult to focus on the actual asked questions. These "seven sins" thoroughly illustrate the issues that might disturb the functioning of the human mind in a general setting. Nevertheless, these obstacles should also hold true in organization research. For instance, Holan and Phillips (2004) suggest that organizational members usually forget particular phenomena to prevent an information overload. Likewise, it is a common occurrence that the construction of reality in organizations is influenced by retrospective sensemaking practices (see Weick et al. 2005; Weick, 1995a).

Bibliography

Acharya, V. V., M. Hahn, and C. Kehoe. 2009. *Corporate governance and value creation: evidence from private equity.* Working Paper, London Business School.

Achleitner, A. K. 2002. *Handbuch Investment Banking* (3rd ed.). Wiesbaden: Gabler.

Achleitner, A. K., K. Herman, J. Lerner, and E. Lutz. 2010. Family business and private equity: Conflict or collaboration? The case of Messer Griesheim. *Journal of Private Equity,* 13: 7 – 20.

Achleitner, A. K., A. Poech, and M. Burger-Calderon. 2008c. Private Equity und Mittelstand -Wege zu einem konstruktiven Dialog. In P. May (Ed.), *Das INTES-Handbuch Familienunternehmen.* Bonn: INTES Akademie.

Achleitner, A. K., S. C. Schraml, and F. Tappeiner. 2008a. *Private Equity in Familienunternehmen – Erfahrungen mit Minderheitsbeteiligungen.* Norderstedt: Books on Demand.

Achleitner, A.K., S.C. Schraml, and F. Tappeiner. 2008b. *Private equity minority investments in large family firms: What influences the attitude of family firm owners?* Working Paper, Technische Universität München.

Adler, P. S., B. Goldoftas, and D. Levine. 1999. Flexibility versus efficiency? A case study of model changeovers in the Toyota production system. *Organization Science,* 10: 43 – 68.

Aiken, M. and J. Hage. 1971. The organic organization and innovation. *Sociology,* 5: 63 – 82.

Aldrich, H. A. and J. Pfeffer. 1976. Environments of organizations. *Annual Review of Sociology,* 2: 121 – 140.

Ambert, A. M., P. A. Adler, P. Adler, and D. F. Detzner. 1995. Understanding and evaluating qualitative research. *Journal of Marriage and Family,* 57: 879 – 893.

Ambos, T. C., K. Makela, J. Birkinshaw, and P. D'este. 2008. When does university research get commercialized? Creating ambidexterity in research institutions. *Journal of Management Studies,* 45: 1424 – 1447.

Amess, K. 2002. Management buyouts and firm-level poductivity: Evidence from a panel of U.K. manufacturing firms. *Scottish Journal of Political Economy,* 49: 304 – 317.

Amess, K. 2003. The effect of management buyouts on firm-level technical efficiency: Evidence from a panel of UK machinery and equipment manufacturers. *Journal of Industrial Economics,* 51: 35 – 44.

Ancona, D. G., P. S. Goodman, B. S. Lawrence, and M. L. Tushman. 2001. Time: A new research lens. *Academy of Management Review,* 26: 545 – 653.

Anderson, P. 1999. Complexity theory and organizational science. *Organization Science,* 10: 216 – 232.

Anderson, P., A. Meyer, K. Eisenhardt, K. Carley and A. Pettigrew. 1999. Introduction to the Special Issue: Applications of complexity theory to organization science. *Organization Science,* 10: 233 – 236.

Anderson, R. C. and D. M. Reeb. 2003. Founding family ownership and firm performance: Evidence from the S&P 500. *Journal of Finance,* 58: 1301 – 1328.

Andriopoulos, C. and M. W. Lewis. 2009. Exploration-exploitation tensions and organizational ambidexterity: Managing paradoxes of innovation. *Organization Science,* 20: 696 717.

Arthur, W. B. 1995. Positive feedbacks in the economy. In T. Kuran (Ed.), *Increasing returns and path dependence in the economy.* Ann Arbor: University Michigan Press.

Astrachan, J. H. and P. Jaskiewicz. 2008. Emotional returns and emotional costs in privately held family businesses: Advancing traditional business valuation. *Family Business Review,* 21: 139 – 149.

Astrachan, J. H., S. B. Klein and K. X. Smyrnios. 2002. The F-PEC scale for solving the family business definition. *Family Business Review,* 15: 45 – 58.

Astrachan, J. H. and T. A. Kolenko. 1994. A neglected factor explaining family business success: Human resource practices. *Family Business Review,* 7: 251 – 262.

Atuahane-Gima, K. 2005. Resolving the capability-rigidity paradox in new product innovation. *Journal of Marketing,* 69: 61 – 83.

Auh, S. and B. Menguc. 2005. Balancing exploration and exploitation: The moderating role of competitive intensity. *Journal of Business Research,* 58: 1652 – 1661.

Avital, M. 2000. Dealing with time in social inquiry: A tension between method and lived experience. *Organization Science,* 11: 665 – 673.

Axelson, U., P. Strömberg, and M. S. Weisbach. 2009. Why are buyouts levered? The financial structure of Private Equity funds. *Journal of Finance,* 64: 1549 – 1582.

Bacharach, S. B. 1989. Organizational theories: Some criteria for evaluation. *Academy of Management Review,* 4: 469 – 515.

Backhaus, D. 2009. Frisches Geld, das keiner will. *Financial Times Deutschland,* October 18. Retrieved from: http://www.ftd.de

Bain & Company. 2010. *Global private equity report.* Retrieved from: http://www.bain.-com

Baldridge, D. C., S. W. Floyd, and L. Markóczy. 2004. Are managers from Mars and academicians from Venus? Toward an understanding of the relationship between academic quality and practical relevance. *Strategic Management Journal,* 25: 1063 – 1074.

Bargeron, L., F. Schlingemann, R. Stulz, and C. Zutter. 2008. Why do private acquirers pay so little compared to public acquirers? *Journal of Financial Economics,* 89: 375 – 390.

Barnett, W. P. and R. A. Burgelman. 1996. Evolutionary perspectives on strategy. *Strategic Management Journal,* 17: 5 – 19.

Barnett, W. P. and G. R. Carroll. 1995. Modeling internal organizational change. *Annual Review of Sociology,* 21: 217 – 236.

Barnett, W. P. and M. T. Hansen. 1996. The red queen in organizational evolution. *Strategic Management Journal,* 17: 139 – 157.

Bartunek, J. M., S. L. Rynes and R. D. Ireland. 2006. What makes management research interesting and why does it matter? *Academy of Management Journal*, 49: 9 – 15.

Baum, J. A. C. 1996. Organizational ecology. In C. Hardy, W. R. Nord, and S. R. Clegg (Eds.), *Handbook of Organization Studies*. London: Sage.

Baum, J. A. C., S. X. Li, and J. M. Usher. 2000. Making the next move: How experiential and vicarious learning shape the locations of chains' acquisitions. *Administrative Science Quarterly*, 45: 766 – 801.

Baum, J. A. C. and J. V. Singh. 1994. *Evolutionary dynamics of organizations*. New York: Oxford University Press.

Baum, J. R. and S. Wally. 2003. Strategic decision speed and firm performance. *Strategic Management Journal*, 24: 1107 – 1129.

Bayus, B. L., G. Erickson, and R. Jacobson. 2003. The financial rewards of new product introductions in the personal computer industry. *Management Science*, 49: 197 – 210.

Beckman, C. M. 2006. The influence of founding team company affiliations on firm behavior. *Academy of Management Journal*, 49: 741 – 758.

Beinhocker, E. 1997. Strategy at the edge of chaos. *McKinsey Quarterly*, 1: 25 – 39.

Bem, D. J. 1987. Writing the empirical journal article. In M. P. Zanna and J. M. Darley (Eds.), *The compleat academic*. New Jersey: Lawrence Erlbaum Associates.

Benner, M. J. and M. L. Tushman. 2003. Exploration, exploitation, and process management: The productivity dilemma revisited. *Academy of Management Review*, 28: 238 – 256.

Bennett, A. and C. Elman. 2006. Qualitative research: Recent developments in case study methods. *Annual Review of Political Sciences*, 9: 455 – 476.

Bennis, W. G. and J. O'Toole. 2005. How business schools lost their way. *Harvard Business Review*, 83: 96 – 105.

Benson, J. K. 1977. Organizations: A dialectic view. *Administrative Science Quarterly*, 22: 1 – 21.

Berger, P. L. and T. Luckmann. 1967. *The social construction of reality*. New York: Doubleday.

Bergh, D. D. and J. F. Fairbank. 2002. Measuring and testing change in strategic management research. *Strategic Management Journal*, 23: 359 – 366

Bergmann, B., H. Christophers, M. Huss, and H. Zimmermann. 2009. *Listed Private Equity*. Working Paper, University of Basel.

Bernstein, R. J. 1971. *Praxis and action: Contemporary philosophies of human activity*. Philadelphia: University of Pennsylvania Press.

Berson, Y., S. Oreg, and T. Dvir. 2008. CEO values, organizational culture and firm outcomes. *Journal of Organizational Behavior*, 29: 615 – 633.

Bertalanffy, L. v. 1950. An outline of general systems theory. *British Journal for the Philosophy of Science*, 1: 134 – 165.

Bertalanffy, L. v. 1968. *Organismic psychology and systems theory*. Worchester: Clark University Press.

Bettis, R.A. 1991. Strategic management and the straightjacket: An editorial essay. *Organization Science*, 2: 315 – 319.

Beyerle, H. 2010. Neuer Anlauf nach der Krise. *Financial Times Deutschland*, June 18. Retrieved from: http://www.ftd.de

Bierly, P. and A. Chakrabarti. 1996. Generic knowledge strategies in the U.S. pharmaceutical industry. *Strategic Management Journal,* 17: 123 – 137.

Bierly, P. and P. S. Daly. 2007. Alternative knowledge strategies, competitive environment, and organizational performance in small manufacturing firms. *Entrepreneurship: Theory and Practice,* 31: 493 – 516.

Bird, B., H. Welsch, J. H. Astrachan, and D. Pistrui. 2002. Family business research: The evolution of an academic field. *Family Business Review,* 15: 337 – 350.

Birkinshaw, J. and C. Gibson. 2004. Building ambidexterity into an organization. *MIT Sloan Management Review,* Vol. 45: 47 – 55.

Birley, S. 2001. Owner-manager attitudes to family and business issues: A 16 country study. *Entrepreneurship: Theory and Practice,* 26: 63 – 76.

Bishop, M. 2004. The new kings of capitalism. *The Economist,* November 27. Retrieved from http://www.economist.com

Black, B. and R. Gilson. 1998. Venture Capital and the structure of capital markets: Banks versus stock markets. *Journal of Financial Economics,* 47: 243 – 277.

Blanco-Mazagatos, V., E. de Quevedo-Puento, and L. A. Castrillo. 2007. The trade-off between financial resources and agency costs in the family business: An exploratory study. *Family Business Review,* 20: 199 – 213.

Böhler, C. 2006. Private Equity für Privatinvestoren. *Neue Zürcher Zeitung,* November 06. Retrieved from: http://www.nzz.ch

Bogner, W. C. and P. S. Barr. 2000. Making sense in hypercompetitive environments: A cognitive explanation of persistence of high velocity competition. *Organization Science,* 11: 212 – 226.

Bourgeois, L. J. and K. M. Eisenhardt. 1988. Strategic decision processes in high velocity environments: Four cases in the microcomputer industry. *Management Science,* 34: 816 – 835.

Bowen, D. D., R. Perloff, and J. Jacoby. 1972. Improving manuscript evaluation procedures. *American Psychologist,* 27: 221 – 275.

Bower, J. L. 1982. Business policy in the 1980s. *Academy of Management Review,* 7: 630 – 638.

Boyd, B. K., S. Gove and M. A. Hitt. 2005. Construct measurement in strategic management research: Illusion or reality? *Strategic Management Journal,* 26: 239 – 257.

Brown, S. J., W. Goetzmann, R. G. Ibbotson, and S. A. Ross. 1992. Survivorship bias in performance studies. *Review of Financial Studies,* 5: 553 – 580.

Brown, S. L. and K. M. Eisenhardt. 1997. The art of continuous change: Linking complexity theory and time-paced evolution in relentlessly shifting organizations. *Administrative Science Quarterly,* 42: 1 – 34.

Bruining, H. and M. Wright. 2002. Entrepreneurial orientation in management buyouts and the contribution of venture capital. *Venture Capital,* 4: 147 – 168.

Bull, I. 1989. Management performance in leveraged buyouts: An empirical analysis. *Journal of Business Venturing,* 3: 263 – 278.

Bundesverband Deutscher Kapitalbeteiligungsgesellschaften. 2011. *BVK Statistik: Das Jahr 2010 in Zahlen.* Retrieved from: http://www.bvkap.de

Burchell, N. and D. Kolb. 2006. Stability and change for sustainability. *University of Auckland Business Review,* Vol 8: 33 – 44.

Burgelmann, R. A. 1983. A model of the interaction of strategic behavior, corporate context and the concept of strategy. *Academy of Management Review,* 8: 61 – 70.
Burgelmann, R. A. 1991. Intraorganizational ecology of strategy-making and organizational adaptation: Theory and field research. *Organization Science,* 2: 239 – 262.
Burgelmann, R. A. 2002. Strategy as vector and the inertia of coevolutionary lock-in. *Administrative Science Quarterly,* 47: 325 – 357.
Burgelmann, R. A. 2004. Fading memories: A process theory of strategic business exit in dynamic environments. *Administrative Science Quarterly,* Vol. 39: 24 – 56.
Burrough, B. and J. Helyar. 1989. *Barbarians at the gate: The fall of RJR Nabisco.* New York: Harper and Row.
Buttignon, F., M. Vedovato, and P. Bortoluzzi. 2005. *Family business investor buyouts: The Italian case.* Working Paper, University of Padova.
Cameron, K. S. and S. J. Freeman. 1991. Cultural congruence, strength, and type: Relationships to effectiveness. *Research in Organizational Change and Development,* 5: 23 – 58.
Cameron, K. S. and R. E. Quinn. 2006. *Diagnosing and Changing Organizational Culture* (revised ed.). San Francisco: Jossey-Bass.
Campbell, D. T. and D. W. Fiske. 1959. Convergent and discriminant validation by the multitrait multimethod matrix. *Psychological Bulletin,* 56: 81 – 105.
Cao, Q., E., Gedajlovic, and H. Zhang. 2009. Unpacking organizational ambidexterity: Dimensions, contingencies, and synergistic effects. *Organization Science,* 20: 781 – 796.
Cao, Q., Z. Simsek, and H. Zhang. 2010. Modelling the joint impact of the CEO and the TMT on organizational ambidexterity. *Journal of Management Studies,* 47: 1272 – 1296.
Capron, L. and J. C. Shen. 2007. Acquisitions of private vs. public firms: Private information, target selection, and acquirer returns. *Strategic Management Journal,* 28: 891 – 911.
Cardieux, L. J. Lorrain, P. Hugron. 2002. Succession in women-owned family businesses: A case study. *Family Business Review,* 15: 17 – 30.
Carmeli, A. and M. Y. Halevi. 2009. How top management team behavioral integration and behavioral complexity enable organizational ambidexterity: The moderating role of contextual ambidexterity. *Leadership Quarterly,* 20: 207 – 218.
Cater, J. and A. Schwab. 2008. Turnaround strategies in established small family firms. *Family Business Review,* 21: 31 – 50.
Chaganti, R. and R. Sambharya. 2006. Strategic orientation and characteristics of upper management. *Strategic Management Journal,* 8: 393 – 401.
Chambliss, D. F. and R. K. Schutt. 2006. *Making sense of the social world: Methods of investigation* (2nd ed.). Thousand Oaks, CA: Sage.
Chatman, J. and F. Flynn. 2006. Full-cycle micro-organizational behavior research. *Organization Science,* 16: 434 – 447.
Cheffins, B. and J. Armour. 2008. The eclipse of private equity. *Delaware Journal of Corporate Law,* 33: 1 – 67.
Chen, A. H., J. A. Conover, and J. W. Kensinger. 2011. Private equity arrangements a real options. In J. W. Kensinger (Ed.), *Research in Finance, Volume 27.* Bingley: JAI Press.
Child, J. 1972. Organizational structure, environment and performance: The role of strategic choice. *Sociology,* 6: 1 – 22.
Chrisman, J. J., J. H. Chua, and R.A. Litz. 2004. Comparing agency costs of family and non

family firms: Conceptual issues and explanatory evidence. *Entrepreneurship: Theory and Practice,* 28: 335 – 354.

Chrisman, J. J., J. H. Chua, A. W. Pearson, and T. Barnett. 2010. Family involvement, family influence, and family-centered non-economic goals in small firms. *Entrepreneurship: Theory and Practice,* forthcoming.

Chrisman, J. J., J. H. Chua, and P. Sharma. 2005. Trends and directions in the development of a strategic management theory of the family firm. *Entrepreneurship: Theory and Practice,* 29: 555 – 575.

Chrisman, J. J., J. H. Chua, and S. A. Zahra. 2003. Creating wealth in family firms through managing resources: Comments and extensions. *Entrepreneurship: Theory and Practice,* 27: 359 – 365.

Chua, J. H., J. J. Chrisman, and P. Sharma. 1999. Defining the family business by behavior. *Entrepreneurship Theory and Practice,* 23: 19 – 37.

Cohen, W. M. and D. A. Levinthal. 1989. Innovation and learning: Two faces of R&D. *Economic Journal,* 99: 569 – 596.

Coleman, S. and M. Carsky. 1999. Sources of capital for small family-owned businesses. *Family Business Review,* 12: 73 – 86.

Collins, J. and J. Porras. 1994. *Built to last: Successful habits of visionary companies.* New York: Harper.

Collis, D. J. 1994. Research note: How valuable are organizational capabilities? *Strategic Management Journal,* 15: 143 – 152.

Conner, K. R. and C. K. Prahalad. 1996. A resource-based theory of the firm: Knowledge versus opportunism. *Organization Science,* 7: 477 – 501.

Connor, P. E. 1992. Decision-making participating patterns: The role of organizational context. *Academy of Management Journal,* 35: 218 – 231.

Connor, T. 2007. Market orientation and performance. *Strategic Management Journal,* 28: 957 – 959.

Cook, T. D. and D. T. Campbell. 1979. *Quasi-Experimentation: Design and analysis issues for field settings.* Boston: Houghton Mifflin.

Corbetta, G. and C. Salvato. 2004. Self-serving or self-acutalizing? Models of man and agency costs in different types of family firms: A commentary on "Comparing agency costs of family and non-family firms: Conceptual issues and exploratory evidence". *Entrepreneurship: Theory and Practice,* 28: 355 – 362.

Corso, M. and L. Pelligrini. 2007. Continuous and discontinuous innovation: Overcoming the innovator dilemma. *Creativity and Innovation Management,* 16: 333 – 347.

Cross, R., W. Baker, and A. Parker. 2003. What creates energy in organizations? *MIT Sloan Management Review,* 44: 51 – 56.

Cumming, D., D. S. Siegel, and M. Wright. 2007. Private equity, leveraged buyouts and governance. *Journal of Corporate Finance,* 13: 439 – 460.

Cummings, L. L. and P. J. Frost. 1995. *Publishing in the organizational sciences.* Thousand Oaks, CA: Sage.

Cyert, R. M. and J. G. March. 1963. *A behavioral theory of a firm.* New Jersey: Prentice-Hall.

Czarniawska, B. 1997. *Narrating the organization: Dramas of institutional identity.* Chicago: University Chicago Press.

Czarniawska, B. 1998. Who is afraid of incommensurability? *Organization,* 5: 273 – 275.

Czarniawska, B. and G. Sevon. 1996. *Translating organization change.* Berlin: Walter de Gruyter.

Daft, R. L. 1983. Learning the craft of organization research. *Academy of Management Review,* 4: 539 – 546.

Daft, R. L. 1995. Why I recommend that your manuscript should be rejected and what you can do about it. In L. L. Cummings and P. J. Frost (Eds.), *Publishing in the organizational sciences.* Thousand Oaks, CA: Sage.

Daft, R. L. 2004. *Organization theory and design* (8th ed.). Natorp Boulevard: Thomson.

Daft, R. L. and A. Y. Lewin. 1990. Can organizational studies begin to break out of the normal science straitjacket? An editorial essay. *Organization Science,* 1: 1 – 9.

Daft, R. L. and A. Y. Lewin. 2008. Rigor and relevance in organization studies: Idea migration and academic journal evolution. *Organization Science,* 19: 177 – 183.

Dalton, D. R. and I. F. Kesner. 1983. Inside/ outside succession and organization science: The pragmatics of executive replacement. *Academy of Management Journal,* 26: 736 – 742.

Danneels, E. 2002. The dynamics of product innovation and firm competences. *Strategic Management Journal,* 23: 1095 – 1121.

Danneels, E. 2008. Organizational antecedents of second-order competences. *Strategic Management Journal,* 29: 519 – 543.

D'Aveni, R. 1994. *Hypercompetition: Managing the dynamics of strategic maneuvering.* New York: Free Press.

David, P. A. 1985. Clio and the economics of QWERTY. *American Economic Review,* 75: 332 – 337.

Davis, G. F. 2005. Firms and environments. In N. Smelser and R. Swedberg (Eds.). *Handbook of Economic Sociology.* Princeton: Sage / Princeton University Press.

Davis, G. F. and C. Marquis. 2005. Prospects for organization theory in the early twenty-first century: Institutional fields and mechanisms. *Organization Science,* 16: 332 – 343.

Davis, J. A. and R. Tagiuri. 1989. The influence of life-stage on father-son work relationship in family companies. *Family Business Review,* 2: 47 – 74.

Davis, P. and P. Harvestone. 1998. The influence of family on the family business succession process: A multigenerational perspective. *Entrepreneurship: Theory and Practice,* 22: 31 – 53.

Debicki, B. J., C. F. Matherne, F. W. Kellermanns, and J. J. Chrisman. 2009. Family business research in the new millennium: An overview of the Who, the Where, the What, and the Why. *Family Business Review,* 22: 151 – 166.

Deissler, K. G. 1988. Erfinderisches Interviewen. *Familiendynamik,* 13: 345 – 363.

De Massis, A., J. H. Chua, and J. J. Chrisman. 2008. Factors preventing intra-family succession. *Family Business Review,* 21:183 – 199.

Denison, R. D. 1990. *Corporate culture and organizational effectiveness.* New York: Wiley.

Deshpande, R. and F. E. Webster. 1989. Organizational culture and marketing: Defining the research agenda. *Journal of Marketing,* 53: 3 – 15.

Dierig, C. 2007. Kontrolle bleibt Familiensache. *Die Welt,* October 30. Retrieved from: http://www.welt.de

Dirks, K. T. and D. L. Ferrin. 2001. The role of trust in organizational settings. *Organization Science,* 12: 450 – 467.

Donaldson, L. 1995. *American anti-management theories of organization: A critique of paradigm proliferation.* Cambridge: Cambridge University Press.

Dostert, E. 2009. Beteiligung auf Dauer. *Süddeutsche Zeitung,* October 29. Retrieved from: http://www.sueddeutsche.de

Drozdow, N. 1998. What is continuity? *Family Business Review,* 11: 337 – 348.

Dul, J. and T. Hak. 2008. *Case Study methodology in business research.* Oxford: Butterworth-Heinemann.

Duncan, R. B. 1976. The ambidextrous organization: Designing dual structures for innovation. In L. R. Pondy, D. P. Slevin, and R. H. Kilmann (Eds.), *The management of organization design.* New York: North Holland.

Dunn, B. 1995. Success themes in Scottish family enterprises: Philosophies and practices through the generations. *Family Business Review,* 8: 17 – 28.

Dutton, J. E., S. J. Ashford, R. M. O'Neill, and K. A. Lawrence. 2001. Moves that matter: Issue selling and organizational change. *Academy of Management Journal,* 44: 716 – 736.

Dyer, W. G. 2006. Examining the "family effect" on performance. *Family Business Review,* 19: 253 – 273.

Dyer, W. G. and M. Sanchez. 1998. Current state of family business theory and practice as reflected in family business review 1988 – 1997. *Family Business Review,* 11: 287 – 295.

Dyer, W. G. and A. L. Wilkins. 1991. Better stories, not better constructs, to generate better theory: A rejoinder to Eisenhardt. *Academy of Management Review,* 16: 613 – 619.

Edmonson, A. C. and S. E. McManus. 2007. Methodological fit in management field research. *Academy of Management Review,* 32: 1155 – 1179.

Einhorn, H. J. and R. M. Hogarth. 1986. Judging probable cause. *Psychological Bulletin,* 99: 3 – 19.

Eisenhardt, K. M. 1989a. Building theories from case study research. *Academy of Management Review,* 14: 532 – 550.

Eisenhardt, K. M. 1989b. Making fast decisions in high-velocity environments. *Academy of Management Journal,* 32: 543 – 576.

Eisenhardt, K. M. 1991. Better stories and better constructs: The case for rigor and comparative logic. *Academy of Management Review,* 16: 620 – 627.

Eisenhardt, K. M. 2000. Paradox, spirals, ambivalence: The new language of change and pluralism. *Academy of Management Review,* 25: 703 – 705.

Eisenhardt, K. M. and J. A. Martin. 2000. Dynamic capabilities: What are they? *Strategic Management Journal,* 21: 1105 – 1121.

Eisenhardt, K. M. and M. E. Graebner. 2007. Theory building from cases: Opportunities and challenges. *Academy of Management Journal,* 50: 25 – 32.

Erikson, T., R. Sorheim, and B. Reitan. 2003. Family angels vs. other informal investors. *Family Business Review,* 16: 163 – 171.

Ethiraj, S. K., P. Kale, M. S. Krishnan, and J. V. Singh. 2004. Where do capabilities come from and how do they matter? A study in the software services industry. *Strategic Management Journal,* 26: 25 – 45.

Engel, D. and M. Keilbach. 2007. Firm-level implications of early stage venture capital investment – An empirical investigation. *Journal of Empirical Finance,* 14: 150 – 167.

Fama, E. and M. C. Jensen. 1983. Seperation of ownership and control. *Journal of Law and Economics,* 26: 301 – 325.

Farjoun, M. 2002. Toward an organic perspective on strategy. *Strategic Management Journal,* 23: 561 – 594.

Feldman, M. S. 2000. Organizational routines as a source of continuous change. *Organization Science,* 11: 611 – 629.

Fenn, G. W., N. Liang, and S. Prowse. 1997. The private equity market: An overview. *Financial Markets, Institutions, and Instruments,* 6: 1 – 106.

Ferlie, E., L. Fitzegerald, M. Wood, and C. Hawkins. 2005. The nonspread of innovations: The mediating role of professionals. *Academy of Management Journal,* 48: 117 – 134.

Fernandez, Z. and M. J. Nieto. 2005. Internationalization strategy of small and medium-sized family businesses: Some influential factors. *Family Business Review,* 18: 77 – 89.

Fettermann, D. M. 2010. *Ethnography: Step-by-step* (3rd ed.). Thousand Oaks, CA: Sage.

Filbeck, G. and S. Lee. 2000. Financial management techniques in family business. *Family Business Review,* 13: 201 – 216.

File, K., R. Prince, and M. Rankin. 1994. Organizational buying behavior of the family firm. *Family Business Review,* 7: 263 – 272.

Financial Times Deutschland. 2010a. Private Equity umwirbt deutschen Mittelstand. June 14. Retrieved from: http://www.ftd.de

Financial Times Deutschland. 2010b. Private Equity investiert zaghaft wieder mehr. August 25. Retrieved from: http://www.ftd.de

Finkelstein, D. and D. C. Hambrick. 1990. Top management team tenure and organizational outcomes: The moderating role of managerial discretion. *Administrative Science Quarterly,* 35: 484 – 503.

Firestone, W. A. 1993. Alternative arguments for generalizing from data as applied to qualitative research. *Educational Researcher,* 7: 437 – 466.

Fleming, L. 2001. Recombinant uncertainty in technological search. *Management Science,* 47: 117 – 132.

Floyd, S. W. and B. Wooldridge. 1992. Middle management involvement in strategy and its association with strategic type: A research note. *Strategic Management Journal,* 13: 153 – 167.

Floyd, S. W. and P. J. Lane. 2000. Strategizing throughout the organization: Managing role conflict in strategic renewal. *Academy of Management Review,* 25: 154 – 177.

Flyvbjerg, B. 2006. Five misunderstandings about case-study research. *Qualitative Inquiry,* 12: 219 – 245.

Folger, R. and C. J. Turillo. 1999. Theorizing as the thickness of thin abstraction. *Academy of Management Review,* 24: 742 – 758.

Ford, J. D. and L. W. Ford. 1995. The role of conversations in producing intentional change in organizations. *Academy of Management,* 20: 541 – 570.

Forst, M. 1992. *Management Buy-Out und Buy-In als Form der Übernahme mittelständischer Unternehmen.* Stuttgart: Schaeffer-Poeschel.

Frank, H., W. H. Güttel, and D. Weismeier-Sammer. 2011. Ambidexterity in Familienunternehmen: Die Top-Management-Familie als Innovationsinkubator. In G. Schreyögg and P. Conrad (Eds.), *Managementforschung, Band 20: Organisation und Strategie.* Wiesbaden: Gabler.

Friedman, S. D. and K. Saul. 1991. A leader's wake: Organization members reactions to CEO succession. *Academy of Management Journal,* 17: 619 – 642.

Galbraith, J. R. 1973. *Designing complex organizations.* Reading: Addison-Wesley.

Gallo, M.A. and J. Sveen. 1991. Internationalizing the family business: Facilitating and restraining factors. *Family Business Review,* 4: 181 – 190.

Gallo, M. A. and A. Vilaseca. 1996. Finance in Family Business. *Family Business Review,* 9: 387 – 401.

Garcia-Alvarez, E. and J. Lopez-Sintas. 2001. A taxonomy of founders based values: The root of family business heterogeneity. *Family Business Review,* 14: 209 – 230.

Gebhardt, G. F., G. S. Carpenter, and J. F. Sherry. 2006. Creating a market orientation: A longitudinal, multiform, grounded analysis of cultural transformation. *Journal of Marketing,* 70: 37 – 55.

George, J. M. and G. R. Jones. 2000. The role of time in theory and theory building. *Journal of Management,* 26: 657 – 684.

Gephart, R. P. 2004. Qualitative research and the Academy of Management Journal. *Academy of Mangement Journal,* 47: 454 – 462.

Gergen, K. J. 2002. *Konstruierte Wirklichkeiten: Eine Hinführung zum sozialen Konstruktionismus.* Stuttgart: Kohlhammer.

Gerring, J. 2004. What is a case study and what is it good for? *American Political Science Review,* 98: 341 – 354.

Gerring, J. 2007. *Case study research: Principles and practices.* Cambridge: Cambridge University Press.

Gersick, C. J. G. 1991. Revolutionary change theories: A multilevel exploration of the punctuated equilibrium paradigm. *Academy of Management Review,* 16: 10 – 36.

Gersick, C. J. G. 1994. Pacing strategic change: The case of a new venture. *Academy of Management Review,* 37: 9 – 45.

Gersick, K. E., J. A. Davis, M. McCollom Hampton, and I. Lansberg. 1997. *Generation to generation: Life cycles of the family business.* Boston: Harvard Business School Press.

Ghoshal, S. 2005. Bad management theories are destroying good management practices. *Academy of Management Learning and Education,* 4: 75 – 91.

Ghoshal, S. and C. A. Bartlett. 1994. Linking organizational context and managerial action: The dimension of quality of management. *Strategic Management Journal,* 15: 91 – 112.

Gibbert, M., W. Ruigrok and B. Wicki. 2008. What passes as a rigorous case study. *Strategic Management Journal,* 29: 1465 – 1474.

Gibson, C. B. and J. Birkinshaw. 2004. The antecedents, consequences, and mediating role of organizational ambidexterity. *Academy of Management Journal,* 47: 209 – 226.

Gibson, J. L. 1966. Organization theory and the nature of man. *Academy of Management Journal,* 9: 233 – 245.

Gilbert, C. G. 2005. Unbundling the structure of inertia: Resource versus routine rigidity. *Academy of Management Journal,* 48: 741 – 763.

Gilbert, N. 2008. *Resarching social life* (3rd ed.). London: Sage.

Gilovich, T. 1991. *How we know what isn't so: The fallibility of human reason in everyday life.* New York: Free Press.

Gilovich, T, D. Griffin, and D. Kahnemann. 2002. *Heuristics and biases – The psychology of intuitive judgement.* Cambridge: Cambridge University Press.

Gimeno, A., G. Baulenas, and J. Coma-Cros. 2010. *Familienunternehmen führen Komplexität managen: Mentale Modelle und praktische Lösungen.* Göttingen: Vandenhoeck und Ruprecht.

Ginsberg, A. and N. Venkatraman. 1995. Institutional initiatives for technological change: From issue interpretation to strategic choice. *Organizational Studies,* 16: 425 – 448

Gioia, D. A. 1992. Pinto fires and personal ethics: A script analysis of missed opportunities. *Journal of Business Ethics,* 11: 379 – 389.

Gioia, D. A. and E. Pitre. 1990. Multiparadigm perspectives on theory building. *Academy of Management Review,* 15: 584 – 602.

Glaser, B. and A. Strauss. 1967. *The discovery of grounded theory: Strategies in qualitative research.* London: Wiedenfeld and Nicholson.

Glaser, B. 1978. *Theoretical sensitivity: Advances in the methodology of grounded theory.* Mill Valley: Sociology Press.

Godfrey, P. C. and C. W. L. Hill. 1995. The problem of unobservables in strategic management research. *Strategic Management Journal,* 16: 513 – 533.

Goel, A. M. and A. V. Thakor. 2008. Overconfidence, CEO selection, and corporate governance. *Journal of Finance,* 63: 2737 – 2784.

Gompers, P. 1996. Grandstanding in the venture capital industry. *Journal of Financial Economics,* 42: 133 – 156.

Gompers, P. and J. Lerner. 2000. Money chasing deals? The impact of fund inflows on private equity valuations. *Journal of Financial Economics,* 55: 281 – 325.

Gompers, P. and J. Lerner. 2001. The venture capital revolution. *Journal of Economic Perspectives,* 15: 145 – 168.

Goode, W. J. and D. F. Mitchell. 1952. *Methods of social research.* New York: McGraw-Hill.

Goossens, L. S. Manigart, and M. Meuleman. 2008. The change in ownership after a buyout: Impact on performance. *Journal of Private Equity,* 12: 31 – 41.

Gordon G. and N. Nicholson. 2008. *Family wars: Classic conflicts in family business and how to deal with them.* London, Philadelphia: Kogan Page.

Grant, R.M. 2005. *Contemporary strategy analysis* (5th ed.). Oxford: Blackwell.

Greiner, L. E. 1972. Evolution and revolution as organizations grow. *Harvard Business Review,* 50: 37 – 46.

Grifell-Tatje, E. and C. A. K. Lovell. 1999. Profits and productivity. *Management Science,* 45: 1177 – 1193.

Groth, T. 2008. Gute Lösungen von Generation zu Generation: Langlebige Familienunternehmen. In A. Nischak, M.E. Hachimi, and A.v. Schlippe (Eds.), *Familienunternehmen verstehen: Gründer, Gesellschafter und Generationen.* Göttingen: Vandenhoeck and Ruprecht.

Groysberg, B. and L.-E. Lee. 2009. Hiring stars and their colleagues: Exploration and exploitation in professional service firms. *Organization Science,* 20: 740 – 758.

Guest, R. 1962. Managerial succession in complex organizations. *American Journal of Sociology,* 68: 47 – 56.

Gulati, R. and P. Puranam. 2009. Renewal through reorganization: The value of inconsistencies between formal and informal organization. *Organization Science,* 20: 422 – 440.

Gupta, A. K., K. G. Smith, and C. A. Shalley. 2006. The interplay between exploration and exploitation. *Academy of Management Journal,* 49: 693 – 706.

Habbershon, T. G. and M. L. Williams. 1999. A resource-based framework for assessing the strategic advantages of family firms. *Family Business Review,* 12: 1 – 26.

Habbershon, T. G., M. L. Williams, and M. MacMillan. 2003. A unified systems perspective of family firm performance. *Journal of Business Venturing,* 18: 451 – 465.

Hage, J. and B. Meeker. 1987. *Social causality.* Boston: Unwin Hyman.

Hambrick, D. C. 1994. 1993 Presidantial address: What if the academy actually mattered? *Academy of Management Review,* 19: 11 – 16.

Hambrick, D. C. 2007. Upper echelons theory: An update. *Academy of Management Review,* 32: 334 – 343.

Hambrick, D. C. and P. A. Mason. 1984. Upper echelons: The organization as a reflection of its top management. *Academy of Management Review,* 9: 193 – 206.

Hamel, J., S. Dufour and D. Fortin. 1993. *Case study methods.* Newbury Park Sage.

Hannan, M. and J. Freeman. 1977. The population ecology of organizations. *American Journal of Sociological Review,* 82: 929 – 964.

Hanssen-Bauer, J. and C. C. Snow. 1996. Responding to hypercompetition: The structure and processes of a regional learning network organization. *Organization Science,* 7: 413 – 427.

Harris, R., D. S. Siegel, and M. Wright. 2005. Assessing the impact of management buyouts on economic efficiency: Plant level evidence from the United Kingdom. *The Review of Economics and Statistics,* 87: 148 – 153.

Hatch, M. J. 2006. *Organization Theory: Modern, symbolic, and postmodern perspective* (2nd ed.). Oxford: Oxford University Press.

Hatum, A. and A. Pettigrew. 2004. Adaptation under environmental turmoil: Organizational flexibility in family-owned firms. *Family Business Review,* 17: 237 – 258.

Hayward, M. L. A., V. P. Rindova, and T. G. Pollock. 2004. Believing one's own press: The causes and consequences of CEO celebrity. *Strategic Management Journal,* 25: 637 – 653.

He, Z. L. and P. K. Wong. 2004. Exploration vs. exploitation: An empirical test of the ambidexterity hypothesis. *Organization Science,* 15: 481 – 494.

Heaton, J. B. 2002. Managerial optimism and corporate finance. *Financial Management,* 31: 33 – 45.

Heckel, M. 2010. Eine Partnerschaft, die ihren Preis hat. *Financial Times Deutschland,* September 21. Retrieved from: http://www.ftd.de

Hehn, M. 2011. *Auswirkungen der Beteiligungen von Private Equity Gesellschaften auf die Governance von Familienunternehmen in Deutschland.* Lohmar: Josef Eul.

Heider, J. and B. Rendner. 2004. *Operations Management* (7th ed.). New Jersey: Pearson.

Hellmann, T. and M. Puri. 2000. The interaction between product market and financing strategy: The role of venture capital. *Review of Financial Studies,* 13: 959 – 984.

Helmich, D. L. and W. B. Brown. 1972. Successor type and organizational change in the corporate enterprise. *Administrative Science Quarterly,* 17: 371 – 381.

Henderson, A. D. and I. Stern. 2004. Selection-based learning: The coevolution of internal and external selection in high-velocity environments. *Administrative Science Quarterly,* 49: 39 – 75.

Herriott, R. E. and W. A. Firestone. 1983. Multisite qualitative policy research: Optimizing description and generalizability. *Educational Researcher,* 12: 14 – 19.

Herzberg, F. 1959. *The motivation to work.* New York: John Wiley and Sons.

Hiennerth, C. and A. Kessler. 2006. Measuring success in family businesses: The concept of configurational fit. *Family Business Review,* 19: 115 – 134.

Hodgkinson, G. P., P. Herriot, and N. Anderson. 2001. Realigning the stakeholders in management research: Lessons from industrial, work and organizational psychology. *British Journal of Management,* 12: 41 - 48.

Hodgson, G. 2002. Darwinism in economics: From analogy to ontology. *Journal of Evolutionary Economics,* 12: 259 - 281.

Höppner, D. 2008. Private-Equity-Landschaft 2008: Fruchtbares Land oder verbrannte Erde? In Handelsblatt (Ed.), *Private Equity Handbuch 2008.* Frankfurt am Main: Verlag für Wirtschaftsinformationen

Ho T.-H. and K. Weigelt. 2005. Trust building among strangers. *Management Science,* 51: 519 - 530.

Hoerster, N. 2010. *Was können wir wissen?* München: Beck.

Hofstede, G. H. and G. J. Hofstede. 2005. *Cultures and organizations: Software of the mind* (2nd ed.). New York: McGraw-Hill.

Holan, P. M. and N. Phillips. 2004. Remembrance of things past? The dynamics of organizational forgetting. *Management Science,* 50: 1603 - 1613.

Holderness, C. G. and D. P. Sheehan. 1988. The role of majority shareholders in publicly held corporations. *Journal of Financial Economics,* 20: 317 - 346.

Howard-Grenville, J. A. 2005. The persistence of flexible organizational routines: The role of agency and organizational context. *Organization Science,* 16: 618 - 636.

Howorth, C., P. Westhead, and M. Wright. 2004. Buyouts, information asymmetry and the family management dyad. *Journal of Business Venturing,* 19: 509 - 534.

Howorth, C., M. Wright, and P. Westhead. 2008. *Succession, professionalization and the staying power of "familiness": A longitudinal study of management buyouts of family firms.* Working Paper, Nottingham University.

Huber, G. P. 1991. Organizational learning: The contributing processes and the literatures. *Organization Science,* 2: 88 - 115.

Huff, A. S. 1999. *Writing for scholarly publication.* Thousand Oaks, CA: Sage.

Hult, G. T. M. and D. J. Ketchen. 2001. Does market orientation matter? A test of the relationship between positional advantage and performance. *Strategic Management Journal,* 22: 899 - 906.

Hult, G. T. M., D. J. Ketchen, and S. F. Slater. 2005. Market orientation and performance: An integration of disparate approaches. *Strategic Management Journal,* 26: 1173 - 1181.

Hunter, J. E. and F. L. Schmidt. 2004. *Methods of meta-analysis: Correcting error and bias in research findings* (2nd ed.). Thousand Oaks, CA: Sage.

Huntington, S.P. 1996. *The clash of civilizations and the remaking of world order.* New York: Simon and Schuster.

Huy, Q. N. 2002. Emotional balancing of organizational continuity and radical change: The contribution of middle managers. *Administrative Science Quarterly,* 47: 31 - 69.

Huydts, H. J. 1992. *Management Buyout als strategische Option zur Regelung der Nachfolge in mittelgroßen Familienunternehmen.* Frankfurt am Main: Broenners.

IFERA. 2003. Quality research guidelines. *Family Business Review,* 16: 109 - 111.

Ilinitch, A. Y., R. A. D'Aveni, and A. Y. Lewin. 1996. New organizational forms and strategies for managing in hypercompetitive environments. *Organization Science,* 7: 211 - 220.

Ireland, R. D., M. A. Hitt, R. A. Bettis, and D. A. de Porras. 1987. Strategy formulation processes: Differences in perceptions of strength and weaknesses indicators and environmental uncertainty by managerial level. *Strategic Management Journal,* 8: 469 – 485.

Jackson, N. and P. Carter. 1991. In defence of paradigm incommensurability. *Organization Studies,* 12: 109 – 127.

James, C. and U. Connolly. 2000. *Effective change in schools.* London: RoutledgeFalmer.

Jansen, J. J. P., G. George, F. A. J. van den Bosch, and H. W. Volberda. 2008. Senior team attributes and organizational ambidexterity: The moderating role of transformational leadership. *Journal of Management Studies,* 45: 982 – 1007.

Jansen, J. J. P., F. A. J. Van den Bosch, and H. W. Volberda. 2005. Exploratory innovation, exploitative innovation, and ambidexterity: The impact of environmental and organizational antecedents. *Schmalenbach Business Review,* 57: 351 – 363.

Jansen, J. J. P., F. A. J. Van den Bosch, and H. W. Volberda. 2006. Exploratory innovation, exploitative innovation, and performance: Effects of organizational antecedents and environmental moderators. *Management Science,* 52: 1661 – 1674.

Jansen, K. J. 2004. From persistence to pursuit: A longitudinal examination of momentum during early stages of strategic change. *Organization Science,* 15: 276 – 294.

Jaspers, F. and J. Van den Ende. 2006. The organizational form of vertical relations: dimensions of integration. *Industrial Marketing Management,* 35: 819 – 828.

Jauch, L. R., R. N. Osborn, and T. N. Martin. 1980. Structured content analysis of cases: A complementary method for organizational research. *Academy of Management Review,* 5: 517 – 525.

Jauch, L. R. and J. L. Wall. 1989. What they do when they get your manuscript: A survey of academy of management reviewer practices. *Academy of Management Journal,* 32: 157 – 173.

Jensen, M.C. 1968. The performance of mutual funds in the period 1945 – 1964. *Journal of Finance,* 23: 389 – 416.

Jensen, M. C. 1986. Agency costs of free cash flows, corporate finance, and takeovers. *American Economic Review,* 76: 323 – 329.

Jensen, M. C. 1989. Eclipse of the public corporation. *Harvard Business Review,* 67: 61 – 74.

Jensen, M. C. and W. H. Meckling. 1976. Theory of a firm: managerial behavior, agency costs, and ownership structure. *Journal of Financial Economics,* 3: 305 – 360.

Jensen, S. 1999. *Erkenntnis, Konstruktivismus, Systemtheorie.* Wiesbaden: Verlag für Sozialwissenschaften.

Jick, T. D. 1979. Mixing qualitative and quantitative methods: Triangulation in action. *Administrative Science Quarterly,* 24: 602 – 611.

Johns, G. 2006. The essential impact of context on organizational behavior. *Academy of Management Review,* 31: 386 – 408.

Jones, G.R. 1983. Transaction costs, property rights, and organizational culture: An exchange perspective. *Administrative Science Quarterly,* 28: 454 – 467.

Jones, S. 1985. Depth interviewing. In R. Walker (Ed.), *Applied Qualitative Research.* Aldershot: Gower.

Kahneman, D. and A. Tversky. 1972. Subjective probability: A judgement of representativeness. *Cognitive Psychology,* 3: 430 – 454.

Kaplan, A. 1964. *The conduct of inquiry.* San Francisco: Chandler.

Kaplan, B. and D. Duchon. 1988. Combining qualitative and quantitative methods in information systems research: A case study. *MIS Quarterly,* 12: 571 – 586.

Kaplan, R. S. and D. P. Norton. 1992. The Balanced Scorecard: Measures that drive performance. *Harvard Business Review*, January-February: 71 – 80.

Kaplan, R. S. and D. P. Norton. 1993. Putting the Balanced Scorecard to work. *Harvard Business Review*, September-October: 2 – 16.

Kaplan, S. and R. Henderson. 2005. Inertia and incentives: Bridging organizational economics and organizational theory. *Organization Science*, 16: 509 – 521.

Kaplan, S.N. 1989. The effects of management buyouts on operating performance and value. *Journal of Financial Economics*, 24: 217 – 254.

Kaplan, S. N. and A. Schoar. 2005. Private Equity performance: Returns, persistence, and capital flows. *Journal of Finance*, 60: 1791 – 1823.

Kaplan, S.N. and P. Strömberg. 2009. Leveraged buyouts and private equity. *Journal of Economic Perspectives*, 22: 121 – 146.

Karra, N., P. Tracey, and N. Phillips. 2006. Altruism and agency in the family firm: Exploring the role of family, kinship, and ethnicity. *Entrepreneurship: Theory and Practice*, 30: 861 – 877.

Kaserer, C., A. K. Achleitner, C. von Einem, and D. Schiereck. 2007. *Private Equity in Deutschland – Rahmenbedingungen, ökonomische Bedeutung und Handlungsempfehlungen*. Norderstedt: Books on Demand.

Katila, R. and G. Ahuja. 2002. Something old, something new: A longitudinal study of search behavior and new product introduction. *Academy of Management Journal*, 45: 1183 – 1194.

Kaufman, A. and E. Englander. 1993. Kohlberg, Kravis, Roberts & Co. and the restructuring of American Capitalism. *Business History Review*, 67: 52 – 97.

Kelly, L., N. Athanassiou, and W. Crittenden. 2000. Founder centrality and strategic behavior in the family-owned firm. *Entrepreneurship: Theory and Practice*, 25: 27 – 42.

Kennedy, M. M. 1976. Generalizing from single case studies. *Evaluation Quarterly*, 3: 661 – 678.

Kets de Vries, M. 1993. The dynamics of family controlled firms: The good news and the bad news. *Organizational Dynamics*, 21: 59 – 68.

Kimberly, J. R. and R. H. Miles. 1980. *The organizational life cycle*. San Francisco: Jossey Bass.

Kirby, D. A. and T. M. Lee. 1996. Succession management in family firms in the North East of England. *Family Business Review*, 9: 75 – 85.

Kirca, A. H., S. Jayachandran, and W. O. Bearden. 2005. Market orientation: A meta-analytic review and assessment of its antecedents and impact on performance. *Journal of Marketing*, 69: 24 – 41.

Klein, K. J., F. Dansereau, and R. J. Hall. Level issues in theory development, data collection, and analysis. *Academy of Management Review*, 19: 195 – 229.

Klein, S. B. 2000. Family businesses in Germany: Significance and structure. *Family Business Review*, 13: 157 – 182.

Klein, S. B. 2010. *Familienunternehmen: Theoretische und empirische Grundlagen* (3rd. ed.). Lohmar: Josef Eul.

Klein, S. B., J. H. Astrachan, and K. X. Smyrnios. 2005. The F-PEC scale of family influence: Construction, validation, and further implication for theory. *Entrepreneurship: Theory and Practice*, 29: 321 – 329.

Klier, D. O., M. K. Welge, and K. R. Harrigan. 2009. The changing face of private equity:

How modern private equity firms manage investment portfolios. *Journal of Private Equity,* 12: 7 – 13.

Klöckner, O. 2008. Buy-outs/ins in family firms – A statistical overview. In L. Scholes , R. Ball, C. Howorth, O. Klöckner, P. Westhead, A. Burrows, and M. Wright (Eds.), *Private equity in family firms – A report on private equity investments in family firms across Europe.* Nottingham: Centre for Management Buyout Research.

Klöckner, O. 2009. *Buy-outs in family businesses.* Wiesbaden: Gabler.

Kocka, J. 1982. Familie, Unternehmer und Kapitalismus. In H. Reif (Ed.), *Die Familie in der Geschichte.* Göttingen: Vandenhoeck & Ruprecht.

Koene, B. A. S., A. L. W. Vogelaar, and J. L. Soeters. 2002. Leaderhsip effects of organizational climate and financial performance: Local leadership effect in chain organization. *Leadership Quarterly,* 13: 193 – 215.

Kolbeck, C. and R. Wimmer. 2002. *Finanzierung für den Mittelstand: Trends, Unternehmensrating, Praxisfälle.* Wiesbaden: Gabler.

Kortum, S. and J. Lerner. 2000. Assessing the contribution of venture capital to innovation. *RAND Journal of Economics,* 31: 674 – 692.

Kotter, J. P. 1995. The new rules: *How to succeed in today's post-corporate world.* New York: Free Press.

Kotter, J. P. 1996. *Leading change.* Boston: Harvard Business School.

Kotter, J. P. 2007. Leading change. *Harvard Business Review. Special Issue: The test of a leader:* 96 – 103.

Kozlowski, S. W. J. and K. J. Klein. 2000. *Multilevel theory, research, and methods in organizations.* San Francisco: Jossey-Bass.

Kuhn, T. S. 1962. *The structure of scientific revolutions.* Chicago: University of Chicago Press.

Kvale, S. 1996. The 1,000-Page question. *Qualitative Inquiry,* 2: 275 – 284.

LaChapelle, K. and L. B. Barnes. 1998. The trust catalyst in family-owned businesses. *Family Business Review,* 11: 1 – 17.

Lahr, H. and F. T. Herschke. 2009. Organizational forms and risk of listed private equity. *Journal of Private Equity,* 13: 89 – 99.

Lamnek, S. 2005. *Qualitative Sozialforschung* (4th ed.). Weinheim und Basel: Beltz.

Lansberg, I. and J. Astrachan. 1994. Influence of family relationships on succession planning and training: The importance of mediating factors. *Family Business Review,* 7: 39 – 59.

Lansberg, I. 1988. The succession conspiracy. *Family Business Review,* 1: 119 – 143.

Lansberg, I., E. L. Perrow, and S. Rogolsky. 1988. Family business as an emerging field. *Family Business Review,* 1: 1 – 8.

Larsson, R. 1993. Case survey methodology: Quantitative analysis of patterns across case studies. *Academy of Management Journal,* 36: 1515 – 1546.

Lavie, D. and L. Rosenkopf. 2006. Balancing exploration and exploitation in alliance formulation. *Academy of Management Journal,* 49: 797 – 818.

Lawrence, P. R. and J. W. Lorsch. 1967. *Organization and environment: Managing differentiation and integration.* Boston: Harvard Business School Press.

Lee, A.S. 1989. A scientific methodology for MIS case studies. *MIS Quarterly,* 13: 33 – 50.

Lee, A.S. 1991. Integrating positivist and interpretative approaches to organizational research. *Organization Science,* 2: 342 – 365.

Lee, T.L., T.R. Mitchell, and C.J.Sablynski. 1999. Qualitative research in organizational and vocational psychology: 1979 – 1999. *Journal of Vocational Behavior*, 55: 161 – 187.

Lee, J. 2006. Family firm performance: Further evidence. *Family Business Review*, 19: 103 – 114.

Leendertse, J. 2009. Unternehmen finden Alternativen zur Hausbank. *Wirtschaftswoche*, April 16. Retrieved from: http://www.wiwo.de

Leonard-Barton, D. 1990. A dual methodology for case studies: Synergistic use of longitudinal single site studies with replicated multiple sites. *Organization Science*, 1: 248 – 266.

Lerner, J., M. Sorensen, and P. Strömberg. 2008. *Private Equity and long-run investment: The case of innovation.* Working Paper, Harvard University.

Levine, H. G. 1985. Principles of data storage and retrieval for use in qualitative evaluations. *Educational Evaluation and Policy Analysis*, 7: 169 – 186.

Levinthal, D. A. 1991. Organizational adaptation and environmental selection – interrelated processes of change. *Organization Science*, 2: 140 – 145.

Levinthal, D. A. and J. G. March. 1993. The myopia of learning. *Strategic Management Journal*, 14: 95 – 112.

Levinthal, D. A. and J. Myatt. 1994. Co-evolution of capabilities and industry: The evolution of mutual fund processing. *Strategic Management Journal*, 15: 45 – 62.

Levitt, B. and J. G. March. 1988. Organizational learning. In J. Hagan and K. S. Cook (Eds.), *Annual review of sociology.* Palo Alto: Annual Reviews.

Lewin, K. 1947. Frontiers in group dynamics: concept, method, and reality in social science. *Human Relations*, 1: 5 – 42.

Lewin, K. 1952. Field theory in social science: Selected theoretical papers by Kurt Lewin. London: Tavistock.

Lewin, A. and C. Wolf. 1974. When the CEO must go. *Advanced Management Journal*, 39: 59 – 62.

Lewin, A. Y., C.P. Long and T.N. Carroll. 1999. The coevolution of new organizational forms. *Organization Science*, 10: 535 – 550.

Lewin, A. Y. and H. W. Volberda. 1999. Prolegomena on coevolution: A framework for research on strategy and new organizational forms. *Organization Science*, 10: 519 – 534.

Lewins, A. and C. Silver. 2007. *Using software in qualitative research: A step-by-step guide.* Los Angeles: Sage.

Lewis, M. W. 2000. Exploring paradox: Toward a more comprehensive guide. *Academy of Management Review*, 25: 760 – 776.

Lichtenberg, F. and D. S. Siegel. 1990. The effects of leveraged buyouts on productivity and related aspects of firm behavior. *Journal of Financial Economics*, 27: 165 – 194.

Liebhold, R. and R. Trinczek. 2009. Experteninterview. In P. Strodtholz, A. Taffertshofer, and S. Kühl (Eds.), *Handbuch Methoden der Organisationsforschung.* Wiesbaden: Verlag für Sozialwissenschaften.

Lincoln, Y. S. and E. G. Guba. 1985. *Naturalistic inquiry.* Newbury Park: Sage.

Lindell, M. K. and J. A. Drexler. 1974. Issues in using survey methods for measuring organizational change. *Academy of Management Review*, 4: 13 – 19.

Lindsey, D. 1978. *The scientific publication system in social science.* San Francisco: Jossey-Bass.

Lindsey, D. H., D. J. Brass, and J.B. Thomas. 1995. Efficay-performance spirals: A multi-level perspective. *Academy of Management Review,* 20: 645 – 678.

Littunen, H. and K. Hyrsky. 2000. The early entrepreneurial stage in Finnish family and nonfamily firms. *Family Business Review,*14: 41 – 54.

Litz, R. A. 2008. Two sides of a one-sided phenomenon: Conceptualizing the family business and business family as a Möbius strip. *Family Business Review,* 21: 217 – 236.

Ljungqvist, A. and M. P. Richardson. 2003. The investment behavior of Private Equity fund managers. Working Paper, University of New York.

Lounsbury, M. and M. J. Ventresca. 2002. *Social structure and organizations revisited: Research in the sociology of organizations.* Amsterdam: Elsevier.

Lovas, B. and S. Ghoshal. 2000. Strategy as a guided evolution. *Strategic Management Journal,* 21: 875 – 896.

Lubatkin, M. H., Z. Simsek, Y. Ling, and J. F. Veiga. 2006. Ambidexterity and performance in small- to-medium-sized firms: The pivotal role of top management team behavioral integretation. *Journal of Management,* 32: 646 – 672.

Lussier, R. N. and M. C. Sonfield. 2004. Family business management activities, styles, and characteristics: A correlational study. *Mid-American Journal of Business,* 19: 47 – 53.

Maier, A. 2010. Hello again. *Financial Times Deutschland,* August 05. Retrieved from: http://www.ftd.de

Maier, A. 2011. Firmenjäger auf Beutezug in Deutschland. *Financial Times Deutschland,* March 01. Retrieved from: http://www.ftd.de

Malmendier, U. and G. Tate. 2005. CEO overconfidence and corporate investment. *Journal of Finance,* 60: 2661 – 2700

Manchot, P. 2009. *Secondary buyouts: Eine empirische Untersuchung von Werttreibern.* Wiesbaden: Gabler.

Manski, C. F. 1989. Anatomy of the selection problem. *Journal of Human Resources,* 24: 343 – 360.

March, J. C. and J. G. March. 1977. Almost random careers: The Wisconsin school superintendency. *Administrative Science Quarterly,* 22: 377 – 409.

March, J. G. 1991. Exploration and exploitation in organizational learning. *Organization Science,* 2: 71 – 87.

March, J. G., L. S. Sproull, and M. Tamuz. 1991. Learning from samples of one or fewer. *Organization Science,* 2: 1 – 13.

March, J. G. and R. I. Sutton. 1997. Organizational performance as a dependent variable. *Organization Science,* 8: 698 – 706.

Marek, D. 2010. *Unternehmensentwicklung verstehen und gestalten: Eine Einführung.* Wiesbaden: Gabler.

Markman, G., D. Siegel, and M. Wright. 2008. Research and technology commercialization. *Journal of Management Studies,* 45: 1401 – 1423.

Marshak, R. J. 1993. Lewin meets Confucius: a review of the OD models of change. *Journal of Applied Behavioral Science,* 29: 393 – 415.

Marshal, C. and G. B. Rossman. 2010. *Designing qualitative research* (5th ed.). Thousand Oaks, CA: Sage.

Martinez, I. J., B. S. Stöhr, and B. F. Quiroga. 2007. Family ownership and firm performance: Evidence from public companies in Chile. *Family Business Review,* 20: 83 – 94.

Masulis, R. W. and R. S. Thomas. 2009. Does private equity create wealth? The effects of private equity and derivatives on corporate governance. *The University of Chicago Law Review,* 76: 219 – 259.

Maxwell, J. A. 2005. *Qualitative research design: An interactive approach* (2nd ed.). Thousand Oaks, CA : Sage.

Maxwell, J. A. 2004. Causal explanation, qualitative research, and scientific inquiry in education. *Educational Researcher,* 33: 3 – 11.

Mayring, P. 2002. *Einführung in die qualitative Sozialforschung* (5th ed.). Weinheim und Basel: Beltz.

Mayring, P. 2010. *Qualitative Inhaltsanalyse: Grundlagen und Techniken* (11th ed.). Weinheim und Basel: Beltz.

McConaughy, D., C. Matthews, and A. Fialko. 2001. Founding family controlled firms: Performance, risk and value. *Journal of Small Business Management,* 39: 31 – 49

McEvily, B., V. Perrone, and A. Zaheer. 2003. Trust as an organizing principle. *Organization Science,* 14: 91 – 103.

McKelvey, B. 1997. Quasi-natural organization science. *Organization Science,* 8: 352 – 380.

McKinsey & Company. 2010. *Farewell to cheap money? The implications of long-term shifts in global investment and saving.* Retrieved from: http://www.mckinsey.com

McNamara, G., P. M. Vaaler, and C. Devers. 2003. Same as it ever was: The search for evidence of increasing hypercompetition. *Strategic Management Journal,* 24: 261 – 278.

Meredith, J. 2002. Introduction to the special issue: Case study and field research. *Journal of Operations Management,* 20: 415 – 417.

Metrick, A. and A. Yasuda. 2010. Economics of private equity funds. *Review of Financial Studies,* 23: 2303 – 2341.

Meyer, A. D., J. B. Goes, and G. R. Brooks. 1993. Organizations reacting to hyperturbulence. In G. P. Hubner and W. H. Glick (Eds.), *Organizational change and redesign.* New York: Oxford University Press.

Midgley, G. 1995. The nature of critical self-reflection. *Journal of Operational Research Society,* 46: 547 – 548.

Miles, M. B. 1979. Qualitative data as an attractive nuisance: The problem of analysis. *Administrative Science Quarterly,* 24: 590 – 601.

Miles, M. B. 1990. New methods for qualitative data collection and analysis. *Qualitative Studies in Education,* 3: 37 – 51.

Miles, M. B. and A. M. Huberman. 1994. *Qualitative Data Analysis* (2nd ed.). Thousand Oaks, CA: Sage.

Miles, R. E. and C. C. Snow. 1978. *Organizational strategy, structure, and process.* New York: McGraw Hill.

Miller, C. C., L. M. Burke, and W. H. Glick. 1998. Cognitive diversity among upper echelon executives: Implications for the strategic decision process. *Strategic Management Journal,* 19: 39 – 58.

Miller, D. 1982. Evolution and revolution: A quantum view of structural change in organizations. *Journal of Management* , 19: 131 – 151.

Miller, D. and I. Le Breton-Miller. 2005. *Managing for the long rung: Lessons in competitive advantage from great family businesses.* Boston: Harvard Business School Press.

Miller, D., and I. Le Breton-Miller. 2006. Family governance and firm performance: Agency, stewardship, and capabilities. *Family Business Review,* 19: 73 – 87.

Miller, K. D. 2002. Knowledge inventories and managerial myopia. *Strategic Management Journal*, 23: 689 – 706.

Miller, W. L. and B. F. Crabtree. 1999. *Doing qualitative research* (2nd ed.). Thousand Oaks, CA: Sage.

Minichiello, V., R. Aroni, E. Timewell, and L. Alexander. 1990. *In-depth interviewing: Researching people.* Melbourne: Longman Cheshire.

Minichilli, A., G. Corbetta, and I. C. MacMillan. 2009. Top management teams in family controlled companies: 'Familiness', 'faultiness', and their impact on financial performance. *Journal of Management Studies*, 47: 205 – 222.

Mintzberg, H. 1978. Patterns in strategy formulation. *Management Science*, 24: 934 – 948.

Mintzberg, H. 1979. An emerging strategy of "direct" research. *Administrative Science Quarterly*, 24: 580 – 589.

Mintzberg, H. 1985. Of strategies: Deliberate and emergent. *Strategic Management Journal*, 6: 257 – 272.

Mintzberg, H. and A. McHugh. 1985. Strategy formation in adhocracy. *Administrative Science Quarterly*, 30: 160 – 197.

Mintzberg, H. and J. A. Waters. 1982. Tracking strategy in an entrepreneurial firm. *Academy of Management Journal*, 25: 465 – 499.

Mintzberg, H. and F. Westley. 1992. Cycles of organizational change. *Strategic Management Journal*, 13: 39 – 59.

Mir, R. and A. Watson. 2001. Critical realism and constructivism in strategy research: Toward a synthesis. *Strategic Management Journal*, 22: 1169 – 1173.

Mitroff, I. I. and R. H. Kilmann. 1975. Stories managers tell: A new tool for organizational problem solving. *Management Review*, 64: 18 – 28.

Modigiliani, F. and M. Miller. 1958. The cost of capital, corporate finance, and the theory of investments. *American Review*, 48: 261 – 297.

Mohr, L. B. 1982. *Explaining organzational behavior.* San Francisco: Jossey-Bass.

Mom, T. J. M., F. A. J. van den Bosch, and H. W. Volberda. 2007. Investigating managers' exploration and exploitation activities: The influence of top-down, bottom-up, and horizontal knowledge inflows. *Journal of Management Studies*, 44: 910 – 931.

Mom, T. J. M., F. A. J. van den Bosch, and H. W. Volberda. 2009. Understanding variation in managers' ambidexterity: Investigating direct and interaction effects of formal structure and personal coordination mechanisms. *Organization Science*, 20: 812 – 828.

Moorman, C. and A. S. Miner. 1998. Organizational improvisation and organizational memory. *Academy of Management Review*, 23: 698 – 723.

Morgeson, F. P. and D. A. Hofmann. 1999. The structure and function of collective constructs: Implications for multilevel research and theory development. *Academy of Management Review*, 24: 249 – 265.

Morris, L. L., C. T. Fitz-Gibbon, and M. E. Freeman. 1987. *How to communicate evaluation findings.* Thousand Oaks, CA: Sage.

Mowday, R. T. 1997. The quest for relevance: "Down, Simba, down". *Journal of Management Inquiry*, 6: 27 – 30.

Mowday, R. T. and R. I. Sutton. 1993. Organizational behavior: Linking individuals and groups to organizational contexts. *Annual Review of Psychology*, 44: 195 – 229.

Müntefering, F. 2004. *Freiheit und Verantwortung.* Retrieved from: http://www.franz muentefering.de

Myers, I. B. and K. C. Briggs. 1962. *The Myers-Briggs type indicator.* Princeton: Educational Testing Service.

Myers, S. C. and N. S. Majluf. Corporate financing and investment decisions when firms have information that investors do not have. *Journal of Financial Economics,* 13: 187 – 221.

Nadkarni, S. and P. S. Barr. 2008. Environmental context, managerial cognition, and strategic action: An integrated view. *Strategic Management Journal,* 29: 1395 – 1427.

Nag, R., D. C. Hambrick, and M.-J. Chen. 2007. What is strategic management really? Inductive derivation of a consensus definition of the field. *Strategic Management Journal,* 28: 935 – 955.

Nagl, H. G. 2009a. Das Ende der Private Equity-Party. *Handelsblatt,* February 03. Retrieved from: http://www.handelsblatt.de

Nagl. H. G. 2009b. Private Equity greift nach dem Mittelstand. *Handelsblatt,* September 29. Retrieved from: http://www.handelsblatt.de

Nicholson, N. 2008. Evolutionary psychology and family business: A new synthesis for theory, research, and practice. *Family Business Review,* Vol. 21: 103 – 118.

Nicolai, A. T. 2004. The bridge to the "real world": Applied Science or a "Schizophrenic Tour de Force"? *Journal of Management Studies,* 41: 951 – 976.

Numagami, T. 1998. The infeasibility of invariant laws in management studies: A reflective dialogue in defense of case studies. *Organization Science,* 9: 2 – 15.

O'Connor, E. S. 1995. Paradoxes of participation: textural analysis and organizational changes. *Organizational Studies,* 16: 769 – 803.

Odean, T. 1998. Are investors reluctant to realize their losses? *Journal of Financial Economics,* 53: 1775 – 1798.

Ofek, E. 1994. Efficiency gains in unsuccessful management buyouts. *Journal of Finance,* 49: 637 – 654.

Olson, P. D., V. S. Zuiker, S. M. Danes, K. Stafford, R. K. Z. Heck, and K. A. Duncan. 2003. Impact of family and business on family business sustainability. *Journal of Business Venturing,* 18: 639 – 666.

O'Reilly, C. A. and M. L. Tushman. 2004. The ambidextrous organization. *Harvard Business Review,* 82: 74 – 81.

O'Reilly, C. A. and M. L. Tushman. 2008. Ambidexterity as a dynamic capability: Resolving the innovator's dilemma. *Research in Organizational Behavior,* 28: 185 – 206.

Orlikowski, W. J. 1996. Improving organizational transformation overtime: a situated change perspective. *Information Systems Research,* 7: 63 – 92.

Palmer, D. 2006. Taking stock of the criteria we use to evaluate one another's work: ASQ 50 years out. *Administrative Science Quarterly,* 51: 535 – 559.

Papadakis, V. M., S. Lioukas, and D. Chambers. 1998. Strategic decision-making processes: The role of management and context. *Strategic Management Journal,* 19: 115 – 147.

Papendick, U. 2004. Private Equity: Retter oder Räuber? *Manager Magazin,* October 11. Retrieved from: http://www.manager-magazin.de

Payne, P. 1983. Family business in Britain: An historical and analytical survey. In A. Okochi and S. Yasuoko (Eds.), *Family business in the era of industrial growth: Proceedings of the Fuji international conference on business history.* Tokyo: University of Tokyo Press.

Penn, P. 1983. Zirkuläres Fragen. *Familiendynamik,* 8: 198 – 220.

Pentland, B. T. 1999. Building process theory with narrative: From description to explanation. *Academy of Management Review,* 24: 711 – 724.

Peretti, F. and G. Negro. 2006. Filling empty seats: How status and organizational hierarchies affect exploration versus exploitation in team design. *Academy of Management Journal,* 49: 759 – 777.

Pettigrew, A. M. 1990. Longitudinal field research on change: Theory and practice. *Organization Science,* 1: 267 – 292.

Pettigrew, A. M. 1988. Researching strategic change. *The management of strategic change.* Oxford: Blackwell.

Pettigrew, A. M., R. W. Woodman, and K. S. Cameron. 2001. Studying organizational change and development: Challenges for future research. *Academy of Management Journal,* 44: 697 – 713.

Pfeffer, T. 2004. *Das "zirkuläre Fragen" als Forschungsmethode zur Luhmannschen Systemtheorie* (2nd ed.). Heidelberg: Carl-Auer.

Phalippou, L. 2007. *Investing in Private Equity funds: A survey.* Working Paper, University of Amsterdam.

Phalippou, L. and O. Gottschalg. 2009. The performance of private equity funds. *Review of Financial Studies,* 22: 1747 – 1776.

Pieper, T. M. and S. B. Klein. 2007. The bulleye: A systems approach to modeling family firms. *Family Business Review,* 20: 301 – 319.

Pierce, J. L. and A. L. Delbecq. 1977. Organization structure, individual attitude, and innovation. *Academy of Management Review,* 2: 27 – 37.

Plous, S. 1993. *The psychology of judgement and decision-making.* New York: McGraw Hill.

Poech, A., A. K. Achleitner, and M. Burger-Calderon. 2005. Private Equity in Familienunternehmen: Eine empirische Untersuchung zu psychologischen Aspekten der Transaktionsentscheidung. *Finanzbetrieb,* 5: 289 – 295.

Poland, B. D. 1995. Transcription quality as an aspect for rigor in qualitative research. *Qualitative Inquiry,* 1: 290 – 310.

Pollit, C. 1999. *Integrating financial management and performance management.* OECD: Paris.

Popov, A. and P. Roosenboom. 2009. Does Private Equity investment spur innovation? Evidence from Europe. Working Paper, European Central Bank. Retrieved from: http:// www.ecb.europa.eu

Porras, J. I. and R. C. Silvers. 1991. Organizational development and transformation. *Annual Review of Psychology,* 42: 51 – 78.

Porter, M. E. 1980. *Competitive strategy: Techniques for analyzing industries and competitors.* New York: Free Press.

Porter, M. E. 1985. *Competitive advantage: Creating and sustaining performance.* New York: Free Press.

Porter, M. E. 1991. Toward a dynamic theory of strategy. *Strategic Management Journal,* 12: 95 – 117.

Porter, M. E. 1998. Clusters and the new economics of competition. *Harvard Business Review,* November-December: 77 – 90.

Poutziouris, P. Z. 2001. The views of family companies on venture capital: Empirical evidence from the UK small medium-size enterprising economy. *Family Business Review,* 14: 277 – 291.

Pugh, D. S., D. J. Hickson, C. R. Hinings and C. Turner. 1968. Dimensions of organization structure. *Administrative Science Quarterly,* 13: 65 – 105.

Punch, K. F. 2006. *Introduction to social research: Quantitative and qualitative approaches.* Thousand Oaks, CA: Sage.

Purser, R. E., A. C. Bluedorn, and J. Petranker. 2005. The times of cause and flow in organizational change. In R.W. Woodman and W.A. Pasmore (Eds.), *Research in organization change and development.* Oxford: Elsevier.

Prahalad, C. K. and G. Hamel. 1990 The core competence of the corporation. *Harvard Business Review,* May-June: 79 – 91

PricewaterhouseCoopers. 2008. *Familienunternehmen 2008.* Retrieved from: http://www.pwc.de

PricewaterhouseCoopers. 2007. *Chance oder Widerspruch? Beteiliungskapital in deutschen Familienunternehmern: Ergebnisse einer Befragung von Gesellschaftern und Entscheidungsträgern.* Retrieved from: http://www.pwc.de

Prym, C. A. M. 2010. *Private Equity in Familienunternehmen: Eine empirische Fallstudienuntersuchung von Unternehmenswertsteigerungen bei Private-Equity Beteiligungen und die Rolle von nicht-monetären Zielen der Unternehmensfamilie im Beteiligungskontext.* Unpublished doctoral dissertation, University of Witten/ Herdecke.

Quinn, R. E. and K. Cameron. 1983. Organizational life cycles and shifting criteria of effectiveness: Some preliminary evidence. *Management Science,* 29: 33 – 51.

Quinn, R. E. and J. Rohrbaugh. 1983. A spatial model of effectiveness criteria: Toward a competing values approach to organizational analysis. *Management Science,* 29: 363 – 377.

Quinn, R. W. and J. E. Dutton. 2004. Coordination as energy-in-conversation. *Academy of Management Review,* 30: 36 – 57.

Ragin, C. C. 1987. *The comparative method: Moving beyond qualitative and quantitative strategies.* Berkerly: University of California Press.

Raina, V. 2009. Private Equity's future in a deleveraging world. *Bloomberg Businessweek,* March 24. Retrieved from: http://www.businessweek.com

Raisch, S. and J. Birkinshaw. 2008. Organizational ambidexterity: Antecedents, outcomes, and moderators. *Journal of Management,* 34: 375 – 409.

Raisch, S., J. Birkinshaw, G. Probst, and M. L. Tushman. 2009. Organizational ambidexterity: Balancing exploitation and exploration for sustained performance. *Organization Science,* 20: 685 – 695.

Reichenbach, B. R. 2001. *Introduction to critical thinking.* New York: McGraw-Hill.

Reimers, N. 2004. *Private Equity für Familienunternehmen.* Wiesbaden: Gabler.

Richardson, L. 1990. *Writing strategies: Reaching diverse audiences* Newbury Park: Sage.

Riegel, K. F. 1975. From traits and equilibrium toward development dialectics. In J. Cole and W.S. Arnold (Eds.), *Nebraska symposium on motivation.* Lincoln: University of Nebraska Press.

Robbins, M. 2009. 'Half of private equity firms' are ignoring transparency guidelines. *The Independen,* January 13. Retrieved from: http://www.independent.co.uk

Robbins, S. P. and M. Coulter. 2009. *Management* (9th ed.). Sydney: Prentice Hall.

Roberts, P. W. 2001. Innovation and firm-level persistent profitability: A Schumpeterian framework. *Managerial and Decision Economics*, 22: 239 – 250.

Roberts, P. W 1999. Product innovation, product-market competition and persistent profitability in the U.S. pharmaceutical industry. *Strategic Management Journal*, 20: 655 – 670.

Roland Berger Strategy Consultants. 2011. *European private equity outlook 2011*. Retrieved from: http://www.rolandberger.com

Romanelli, E. and M. L. Tushman. 1986. Inertia, environments, and strategic choice: A quasi experimental design for comparative longitudinal research. *Management Science*, 32: 608 – 621.

Romano, C. A., G. A. Tanewski, and K. X. Smyrnios. 2000. Capital structure decision-making: A model for family business. *Family Business Review*, 16: 285 – 310.

Rothermel, A. and R. Feierfeil. 1990. Zirkuläres Fragen als Methode der systemischen Therapie. Eine qualitative Untersuchung zu diesem Konzept. *Familiendynamik*, 15: 330 – 345.

Rutherford, M. W., D. F. Kuratko, and D. T. Holt. 2008. Examining the link between "familiness" and performance: Can the F-PEC untangle the family business theory jungle. *Entrepreneurship: Theory and Practice*, 32: 1089 – 1109.

Sahlman, W. A. 1990. The structure and governance of venture-capital organizations. *Journal of Financial Economics*, 27: 473 – 521.

Schacter, D. L. 2001. *The seven sins of memory*. New York: Houghton Mifflin.

Schalast, C. and B. Barten. 2008. *Private Equity und Familienunternehmen – eine Untersuchung unter besonderer Berücksichtigung deutscher Maschinen- und Anlagebauunternehmen*. Working Paper, Frankfurt School of Finance.

Schatzman, L. and A. L. Strauss. 1973. *Field Research*. New York: Prentice-Hall.

Schein, E. H. 1992. *Organizational culture and leadership: A dynamic view* (2nd ed.). San Francisco: Jossey-Bass.

Schiepek, G. 2010. Systemische Forschung. *Familiendynamik*, 35: 60 – 70.

Schilit, W. K. 1987. An examination of the influence of middle-level managers in formulating and implementing strategic decisions. *Journal of Management Studies*, 24: 271 – 293.

Schlippe, A. v. 2007. Das Balancieren von Paradoxien in Familienunternehmen – Kultur mit Struktur versöhnen. In K. Rausch (Ed.), *Organisationen gestalten*. Lengerich: Pabst.

Schlippe, A. v., C. Buberti, T. Groth, and M. Plate. 2009. Die zehn Wittener Thesen. In A. v. Schlippe, T. Groth, and T.A. Rüsen (Eds.), *Familienunternehmen: Exploration einer Unternehmensform*. Lohmar: Josef Eul.

Schlippe, A.v., A. Nischak, and M.E. Hachimi. 2008. *Familienunternehmen verstehen: Gründer, Gesellschafter und Generationen*. Göttingen: Vandenhoeck and Ruprecht.

Schnell, R., P.B. Hill, and E. Esser. 1995. *Methoden der empirischen Sozialforschung* (5th ed.). München, Wien: Oldenburg.

Scholes, L., M. Wright, P. Westhead, H. Bruining, and O. Klöckner. 2009. Family-firm buyouts, Private Equity, and strategic change. *Journal of Private Equity*, 12: 7 – 18.

Scholes, L. M., P. Westhead, and A. Burrows. 2008. Family firm succession: The management buy-out and buy-in routes. *Journal of Small Business and Enterprise Development*, 15: 8 – 30.

Scholes, L. M., M. Wright, P. Westhead, A. Burrows, and H. Bruining. 2007. Information sharing, price negotiation and management buy-outs of private family-owned firms. *Small Business Economics*, 29: 329 – 349.

Schulze, W., M. Lubatkin, and R. Dino. 2002. Altruism, agency, and the competitiveness of family firms. *Managerial and Decision Economics*, 23: 247 – 259.

Scott, W. R. 1975. Interreferee agreement on characteristics of manuscripts submitted to the Journal of Personality and Social Psychology. *American Psychologist*, 29: 698 – 702.

Scott, W. R. Reflections on a half-century of organizational sociology. 2004. *Annual Review of Sociology*, 30: 1 – 21.

Seawright, J. and J. Gerring. 2008. Case selection techniques in case study research. *Political Research Quarterly*, 61: 294 – 308.

Seet, P. S., C. Graves, M. Hadji, A. Schnackenberg, and P. Gustafson. 2010. The effect of finance, knowledge and empathy gaps on the use of private equity amongst family owned SMEs. *International Journal of Entrepreneurship and Small Business*, 11: 85 – 104.

Sekaran, U. 2003. *Research methods for business: A skill building approach* (4th ed.). New Jersey: John Wiley and Sons.

Selvini Palazolli, M., L. Boscolo, G. Cecchin and G. Prata. 1981. Hypothesieren – Zirkularität – Neutralität: Drei Richtlinien für den Leiter einer Sitzung. *Familiendynamik*, 6: 123 – 139.

Sharma, P. 2004. An overview of the field of family business studies: Current status and directions for the future. *Family Business Review*, 17: 1 – 36.

Sharma, P., J.J. Chrisman, and J.H. Chua. 1996. *A review and annotated bibliography of family business studies.* Boston: Kluwer.

Sharma, P., J. J. Chrisman, and J. H. Chua. 1997. Strategic management of the family business: Past research and future challenges. *Family Business Review*, 10: 1 – 35.

Sharmpa, P., and M. Nordqvist. 2007. A typology for capturing the heterogeneity of family firms. *Academy of Management Proceedings*, 1 – 6.

Shrivastava, P. 1987. Rigor and practical usefulness of research in strategic management. *Strategic Management Journal*, 8: 77 – 92.

Sidhu, J. S., H. R. Commandeur, and H. W. Volberda. 2007. The multifaceted nature of exploration and exploitation: Value of supply, demand, and spatial search for innovation. *Organization Science*, 18: 20 – 40

Sieber, S. D. 1973. The integration of fieldwork and survey methods. *American Journal of Sociology*, 78: 1335 – 1359.

Siggelkow, N. 2007. Persuasion with case studies. *Academy of Management Journal*, 50: 20 – 24.

Siggelkow, N. and D. A. Levinthal. 2003. Temporarily divide to conquer: Centralized, decentralized, and reinegrated approaches to exploration and adaptation. *Organization Science*, 14: 650 – 669.

Simon, F. B. 2005. *Die Familie das Familienunternehmens: Ein System zwischen Gefühl und Geschäft.* Heidelberg: Carl-Auer.

Simon, F. B. 2007. *Einführung in die systemische Organisationstheorie.* Heidelberg: Carl Auer.

Simon, F. B., R. Wimmer, and T. Groth. 2005. *Mehr-Generationen-Familienunternehmen. Erfolgsgeheimnisse von Oetker, Haniel, Merck u. a.* Heidelberg: Carl-Auer.

Simons, R. 1994. How new top managers use control systems as levers of strategic renewal. *Strategic Management Journal*, 15: 169 – 189.

Simsek, Z. 2009. Organizational ambidexterity: Toward a multilevel understanding. *Journal of Management Studies*, 46: 597 – 624.

Simsek, Z., C. Heavey, J. F. Veiga, and D. Souder. 2009. A typology for aligning organizational ambidexerity's conceptualizations, antecedents, and outcomes. *Journal of Management Studies*, 46: 864 – 894.

Singh, J. V., D. J. Tucker, and A. G. Meinhard. 1986. Organizational change and mortality. *Administrative Science Quarterly*, 31: 587 – 611.

Singleton, R. A. and B. C. Straits. 1999. *Approaches to social research* (3rd ed.). New York and Oxford: Oxford University Press.

Sitkin, S. B., K. M. Sutcliffe and K. E. Weick. 1998. Organizational learning. In R. Dorf (Ed.), *The technology management handbook*. Boca Raton: CRC Press.

Slater, S. F. and J. C. Narver. 1995. Market orientation and the learning orientation. *Journal of Marketing*, 59: 63 – 74.

Slater, S. F. and J. C. Narver. 1999. Market-oriented is more than being cutomer-led. *Strategic Management Journal*, 20: 1165 – 1168.

Sloman, J. 2007. *Essentials of Economics* (4th ed.). Edinburgh: Financial Times / Prentice Hall.

Smircich, L. 1983. Concepts of culture and organizational analysis. *Administrative Science Quarterly*, 28: 339 – 358.

Smith, P. C. and M. Goddard. 2002. Performance management and operational research: A marriage in heaven? *Journal of Operational Research Society*, 53: 247 – 255.

Smith, W. K. and M. W. Lewis. 2011. Toward a theory of paradox: A dynamic equilibrium model of organizing. *Academy of Management Review*, 36: 381 – 403.

Smith, W. K. and M. L. Tushman. 2005. Managing strategic contradictions: A top management model for managing innovation streams. *Organization Science*, 16: 522 – 536.

Snyder, A. W. 2001. Paradox of the savant mind. *Nature*, 413: 251 – 252.

Snyder, A. W. 2003. Savant-like skills exposed in normal people by suppression of the left fronto-temporal lobe. *Journal of Integrative Neuroscience*, 2: 149 – 158.

Sonfield, M. C. and R. N. Lussier. 2004. First-, second-, and third-generation family firms: A comparison. *Family Business Review*, 17: 189 – 202.

Sorenson, O. and T. E. Stuart. 2001. Syndication networks and the spatial distribution of venture capital investments. *American Journal of Sociology*, 106: 1546 – 1588.

Sorenson, R. L. 2000. The contribution of leadership style and practices to family and business success. *Family Business Review*, 13: 183 – 200.

Spradley, J. P. 1980. *Participant observation*. New York: Holt, Rineheart and Winston.

Stake, R. E. 1994. Case Studies. In N.K. Denzin and Y.S. Lincoln (Eds.), *Handbook of qualitative research*. Thousand Oaks, CA: Sage.

Staw, B. M., P. I. McKechnie, and S. M. Puffer. 1983. The justification of organizational performance. *Administrative Science Quarterly*, 28: 582 – 600.

Steier, L. 2001. Family firms, plural forms of governance and the evolving role of trust. *Family Business Review*, 14: 353 – 367.

Stoelhorst, J. W. and A. Huizing. 2006. *Why the adaptation-selection debate is miscontrued: a Darwinian view of organizational change*. Working Paper, University of Amsterdam.

Stokes, D. E. 1997. *Pasteur's quadrant: Basic science and technological innovation.* Washington D.C.: Brookings Institution Press.

Stone, O. (Director). 1987. *Wall Street [DVD].* United States: Twentieth Century Fox.

Strauss, A. and J. Corbin. 1998. *Basics of qualitative research: Techniques and procedures for developing grounded theory.* Thousand Oaks, CA: Sage.

Stuart, I., D. McCutcheon, R. Handfield, R. McLachlin, and D. Samson. 2002. Effective case research in operations management: A process perspective. *Journal of Operations Management*, 20: 419 – 433.

Sundaramurthy, C. 2008. Sustaining trust within family businesses. *Family Business Review*, 21: 89 – 102.

Susman, G. I. and R. D. Evered. 1978. An assessment of the scientific merits of action research. *Administrative Science Quarterly*, 23: 582 – 603.

Sutcliffe, K. M. and G. P. Huber. 1998. Firm and industry as determinants of executive perceptions of the environment. *Strategic Management Journal*, 19: 793 – 807.

Sutton, R. I. 1997. The virtues of closet qualitative research. *Organization Science*, 8: 97 – 106.

Sutton, R. I. and B. M. Staw. 1995. What theory is not. *Administrative Science Quarterly*, 40: 371 – 384.

Swensen, D.F. 2000. *Pioneering portfolio management.* New York: Free Press.

Sydow, J., G. Schreyögg, and J. Koch. 2009. Organizational path dependence: Opening the black box. *Academy of Management Review*, 34: 689 – 709.

Szulanski, G. and S. Winter. 2002. Getting it right the second time. *Harvard Business Review*, 80: 62 – 69.

Tagiuri, R. and J. Davis. 1992. On the goals of successful family companies. *Family Business Review*, 5: 43 – 62.

Tagiuri, R. and J. Davis. 1996. Bivalent attributes of the family firm. *Family Business Review*, 9: 199 – 208.

Tan, W. and T. Fock. 2001. Coping with growth transitions: The case of Chinese family business in Singapore. *Family Business Review*, 14: 123 – 140.

Taylor, A. and C. E. Helfat. 2009. Organizational linkages for surviving technological change: Complementary assets, middle management, and ambidexterity. *Organization Science*, 20: 718 – 739.

Teece, D. J., G. Pisano, and A. Shuen. 1997. Dynamic capabilities and strategic management. *Strategic Management Journal*, 18: 509 – 533.

Tellis, W. 1997. Introduction to case study. *Qualitative Report*, 3: 49 – 61.

Timmons, H. 2006. Private Equity goes public for $5 billion. Its investors ask, 'What's next?' *New York Times*, November 10. Retrieved from: http://www.nytimes.com

Tiwana, A. 2007. Do bridging ties complement strong ties? An empirical examination of alliance ambidexterity. *Strategic Management Journal*, 29: 251 – 272.

Tomm, K. 1987. Das systemische Interview als Intervention: Teil I. Strategisches Vorgehen als vierte Richtlinie für Therapeuten. *System Familie*, 1: 145 – 159.

Trochim, W. 1985. Pattern matching, validity, and conceptualization in program evaluation. *Evaluation Review*, 9: 575 – 604.

Trochim, W. 1989. Outcome pattern matching and program theory. *Evaluation and Program Planning*, 12: 355 – 366.

Tsao, C.-W., S.-J. Chen, C.-H. Lin, and W. Hyde. 2009. Founding-family ownership and firm performance: The role of high-performance work systems. *Family Business Review*, 22: 319 - 322.

Tsoukas, H. and R. Chia. 2002. On organizational becoming: Rethinking organizational change. *Organization Science*, 13: 567 - 582.

Tukey, J. W. 1977. *Exploratory Data Analysis.* Boston: Addison-Wesley.

Tushman, M. L. and C. A. O'Reilly.1996. The ambidextrous organization: managing evolutionary and revolutionary change. *California Management Review*, 38: 1 - 23.

Tushman, M. L. and C. A. O'Reilly. 2007. Research and relevance: Implications of Pasteur's Quadrant for doctoral programs and faculty development. *Academy of Management Journal*, 50: 769 - 774.

Tushman, M.L. and C. A. O'Reilly. 2008. Ambidexterity as a dynamic capability: Resolving the innovator's dilemma. *Research in Organizational Behavior*, 185 - 206.

Tushman, M. L. and E. Romanelli. 1985. Organizational evolution: A metamorphosis model of convergence and reorientation. In B.M. Staw and L.L. Cummings (Eds.), *Research in organizational behavior.* Greenwich: JAI Press.

Tushman, M. L. and L. Rosenkopf. 1992. Organizational determinants of technological change: toward a sociology of technological evolution. *Research in Organizational Behavior*, 14: 311 - 347.

Ughetto, E. 2010. Assessing the contribution to innovation of private equity investors: A study on European buyouts. *Research Policy*, 39: 126 - 140.

Uotila, J., M. Maula, T. Keil, and S. Zahra. 2009. Exploration, exploitation, and financial performance: Analysis of S&P 500 corporations. *Strategic Management Journal*, 30: 221 - 231.

Upton, N. and W. Petty. 2000. Venture capital investment and US family business. *Venture Capital*, 2: 27 - 39.

Useem, M., E. H. Bowmann, and C. W. Irvine. 1996. U.S. institutional investors look at corporate governance in the 1990s. *European Management Journal*, 11: 175 - 189.

Van de Ven, A. H. and M. S. Poole. 1995. Explaining development and change in organizations. *Academy of Management Review*, 20: 510 - 540.

Van de Ven, A. H. 1992. Suggestions for studying strategy processes: A research note. *Strategic Management Journal*, 13: 169 - 188.

Van Maanen, J. 1979. Reclaiming qualitative methods for organizational research: A preface. *Administrative Science Quarterly*, 24: 520 - 526.

Van Maanen, J. 1988. *Tales of the field: On writing ethnography.* Chicago: University of Chicago Press.

Vermeulen, F. 2005. On rigor and relevance: Fostering dialectic progress in management research. *Academy of Management Journal*, 48: 978 - 982.

Vermeulen, F. 2007. "I shall not remain insignificant": Adding a second loop to matter more. *Academy of Management Journal*, 50, 4: 754 - 761.

Vermeulen, F. and H. G. Barkema. 2002. Pace, rhythm, and scope: Process dependence in building a profitable multinational corporation. *Strategic Management Journal*, 23: 37 - 653.

Verona, G. 1999. A resource-based view of product development. *Academy of Management Review*, 24: 132 - 142.

Verschuren, P. and H. Doorenwaard. 1999. *Designing a Research Project.* Utrecht: Lemma.

Villalonga, B. and R. Amit. 2006. How do family ownership, control and management affect firm value? *Journal of Financial Economics*, 80: 385 – 417.

Volberda, H. 1996. Toward the flexible form: How to remain vital in hypercompetitive environments. *Organization Science*, 7: 359 – 374.

Vorhies, D. W. and N. A. Morgan. 2005. Benchmarking marketing capabilities for sustainable competitive advantage. *Journal of Marketing*, 69: 80 – 94.

Wadhwa, A. and S. Kotha. 2006. Knowledge creation through external venturing: Evidence from the telecommunications equipment manufacturing industry. *Academy of Management Journal*, 49: 819 – 835.

Walker, J. S. 1992. "Greed is good" … or is it? Economic ideology and moral tension in a graduate school of business. *Journal of Business Ethics*, 11: 273 – 283.

Wallau, F., L. Haunschild, H. E. Hause, and H. J. Wolter. 2007. Die volkswirtschaftliche Bedeutung von Familienunternehmen. Working Paper, Institut für Mittelstandsforschung Bonn.

Ward, J. L. 1990. What is a family business? And how can we help? *Small Business Forum*, 8: 63 – 71.

Ward, J. L. 1997. Growing the family business: Special challenges and best practices. *Family Business Review*, 10: 323 – 338.

Watzlawik, P., J. H. Weakland, and R. Fisch. 1974. *Change: Principles of problem formation and problem resolution*. New York: Norton.

Weick, K. E. 1989. Theory construction as disciplined imagination. *Academy of Management Review*, 14: 516 – 531.

Weick, K. E. 1993. The collapse of sensemaking in organizations: The Mann Gulch Disaster. *Administrative Science Quarterly*, 38: 628 – 652.

Weick, K. E. 1995a. *Sensemaking in organizations*. Thousand Oaks, CA: Sage.

Weick, K. E. 1995b. What theory is not, theorizing is. *Administrative Science Quarterly*, 40: 385 – 390.

Weick, K. E. 1996. Drop your tools: An allegory for organizational studies. *Administrative Science Quarterly*, 41: 301 – 313.

Weick, K. E. 1998. Improvisation as a mindset for organizational analysis. *Organization Science*, 9: 543 – 555.

Weick, K. E. 1999. Conclusion: Theory construction as disciplined reflexivity: Tradeoffs in the 90s. *Academy of Management Review*, 24: 797 – 806.

Weick, K. E. 2001. Gapping the relevance bridge: Fashions meet fundamentals in management research. *British Journal of Management*, 12: 71 – 75.

Weick, K. E. 2007. The generative properties of richness. *Academy of Management Journal*, 50: 14 – 19.

Weick, K. E. and R. E. Quinn. 1999. Organizational change and development. *Annual Review of Psychology*, 50: 361 – 386.

Weick, K. E., K. M. Sutcliffe, and D. Obstfeld. 2005. Organizing and the process of sensemaking. *Organization Science*, 16: 409 – 421.

Weisbord, M. 1988. Toward a new practice theory of OD: Notes on snapshooting and moviemaking. In W. Pasmore and R. Woodmand (Eds.), *Research in organizational change and development* (2nd ed.). Greenwich: JAI Press.

Werner, O. and G. M. Schoepfle. 1987. *Systematic Fieldwork: Vol 2. Ethnographic analysis and data management*. Newbury Park: Sage.

Westhead, P. and C. Howorth. 2006. Identification of different types of private family firms. In P.Z. Poutziouris, K. X. Smyrnios, and S.B. Klein (Eds.), *Handbook of research on family business.* Cheltenham: Elgar Edward.

Whetten, D. A. 1989. What constitutes a theoretical contribution. *Academy of Management Review,* 12: 490 – 495.

Wiggins, R. R. and T. W. Ruefli. 2005. Schumpeter's ghost: Is hypercompetition making the best of times shorter? *Strategic Management Journal,* 26: 887 – 911.

Williamson, O. E. 1975. *Markets and hierarchies: Analysis of antitrust and implications.* New York: Free Press.

Williamson, O.E. 1985. *The economic institutions of capitalism.* New York : Free Press.

Willke, H. 2001. *Systemtheorie: Systemtheorie 3. Steuerungstheorie: Grundzüge einer Theorie der Steuerung komplexer Sozialsysteme: III* (3rd ed.). Stuttgart: UTB.

Willke, H. 2005. *Systemtheorie: Systemtheorie 2. Interventionstheorie: Grundzüge einer Theorie der Intervention in komplexe Systeme: II* (4th ed.). Stuttgart: UTB.

Wilson, E.O. 1998. *Consilience: The unity of knowledge.* New York: Random House.

Wimmer, R. 1989. Die Steuerung komplexer Organisationen. In K. Sandner (Ed.), *Politische Prozesse in Unternehmen.* Berlin/Heidelberg: Springer-Verlag.

Wimmer, R. 2009. Familienunternehmen. In A. v. Schlippe and T. Rüsen (Eds.), *Beiträge zur Theorie des Familienunternehmens.* Lohmar: Josef Eul.

Winship, C. and R. D. Mare. 1992. Models for sample selection bias. *Annual Review of Sociology,* 18: 327 – 350.

Winter, M., M. A. Fitzgerald, R. K. Z. Heck, G. W. Haynes, and S. M. Danes. 1998. Revisiting the study of family businesses: Methodological challenges, dilemmas, and alternative approaches. *Family Business Review,* 11: 239 – 252.

Winter, S. G. and G. Szulanski. 2001. Replication as strategy. *Organization Science,* 12: 730 – 743.

Witt-Hansen, J. and. H. C. Ørsted. 1976. Immanuel Kant and the thought experiment. *Danish Yearbook of Philosophy,* 13: 48 – 65.

Wolcott, H. F. 1982. Differing styless of on-site research, or "If it isn't ethnography, what is it?". *Review of Journal of Philosophy and Social Science,* 7: 154 – 169.

Woodward, J. 1958. *Management and technology.* London: HMSO.

Wright, M., K. Amess, C. Weir, and S. Girma. 2009. Private equity and corporate governance: Retrospect and prospect. *Corporate Governance: An International Review,* 17: 353 – 375.

Wright, M., R. E. Hoskisson, and L. W. Busenitz. 2001a. Firm rebirth: Buyouts as facilitators of strategic growth and entrepreneurship. *Academy of Management Executive,* 15: 111 – 125.

Wright, M., R. E. Hoskisson, and L. W. Busenitz. 2001b. Finance and management buyouts: Agency versus entrepreneurship perspectives. *Venture Capital,* 3: 239 – 261.

Wright, M., R. E. Hoskisson, L. W. Busenitz, and J. Dial. 2000. Entrepreneurial growth through privatization: The upside of management buyouts. *Academy of Management Review,* 25: 591 – 601.

Wright, M. and K. Robbie. 1998. Venture capital and private equity: A review and synthesis. *Journal of Business Finance & Accounting,* 25: 521 – 570.

Wright, M., S. Thompson, and K. Robbie. 1992. Venture capital and management-led leveraged buyouts: A European perspective. *Journal of Business Venturing,* 7: 47 – 71.

Wulf, T., S. Stubner, R. Gietl, and C. Landau. 2010. *Private Equity and family business – Can Private Equity investors add to the success of formerly owned family firms?* Working Paper, Leipzig Graduate School of Management.

Yeung, A. K. O., J. W. Brockbank, and D. O. Ulrich. 1991. Organizational culture and human resources practices: An empirical assessment. In R. W. Woodman and W. A. Pasmore (Eds.), *Research in organizational change and development*. Greenwich: JAI Press.

Yin, R. K. 1981. The case study crisis: Some answers. *Administrative Science Quarterly*, 26: 58 – 65.

Yin, R. K. 2000. Rival explanations as an alternative to "reforms as experiments". In L. Bickman (Ed.), *Validity & social experimentation: Donald Campbell's legacy*. Thousand Oaks, CA: Sage.

Yin, R. K. 2003. *Case Study Research: Design and Methods* (3rd ed.). Thousand Oaks, CA: Sage.

Yin, R. K. and K. A. Heald. 1975. Using case survey method to analyze policy studies. *Administrative Science Quarterly*, 20: 371 – 381.

Young, F. 1988. Is population ecology a useful paradigm for the study of organizations? *American Journal of Sociology*, 94: 1 – 24.

Zaheer, A., B. McEvily, and V. Perrone. 1998. Does trust matter? Exploring the effects of interorganizational and interpersonal trust. *Organization Science*, 9: 141 – 159.

Zaheer, S., A. Stuart and A. Zaheer. 1999. Time scales and organizational theory. *Academy of Management Review*, 24: 725 – 741.

Zahra, S. A. 1995. Corporate entrepreneurship and financial performance: The case of management leveraged buyouts. *Journal of Business Venturing*, 10: 225 – 247.

Zahra, S. A. 2005. Entrepreneurial risk taking in family firms. *Family Business Review*, 18: 23 – 40.

Zahra, S. A., J. C. Hayton, and C. Salvato. 2004. Entrepreneurship in family vs. non-family firms: A resource based analysis of the effect of organizational culture. *Entrepreneurship: Theory and Practice*, 28: 363 – 381.

Zahra, S. A. and P. Sharma. 2004. Family business research: A strategic reflection. *Family Business Review*, 17: 331 – 346.

Zellmer-Bruhn, M. and C. Gibson. 2006. Multinational organization context: Implications for team learning und performance. *Academy of Management Journal*, 49: 501 – 518.

Zellweger, T. and J. H. Astrachan. 2008. Performance of family firms: A literature review and guidance for future research. *Zeitschrift für KMU und Entrepreneurship*, 56: 83 – 108.

Zerbe, W. J. and D. L. Paulhus. 1987. Socially desirable responding in organizational behavior: A reconception. *Academy of Management Review*, 12: 250 – 264.

Zhang, Y. and N. Rajagopalan. 2004. When the known devil is better than an unknown god: An empirical study of the antecedents and consequences of relay CEO successions. *Academy of Management Journal*, 47: 483 – 500.

Zhou, K. Z., J. J. Li, N. Zhou, and C. Su. 2008. Market orientation, job satisfaction, product quality, and firm performance: Evidence from China. *Strategic Management Journal*, 29: 985 – 1000.

Zhou, K. Z., C. K. Yim, and D. K. 2005. The effects of strategic orientations in technology- and market-based breakthrough innovation. *Journal of Marketing*, 69: 42 – 60.

Zucker, L. G. 1987. Normal change or risky business: Institutional effects on the 'hazard' of change in hospital organizations. *Journal of Management Studies*, 24: 671 – 700.

Das Wittener Institut für Familienunternehmen (WIFU) der Wirtschaftsfakultät der Universität Witten Herdecke ist in Deutschland der Pionier und Wegweiser akademischer Forschung und Lehre zu Besonderheiten von Familienunternehmen. Drei Forschungs- und Lehrbereiche – Betriebswirtschaftslehre, Psychologie/Soziologie und Rechtswissenschaften – bilden das wissenschaftliche Spiegelbild der Gestalt von Familienunternehmen. Dadurch hat sich das WIFU eine einzigartige Expertise im Bereich Familienunternehmen erarbeitet. Seit 2004 ermöglichen die Institutsträger, ein exklusiver Kreis von über 50 Familienunternehmen, dass das WIFU auf Augenhöhe als Institut von Familienunternehmen für Familienunternehmen agieren kann. Mit aktuell zwölf Professoren leistet das WIFU mittlerweile seit fünfzehn Jahren einen signifikanten Beitrag zur generationenübergreifenden Zukunftsfähigkeit von Familienunternehmen.

Das Leiten und Führen von Familienunternehmen stellt eine komplexe und mitunter auch paradoxe Herausforderung dar. Ein neues Studienangebot leistet hier wichtige Unterstützung: Seit Oktober 2010 bietet die Fakultät für Wirtschaftswissenschaft der Universität Witten/Herdecke den als »Land der Ideen« ausgezeichneten Studiengang »Master in Family Business Management (M.Sc.)« an. Hierdurch kann das WIFU seine Expertise an potenzielle Nachfolger, Fach- und Führungskräfte und Berater in Familienunternehmen weitergeben. Daneben gibt es für Studierende im Bachelorstudiengang »Business Economics (B.A.)« sowie im Masterstudiengang »Management (M.A.)« die Möglichkeit, ein Vertiefungsfach im Bereich Familienunternehmen zu belegen.